FELIPE FERNÁNDEZ-
ARMESTO

A FOOT IN
THE RIVER

Why Our Lives Change—and
the Limits of Evolution

OXFORD
UNIVERSITY PRESS

OXFORD
UNIVERSITY PRESS

Great Clarendon Street, Oxford, OX2 6DP,
United Kingdom

Oxford University Press is a department of the University of Oxford.
It furthers the University's objective of excellence in research, scholarship,
and education by publishing worldwide. Oxford is a registered trade mark of
Oxford University Press in the UK and in certain other countries

The moral rights of the author have been asserted

First published 2015
First published in paperback 2017
Impression: 1

Published in the United States of America by Oxford University Press
198 Madison Avenue, New York, NY 10016, United States of America

British Library Cataloguing in Publication Data
Data available

Library of Congress Cataloging in Publication Data
Data available

ISBN 978–0–19–874442–9 (Hbk.)
ISBN 978–0–19–880680–6 (Pbk.)

Printed in Great Britain by
Clays Ltd, St Ives plc

You cannot step twice into the same river.

Heraclitus [Diels and Kranz, fragments 12, 91; ed. T.A. Robinson (Toronto, University of Toronto Press, 1987), 16, 55.]

'*He is entirely human,*' *I replied;* '*the accepted tests of humanity being, as I understand, the habitual adoption of the erect posture in locomotion, and the relative position of the end of the thumb –*'
'*I don't mean that,*' *interrupted Mrs Haldean.* '*I mean human in things that matter.*'

R. Austin Freeman [*The Famous Cases of Dr Thorndyke* (London, Hodder, 1929), 271–2.]

CONTENTS

INTRODUCTION:
THE WEIRD PLANET

We live on a weird planet. As far as we know, all the others are pretty much inert. Gases and dust swirl. Occasional cosmic events—experienced on Earth, too, such as a blip in an orbit, the tilt of an axis, an errant meteor—may alter the environment. But most changes on most planets happen predictably, within a narrow compass, or are measurable on a slow scale of millions of years.

Earth is not like that. Sci-fi writers who strain to imagine strange worlds might as well look inward, at the wild, untrackable, unparalleled oddness of our own.

Earth is, to us, the most interesting large lump in the cosmos, not just because we live on it and it matters most to us, but also because—objectively speaking—a lot happens on it. For two reasons, Earth is the scene of vast, rapid changes, unreplicated anywhere else that we know of: first, because our planet has life, and organic systems are more dynamic than inorganic ones; second, because Earth has us—cultural animals. And culture, which is the subject of this book, is even more volatile than biota.

By 'culture' I mean behaviour—including mental behaviour, such as thoughts and attitudes—acquired by learners, transmitted by teachers or exemplars, and adopted widely. People use the word loosely to mean many different things: civilization; 'high' culture; elaborate social organization; the peculiar features of a particular society; the commonalities that make individuals identify with a group; and hundreds of variants, with many nuances, on all these definitions.

Underlying every usage, however, and uniting them all, is the bedrock of the word: differentiation from 'nature'.

Culture is part of nature, in an unchallengeable sense: it happens inside nature and cannot happen without it. But in equally obvious ways it is useful to distinguish the cultural part of nature from what is merely natural. Some of what we do comes to us without any conscious input of our own. We share it with other creatures in the same measure as we share their ancestry or their physical environment: that is mere nature. Other behaviour can vary from group to group; we learn it from other members of our own group—our parents, for instance, or our professors and peers: that is culture.

It is proper to speak of culture apart from nature, just as it is to speak of Essex, say, apart from England, or of an organ apart from the body to which it belongs, only if one is aware that the larger term always includes the smaller, and that consideration of neither is complete without the other. At times, especially in the West, people have pressed the distinction too far by treating culture as if nature had nothing to do with it, but that is not a reason for refusing to acknowledge that culture might have peculiar features that distinguish it from the rest of nature.[1]

Nature and culture are not mutually independent: each influences the other. But the balance is a battleground. Scholars and scientists fight over it. The answer to the question 'why do we have culture?' lies, I think, in the realm of nature: the simple (but, as we shall see, insufficient) answer is 'it is natural for us to be cultural'. The question 'why do we have cultures?'—in the plural or, to put almost the same question another way, 'why does culture change?'—is, I want to suggest, not answerable in the same way. I propose to explore that question by posing two possibilities: whether evolution or some analogous process is the answer, and whether cultural change happens beyond the limits of evolution's explanatory power. The purpose of this book is to contribute a new response to what perhaps—as we puzzle over strangers' comportment, or ponder alien ways of life, or contemplate the variety of our conduct, or compare the commonalities and curiosities that link and part us from other creatures—is the most perplexing property of human beings: why we behave as we do.

*   *   *

Humans are not the only creatures with culture; over the last sixty years or so, scientists have identified culture among many primate species and claimed it for many others, including examples to be paraded in this book, like the menagerie of some fantastic Barnum or Bailey, such as dolphins, whales, elephants, rats, and even bacteria. Human cultures, however, are different: in comparison with other species, we are strangely unstable. Communities become differentiated, as they change in contrasting and inconsistent ways: that is true, as we shall see, of any cultural species, but the processes involved happen incalculably more often, with a perplexingly greater range of variation, among humans than among any other animals. Human cultures register the constant series of changes that we call 'history'; they self-transform, diverge, and multiply with bewildering and apparently—now and for most of the recent past—accelerating speed. They vary, radically and rapidly, from time to time and place to place.

A lifetime's study of history has convinced me that one of the great problems—unsolved by the scientists and sociologists who have confronted it and rarely even broached among historians—is 'why have human societies grown so different from each other?' Or, to express a similar question with the comparative emphasis that I think will lead us to a solution: 'why, compared with those of other animals who lead social lives, are humans so mutable?' It is one of the most basic and pervasive questions, but we have no agreed answer. The question raises, in turn, a matter of enduring and apparently unclinchable controversy: how far the laws of evolution might provide solutions. Does evolution or something like it regulate culture as well as organic life? Is all behaviour the result of evolved traits? If not, where lie the limits between what evolution can explain and what is beyond evolution? For historians, one might express the subject of this book as 'why do we have history at all? Why do the changes we call history happen? Why do we humans alone have history—or, at least, so much more of it than other animals?' For biologists, a way of putting the same problem might be: 'is culture an effect or aspect of biology? Or is there more to it?' People with no disciplinary bias might put it like this: 'why do humans behave so differently from other animals?'

With some remarkable exceptions, which we shall come to in their place, the lifeways of most extant cultural creatures seem nearly uniform and nearly stagnant by human standards. That does not mean that their cultures are incapable of multiplying and accelerating in the future. Maybe, one day, we will find other species in other worlds with the same propensies as humans' to create highly mutable behaviours. At present, we have no evidence that such beings exist. Part of the message of this book will be (I hope) that we may not need to go as far as outer space to find them: given time, other Earthbound species—chimpanzees, in particular, and perhaps some other primates—could acquire some of the changeable traits in lifestyle and social and political relationships that up to now seem uniquely human. So far, however, although non-human creatures' ways of life—those so far identified and studied, most of which belong to apes, dolphins, and whales—do register measurable changes, the rates at which they diverge and transmute seem infinitesimally small in comparison with the swirl and blur of human spindrift, densely sprayed, widely spattered. The key to understanding why human cultures vary so much therefore lies, I propose, in the comparative study of other cultural creatures. Only when we acknowledge how much we have in common with other animals can we begin to see what, if anything, makes us peculiar.

In the pages that follow, I begin by approaching the subject historically. It is, after all, no sin for a man to labour in his vocation. Chapters 1 to 3 tell the story of how people in the Western tradition have tried to understand the problem of why change happens. In Chapter 1 the focus is on theories of change in general—the ancient debate, and the isolated geniuses who tried to add to it later. I start with the history of this very broad question, partly because, logically, it precedes narrower questions of why specific kinds of change occur, and partly because curiosity about cultural evolution arose from—and in a sense, as we shall see, in aversion from—the stagnation of the debate about change in general. Chapters 2 and 3 narrow the focus, turning to attempts to explain cultural change, in particular, and why and how scientists and scholars have failed to achieve a consensual approach.

While the first three chapters tell a story, the remaining five expound and explore a theory. In Chapter 4 I introduce some of the game-changing research of the last sixty years and explain the scope of the comparative method I follow. In Chapters 5 and 6 I propose a new theory based on recent revelations. Chapter 7 is an attempt to explain why that theory matters now—why recent and current history make it urgent for us to find convincing explanations of the rapid, perplexing changes that befall us. In Chapter 8 I ask how change itself might change and adumbrate possible futures.

*   *   *

In fairness to readers I should declare the assumptions I hope to vindicate. Cultures do not evolve, develop, progress, nor follow any linear, predictable, or regular trajectory. They just change: sometimes more, sometimes less, sometimes for better, sometimes for worse, sometimes (for reasons I intend to explain) accelerating, often in increasing complexity but occasionally in the opposite direction. They change unpredictably, over a range that neither our biological equipment nor our physical environment can fully explain. They change autocatalytically, according to dynamics of their own, or randomly, like the contents of a vast kaleidoscope, shaken without intelligence or purpose or design, in ways that conventional metaphors—of laws, mechanisms, evolutionary trees, descent, and so on—cannot helpfully describe.

Yet, even as I write, between 2011 and 2014, a battery of books fires off what I see as an increasingly desperate bombardment to cover the cultural evolutionists' retreat.[2] Although on the whole the language of debate in the field has got gradually more moderate and conciliatory in recent years, there are still some shrill, aggressive, and uncompromising voices. Their insistence that cultural change is best expressed as evolution and that only evolutionary theory can explain human culture or 'produce a unifying and productive theory'[3] rests—I hope to show—on false assumptions and sometimes on slapdash language. (See below, pp. 146–9.)

I do not have any general theory of change to propose. (I do intend, however, to offer a new way of explaining how and why cultures change: not how and why life changes, but how and why our lives change. I think the theory of evolution describes the former pretty well, but that we need a new approach to the latter.) My explanation serves (and, I should admit, is probably, though not consciously, designed to serve) the cause of freedom. The way we live is up to us, not encoded in our genes or any analogous units, nor implicit in evolution, nor determined by our environment. If we dislike it, we can re-imagine it and strive to refashion it.

Of course, evolutionary explanations of cultural change do not preclude individual freedom. They identify (probably realistically and often accurately) limits to the choices open to us, but leave a lot of possibilities open. On the other hand, by making change seem, to some extent, predictable, they imply that it is controllable: that, I think, is why evolutionary explanations of culture appeal to authoritarian politicians, despite the liberal disavowals of many of the contributing scientists and scholars; I blame the politicians, not the academics. Advocates of Darwinian models for explaining cultural change, moreover, do offend seriously against freedom because, without exception as far as I am aware, they insist that individuals' contributions only come to characterize cultures if some further, impersonal factor intervenes, such as a propitious physical environment, or an inherited trait, or an intrinsic evolutionary advantage in the proposed innovation. The theory I shall put up for readers' consideration will obviate the need to appeal to such factors, and leave cultural change to human behest. According to a famous and almost certainly apocryphal anecdote, Napoleon asked Pierre-Simon Laplace, the astronomer who brilliantly described a mechanistic universe, where God fitted into his system.

'Sire,' the geometrician answered, 'I see no need for that hypothesis.' I imagine some Napoleon of scientism asking me 'and where does cultural evolution fit into your scheme?' Like some anti-materialist mutation of Laplace, I should make the same answer.

Since this book is unprecedented and, I hope, surprising, readers may find it helpful to have an outline at this stage of how I have distributed the material and elaborated the argument. The story I start with is of an ancient debate—well documented in the pre-Socratic West—that addressed the problem of change in very general terms: why does change happen? Why is the cosmos unstable? The debate resumed at intervals, but was largely abandoned in modern times, perhaps because it is irresoluble: we are too enmeshed in change to see it objectively. Instead, enquiry—sporadic in antiquity, renewed in modernity—became focussed on seeking to explain particular kinds of change, especially cultural and biological, and how, if at all, the two are related.

The tendency to treat them apart from each other grew pronounced in the nineteenth century, partly because of the way universities structured and compartmentalized academic disciplines; but efforts persisted to find a level of analysis that embraced both. Darwin largely solved the problem of biological change, inviting attempts to understand cultural change in evolutionary terms, too. In the twentieth century genetics, complementing and completing Darwin's account of how organisms change, excited further efforts and (to over-simplify for purposes of synopsis) four kinds of purported solution: first, that cultural behaviour is largely the product of genetic inheritance and changes accordingly; second, that cultures or the features of cultures operate like organisms, competing to survive; third, that cultural innovations operate like genes, encoding, as it were, evolutionary advantages in successful cases, or spreading in environments to which they are well adapted; and finally, that culture evolves, not in strictly Darwinian terms, but by a 'second inheritance system' or process of 'co-evolution' in which acquired characteristics are passed on by learning as cultures, like species, 'descend' from one another.

I undertake a critique of evolutionary models of cultural change, while conceding roles to evolution as the source of the faculties that dispose some animals to be cultural, and as a relatively minor source of influence on the ways in which cultural creatures behave. I argue that evolution is generally an unhelpful term for representing or understanding how cultures change.

Comparing human cultures with those of other cultural creatures, especially our fellow primates, I propose, first, that culture is a by-product of faculties of memory and anticipation evolved in some species; second, that those faculties predispose cultures to change; third, that humans' faculty of anticipation is exceptionally developed and contributes to making them highly imaginative; fourth, that humans are the most mutable of cultural creatures because in their case peculiar features of memory and imagination make them fertile in ideas (which I understand as ways of re-imagining the world); fifth, that ideas are the main motors of change in human cultures; and finally, that the pace of change is a function of the mutual accessibility of ideas: the more that ideas are exchanged, the more new ideas ensue; and cultural instability increases accordingly. I also suggest that the recent and increasing acceleration of change makes the task of understanding it urgent, and try to connect it with the growth of opportunities for the exchange of culture.

I end with further speculations: that great variety of cultures, such as humans exhibit, may be accessible, albeit not on the same scale, to other species, especially chimpanzees, in future; and that, as opportunities for cultural interchange diminish the acceleration of change will slacken and—even, perhaps—the pace will slow down.

It may seem risky to disclose so much of the end of the book at the outset, rather like revealing that the butler did it in the first pages of a detective story—especially since, as in a whodunnit, I shall unfold in this book, bit by bit, evidence against my case before turning to my own solution. But at least readers with prejudices different from mine are forewarned. A further warning may be in order: this book is an attempt, not to set out a thesis and demonstrate it, but to map a quest, leading to what I hope are suggestive but speculative conclusions. The theory I have to offer must be judged, like all theories including the theory of evolution, not by standards of proof, but according to whether, with elegance and economy, it matches the known facts and achieves its purpose.

The subject transcends every discipline and involves every individual and every species. It ranges over the great battlefield of ideas, joining the conflicts of materialism against metaphysics and determinism against freedom. Big subjects deserve big books but demand short ones: I have tried to keep this one decently trim.

1

CHALLENGING CHANGE

*Thinkers' confrontations with the problem,
from antiquity to modernity*

If we want to understand what is special about our planet and about our own species, we have to begin by confronting an even deeper problem: the problem of change. Why do we not live in a stable—or at least a more stable—world? Why do we have change—or at least so much more of it than other worlds?

These are questions so big and daunting that, in spite of their importance, philosophy has given up trying to deal with them. We hardly ever even crack them open nowadays for close examination. Some questions are hard to answer: all interesting questions, I think, are of that kind. And others—like those that fill the pages that follow—are almost too hard to ask. Change is a difficult subject to address, because everything we say about it is observed from the inside, trapped by a form of uncertainty principle. Change grips us as we try to grasp it. It is almost unimaginably hard to conceive of life without it.

Yet people have tried.

The earliest evidence of their efforts is visible in Ice Age art. The painters of the cave art of northern Spain and southern France, between about twenty- and thirty-thousand years ago, felt drawn to deep, dark places in barely accessible caverns, in the most unchanging environment they could penetrate—made of unyielding rocks. They decorated some of the innermost spaces of the caves with images so enduring that many of them are intact to this day, despite the corruptions of the atmosphere caused in the meantime by natural disasters and the corrosive exhalations of human bodies and breath. No one knows why Ice Age artists made their paintings in such adverse conditions, with painful labour, coarse tools, and limited pigments, in the gloom of flickering torchlight—but only an enterprise of supreme importance can have been worth so much commitment.

The best explanation we have connects their efforts with a need to escape evanescence by reaching for the undying world of gods or spirits or ancestors, locked inside the stone, where shamans could travel imaginatively, on spiritual journeys, propelled by rites and drugs. You can almost see, almost touch those efforts in the hand-prints that smother some of their stones. The attempt to reach the world inside the rock was part of a widespread quest to escape change, perhaps because change is inseparable from mortality. Worshippers have always been drawn, for the same reasons, to mountains, which seem to resist change by outlasting life, or trees, which evade mortality by impressive longevity and incalculable self-renewals.[1]

Change was and is something to fear or flee. We still have a love–hate relationship with it, sometimes embracing it in the hope of improvement, sometimes eschewing it in a spirit of scepticism or despair. Perhaps, if we understood change better, we would cease to fear it. Yet for thousands of years we have been short of new thoughts, almost bereft of new theories about it—so much so that we have pretty much given up on the job.

*   *   *

For an account of systematic enquiry about change in general—rather than about particular changes—we have to go back about two-and-a-half millennia.

There was a time, towards the middle of the millennium before Christ, when the question 'why does change happen?' was the subject of intense debate among schools and sages in the eastern Mediterranean. Thinkers we usually call the pre-Socratics, whose work informed Socrates's thinking (and, therefore, the whole Western tradition ever since) came up with two, mutually contradictory, answers.

Change puzzled the philosophers because it is an apparently universal law—the most obvious feature of how we humans experience the world; but change only makes sense in distinction from a previous, unchanged state against which to recognize it. In that case, what can set it going? Moreover, if something changes, it is different from what it previously was, so how can we continue to speak of it? 'You cannot step twice into the same river' is the aphorism Heraclitus coined around the turn of the fifth and sixth centuries BCE to express this troubling insight. By the time one foot follows another, the stream will have borne its own self away.

The story of the debates these problems ignited is, in a sense, the story of the society that produced the contending ideas; or of the ideas themselves, disembodied from the thinkers who thought them up. But for the sake of convenience, intelligibility, and vividness—and at the risk of seeming to succumb to the fallacy that intellectual history is incarnate in great lives—it may be best to look at the individuals who dominated the discussions. Like almost all the thought of the 'age of sages' in the first millennium, questions about the nature of change arose across Eurasia. Taoists in China, for instance, echoed or antici-pated Heraclitus's conviction that nature was self-transforming. The compiler of the *Chuang Tzu*, around the turn of the fourth and third centuries BCE asked how clouds become rain and what makes winds blow. 'Is there,' he asked ironically, 'someone with nothing to do who shakes the world?' Taoists' generally approved answer was that a universal force or, in most versions, a pair of counterpoised forces called Yin and Yang, drove everything that happened, 'flooding in every direction'.[2] But the story I reconstruct in the pages that follow is a Western one, because Westerners have left most of the relevant texts and inspired all the subsequent prolongations and adumbrations of the debates. The story I tell is of the battles of heroes and giants—and Western giants at that.

Heraclitus, a misanthropic aristocrat of early Ephesus, provided the first general explanation of change that we know of. His life probably overlapped with that of Confucius, but he was much closer to the traditions of orally transmitted wisdom—oracular, bardic, deliberately esoteric—than his great Chinese contemporary. He communicated in figures of speech, images, and imperfect analogies, 'careless,' said his perceptive early twentieth-century German editors, 'of making his meaning clear, perhaps because in his view we ought to seek within ourselves, as he had successfully sought'.[3] He expressed himself with such gnomic obscurity that on the basis of a few surviving fragments he has been hailed as a precursor by a bewilderingly inconsistent range of schools of thought. To Justin Martyr, in the second century CE, he was a prophet of Christianity. He was a Marxist to Lenin and, to German idealists of the nineteenth century, a precursor of German idealism.[4]

His early audiences and readers were less glib in interpreting him, calling him 'the riddler' and 'the darkling'. His thought was like a deep, muddy lake. Socrates, it was said, needed 'a diver to get to the bottom of it'.

He was engaged in a quest for what we would now call a 'theory of everything'. Instead of merely accumulating knowledge, he hoped to think his way through to 'one big thing'—God, or Nature, or some universal principle—that encompasses everything else and makes it intelligible. Understanding change seemed to be the key to the quest.

Heraclitus is often cited as a pluralistic thinker who divided the world into strenuously conflicting particles. Part of his message, however, also seems consistent with a very different commonplace advocated by some of the world's earliest recorded philosophy, encountered, in the late second millennium BCE and the following half-millennium or so, across Eurasia, from China to India, southwest Asia, Egypt, and Greece: 'all things,' as Heraclitus put it, 'are one'.[5] The cosmos is a single, linked system of interdependent parts; how many bits we identify, and how we distinguish them from one another, is not part of objective reality, but merely an effect of our own unreliable perceptions and a technique for coping from day to day. Numbers beyond one have no objective reality: they are devices for classifying perceptions. For convenience, for instance, we might speak of two eyes, but really they are a single pair of eyes. We might speak severally of leaves, stamens, petals—but they form one flower . . . and so on, until you get to the single all that encompasses everything.

The difference between Heraclitus and contemporaries who quarrelled with him was that he thought that the underlying unity of the universe could be compatible with real diversity—rather like the unity of a family, say, tense with squabbles and strained by collisions; or like the Greek world Heraclitus inhabited, riven among inimical cities but conscious of being singly, consistently Greek; or like the environment of his native Ephesus, where earth and sea were in continual conflict, as coasts eroded and silt piled up. He thought the equilibrium of the cosmos was established in strife: a struggle of each constituent part against all the others. Conflict is essential to the system, as Heraclitus understood it, because unity and diversity are inherently conflicting; differences, obviously, make the parts of any system distinguishable from one another, and the reconciliation of those differences is the function of the system.

We can reconstruct—speculatively, at least, or in part—his path to those conclusions. 'The waking,' in Heraclitus's formulation, 'share one common world but when asleep each man turns away to a private one.'[6] He was not speaking literally, I suspect, of wakefulness and dream-worlds: anyone who tries to interpret his sayings has to remember that Heraclitus was not trying to make things easy. On the contrary, like the oracles who were, in one sense, his rivals in the hunt for esteem, for followers, and for material rewards, his job was to 'wrap the truth in obscurity'. He wanted to enhance its mystery, make his own wisdom more esoteric, and gratify his pupils by giving them puzzles to solve—rather like the relationship, alternately maddening and satisfying, of a crossword-deviser and his public today. Paradox was always implicated in Heraclitus's pronouncements. By wakefulness he meant reality, disclosed by thought. By sleep he meant the practical world in which we have to live and act.

He puzzled over the difference between experience and reality and came up with a brilliant solution: reality was inherently dynamic in tension 'like that of the bow or the lyre', when a multitude of infinitesimal throbbings produces harmony. Conflict solders the world together, like a raging fire that fuses rather than consumes. What

Heraclitus called 'God' was the place or agency in which tensions are reconciled. His most striking paradox was 'change is rest'.[7] He meant, I think, that change is what we would now call 'the default system' of the universe. There is no point, Heraclitus thought, in trying to explain it or say what causes it. It just is. It is the sound between the twanging strings—the inescapable state of everything.

Heraclitus's thought survives only in fragments recorded or preserved by commentators; so all reconstructions have to be tentative. But a further way to approach his doctrine of change—and to check on whether we understand it correctly—is via the refutation ascribed to Parmenides, Heraclitus's much younger contemporary and critic.

The young Turks (or, in this case, Greeks) of one generation become the wise old sages of the next or next but one. In the late fifth century BCE Socrates remembered Parmenides as 'an elegant greybeard' of the preceding generation, who philosophized in iambic pentameters.[8] In the way the greybeard used language—striving, by poetry and paradox, to transcend its limitations, to extend its reach—readers can still sense the agonies of a great mind imprisoned in the imperfections of human communication, like an orator frustrated by a defective megaphone. To put ideas into verse is a way of retrieving or continuing the oral flavour of traditional wisdom in an increasingly literate age. Parmenides made the second great contribution in the Western tradition to what we might call a philosophy of change.

In a poem now lost save for fragments transmitted by his students and adversaries he described a spiritual journey along the 'Way of Truth', drawn by the chariot of the daughters of the Sun to the threshold of Night and Day, where the maidens threw back their veils in a dazzling act of revelation. It sounds like a shaman's experience of enlightenment—induced by excitants, perhaps, or glimpsed in a trance—and, in a way, it is. Parmenides was one of the last philosophers in the West to maintain the language of the shamans of the past, who monopolized communication with gods, spirits, and ancestors by dancing, drumming, and drugging themselves into ecstasy. But he broke the bonds of inspired wisdom to reach for truth by unaided reason.

Literary convention demanded that he start with an inspired revelation, a divine message. Then his powers of thought took over.

In some respects, reason confirmed for him insights Heraclitus had already formulated. Parmenides proved the oneness of everything with elegant logic. 'There is,' he taught, 'and will be nothing besides what is,' since, he reasoned, if there were anything else it would be 'what is not'. At this point his train of thought veered from the teaching of the earlier master. As there can be no degrees of existence, Parmenides explained, 'it is all continuous'. The oneness of the universe cannot be divided, because the whole of it is present everywhere.[9] Heraclitus had erred in seeing the unity of everything as a kind of abstraction of its parts because, according to Parmenides's logic, there were no parts—and therefore no conflicts, no tensions for harmony to resolve, only illusions of conflict in our own minds.

Change itself must be an illusion because, in the seamless unity of the universe, there was nothing for anything to change into. Students Parmenides taught in his native colony of Elea (in what is now southern Italy) produced proofs (at least, to their own satisfaction) of the impossibility of change. His favourite pupil, Zeno, wrote his proofs in the form of paradoxes, which became famous in Athens when they circulated among the sages of the city, including Socrates, during a visit of scholars from Elea, probably in 429 BCE. Among those that have survived because Athenian commentators recorded them is the 'arrow paradox', according to which motion is illusory because an arrow is at rest throughout its flight, since it always occupies a space equal to its own size. The 'dichotomy paradox' asserts the impossibility of motion on the ground that a journey can never be completed, since half the remaining distance has always to be crossed first. The 'tortoise paradox' makes the same point by imagining a race in which Achilles gives the tortoise a head-start but can never catch him, because at every moment of the race, when he reaches his rival's point of departure, he will still have a further distance to make up.

In Zeno's world, all was changeless and inert, and all our contrary impressions were delusive. He was candid in admitting that his paradoxes did not prove the reality of his world, but he did insist that the pluralist, restless alternative proposed by Heraclitus was riven with absurdities.[10]

So, for the Eleatics, change was so hard to explain that our sense that it happens must be a mistake, whereas for Heraclitus change was so hard to explain that one just has to accept it as the way things are.

Neither response seems satisfactory—or seemed so to Plato, who continued to worry at the problem for a while. As we have to confront the practical reality of change at every moment of our lives, it is not very helpful to call it illusory. And as every change demands that we imagine unchanged states with which to compare it—implying the reality of changelessness—the temptation to go on asking 'why?' continues to nag. The best solution that thinkers who took the question seriously could come up with was to refer to God, the 'prime mover' who, as if with the jerk of a cosmic fulcrum, flicked time into the midst of eternity and got the first change going—starting a sequence of causes from which all other changes flow. This was not so much a solution to the problem as a displacement of it or another way of putting it; one that closed down debate but left the problem exposed, like a wound bleeding through a patch.

In the shadow of the debate on change, questions arose about the particular kinds of change we now call evolutionary. How did organic life arise? It was always present—according to the pre-Socratic consensus—in the living Earth itself, in dust and water and the mud they spawned when they collided and colluded. It was visible in fossils, vanished fish, monsters, and 'indescribable serpents'—the phrase is Herodotus's—that preceded extant life-forms. But, as distilled in the first century BCE by the great Roman poet of nature, Lucretius, the thinking of the pre-Socratics and their successors in classical Greece did not discern evolutionary links between the species. Rather, Earth 'gave birth' to each in turn until, like an ageing mother, she withdrew, exhausted, from the labour of renewing creation.[11] In a later generation of the same century, Lucretius's successor, Ovid, focussed on sex or mating strategy (or, in evolution's terms, sexual selection): one of the most obvious and puzzling examples of a natural activity, seemingly unified worldwide, that culture shivers into fragments so different from one another that they hardly seem together again. Ovid could see that his own species' lovemaking was connected to patterns common in all organic life, but that its human varieties made it an 'art' rather than a science.[12]

* * *

In the second half of the first millennium BCE, thoughts about change shifted from the problem of how to explain it to the problem of how best to describe it. Of course, without a good description any attempt at explanation could only succeed by accident. So, instead of revolving inconclusively the problem of whether change is explicable in principle, it makes sense to treat as prior the question whether there is a single useful or true way of describing change.

As far as we know, the earliest general descriptions were inspired by the motion of the heavens: cyclical, unending. But since the time of the formulation of the Genesis story, probably around the fifth or sixth century BCE, a linear narrative of change has gradually gained adherents. In the West, linear narrative has become the predominant way of describing history—'one damned thing after another'. The phrase was already popular as a way of describing everyday experience or the plots of picaresque fiction when A.J. Toynbee applied it to history; John Masefield alluded to it in the title of a novel he published in 1926.[13] Against the beauty of a cycle, which has no beginning and no ending, Genesis proposed that change began with a single act of creation, like a loosed arrow or released clockwork. A tempting inference is that change will come to an end when the system winds down or creation reaches its target: a climax—Armageddon or the Millennium—which will re-fuse time with eternity.

* * *

There, with minimal further contributions, rested the debate on the causes of change in general. During the last 2,500 years, as far as

I know, only two ingenious philosophers even returned to the subject in an attempt to devise a new approach. They approached the topic independently, at an interval of 1,500 years. They were both brilliant. They came up with remarkably similar responses to the problem of change. Yet neither, in practice, got us much further forward.

First was St Augustine, around the turn of the fourth and fifth centuries CE. We know a lot about St Augustine's mind, partly because he wrote in a deliberately self-revelatory fashion, candidly trying to disclose his thought processes as he went along, and partly because a good deal of his personal correspondence survives, treasured by recipients and legatees. He also wrote a book of autobiography—the celebrated *Confessions*; and autobiography, however contrived or disguised, always lets slip something of the author's real character, if only between the lines.

He was one of the clearest-headed thinkers ever—remarkably adept in escaping the prejudices with which surrounding culture binds us and the influences in which existing tradition traps us. And yet his was one of the most dispiriting intellects given to man. While Rome burned, Augustine fiddled with philosophy. His tiresome obsessions with sin and sex made the two things seem identical. He was passionate about human freedom in some respects: he insisted, for instance, that sex was deplorable only because the sex-drive is involuntary—as volatile and uncontrollable 'as hot wax'.[14] He argued that God's foreknowledge of our moral choices makes them no less our own. Nonetheless, he preached a bleak doctrine of damnation for most of humankind, which none of us can do anything about.

Though he expressed himself trenchantly, he had a virtue for which every scholar should strive: he was willing to be wrong, explaining that all writers learn as we go along; we write what we think is a description of Truth with one hand, while still tugging at her veil with the other. His work is full of evidence of his genius. He was a great phrasemaker ('make me chaste, but not yet!', 'hate the sin, love the sinner', 'I value my own reputation too much to vouch for that of my friends', 'the feast the rich man eats on Earth he digests in hell'). He more or less beat Descartes to the argument 'I think therefore I am', by more than 1,200 years, and anticipated much modern praise of intuition and mysticism by arguing that knowledge is only imperfectly attainable by observation or authority: it has to be directly present in the mind. His own most stunning intuition pre-empted, in principle but without proof of course, Einstein's key insight: that time is relative.

Augustine shared a form of anxiety intelligible to us, who inhabit a rapidly, bewilderingly changing world. He confronted changes that seemed unprecedented—the fall of Rome, the conflict of new religions, the traumas of great migrations, the cascade of changes that Gibbon famously summed up as 'the triumph of barbarism and Christianity'. He also had strictly intellectual reasons for being anxious about how to measure change, because he was striving to imagine what the world looked like to God, beholding time from outside it—from the perspective of eternity, 'where nothing begins or ceases'.[15] In particular, he was struggling with the problem of how God could know everything—including everything in the future—without foreclosing on humans' freedom to craft their futures for themselves. 'What, then, is time?' he wrote. 'If no one asks me, I think I know what it is. If I try to explain it to an enquirer, I am baffled.'[16]

The past and the future, Augustine felt, were incoherent concepts, as they had no present existence outside memory or anticipation. Nor did the present exist, except as an idea uninstantiated in the world, since 'if the present were always present, and did not pass into past time, it obviously would not be time but eternity'. And yet, Augustine prayed in his perplexity, 'O Lord, we do perceive intervals of time, and we compare them with each other, and we say that some are longer and others are shorter. We even measure how much longer or shorter this time may be than that time.'[17] These reflections seem obvious when one thinks about them and compares them with one's own experience of time. But genius consists in pointing out the obvious that no one else has noticed.

As understanding of time slipped from his grasp, Augustine realized that the nature of time changes with the perspective of the beholder. God, for instance, perceived it differently from His creatures, for he saw everything conspectually, simultaneously, in a single, all-encompassing glance. It takes, perhaps, a mystical insight—a dark night of the soul— to allow a sighted person to imagine the possibility of seeing all times and all places at once, for only the obliteration of sense can fully liberate imagination. The writer who most vividly conjured up a God-like way of looking at the world was blind. The protagonist of Borges's magical story 'The Aleph' faced the threat that his old family home would be demolished for development. 'He could not get along,' Borges wrote, because, secreted in the cellar, was the Aleph he discovered in childhood.

'The Aleph?' I repeated.
'Yes, the only place on earth where all places are—seen from every angle, each standing clear, without any confusion or blending. I kept the discovery to myself and went back every chance I got . . .'
I tried to reason with him. 'But isn't the cellar very dark?' I said.
'Truth cannot penetrate a closed mind. If all places in the universe are in the Aleph, then all stars, all lamps, all sources of light are in it, too.'
'You wait there. I'll be right over to see it.'
I saw the circulation of my own dark blood; I saw the coupling of love and the modification of death; I saw the Aleph from every point and angle, and in the Aleph I saw the earth and in the earth the Aleph and in the Aleph the earth; I saw my own face and my own bowels; I saw your face; and I felt dizzy and wept, for my eyes had seen that secret and conjectured object whose name is common to all men but which no man has looked upon—the unimaginable universe.[18]

Once one has grasped the idea that all places can be visible at once, so that the very notion of place is obliterated, it becomes possible to think of experiencing all time simultaneously.

Borges's, however, was a blind man's vision, which physical powers of sight occlude. To help make Augustine's account of the mind of God intelligible, a less vivid but simpler and more widely accessible analogy is with a journey. To travellers struggling overland from, say, New York to Los Angeles, it seems that they encounter every inter- vening town sequentially, one after the other, and that great distances separate them. To a celestial observer, however, the stations on the journey are all in one place, on a tiny planet, visible, with the right technology, simultaneously. God's perspective on time is equally all-encompassing. All events are discernible at once.

Augustine's conclusion was that time as we understand it—our means of measuring different changes against each other—was what we should now call a mental construct. This was a stunningly radical point—too radical for the following millennium-and-a-half. We now accept that Augustine was right, but in the intervening period hardly anyone else did. The clockwork of the universe, according to assumptions common to every culture that has left us records, seemed definitive, as if wound at creation according to an immutable principle, universally manifest in the rate of progress of spheres and lights across the sky.

Even before he appreciated the relative mutability of time, Augustine had dismissed the notion that it could only be measured in one way, condemning reliance on the motions of the heavens as arbitrary. Practical reasons commended the method, because those movements of Sun, Moon, and stars have, for most of the past, been reliable, unwavering, predictable standards of measurement. Nowadays, for the same reason, we have replaced them with an even more stable technology, based on the slow, relentless, almost perfectly uniform rate at which caesium atoms decay. But there is in principle no reason for preferring any one standard of measurement over another: as Augustine pointed out, 'the motions of all bodies constitute time'.[19]

By implication, therefore, a theory of time is also a theory of change. Time is the rate of change (or, in Augustine's lexicon, 'motion') of one body, measured against that of another. We might time the fall of a leaf, for instance, glimpsed through a window, by the drift of raindrops across the pane, or the painful ageing that turns hair grey in terms of the number of meals we eat meanwhile. The Nuer of Southern Sudan relate major events to the growth-rate of cattle or rites of passage. Famine or war will be dated to 'when my calf was so-high' or when 'such-and-such a generation was initiated into manhood'.[20]

By unwinding the clockwork of the universe, Augustine made the problem of how change happens appear distinct from, independent of, that of time. His only solution was to fall back on God—the old, catch-all explanation—whose omnipotence is such that He can do anything except dispel perplexity. Augustine's interest in change as a general problem, transcending human affairs, was unparalleled among contemporaries and unechoed among successors for centuries, perhaps because Judaism, Christianity, and Islam share a world-view that radically separates humans from the rest of creation, as lords or stewards engaged in a uniquely dynamic relationship with God, whereas the rest of nature had sprung into being, at divine command, all at once. The non-human world would change—the valleys exalted, the lion made to lie down with the lamb—only when the story of salvation was complete.

*   *   *

In effect, the general philosophy of change stayed, defying change's own dynamic, where Augustine left it—not far from the point Heraclitus and the Eleatics reached—until the late nineteenth century, when the world was brimming with new ways of explaining particular kinds of change—geological, biological, and historical, which are subjects of future chapters. At that point, Henri Bergson returned to it.

Today, the curriculum of most schools and universities has edged Bergson to the margins, or even off the page. Most people—even most people who are conventionally well educated—have never even heard of him. Yet he was lionized in his day. Professors who preceded him in his lecture rooms at the École Normale or the Collège de France had to endure impatient audiences who turned up early to be sure of a seat ahead of Bergson's appearance. American ladies who crossed the Atlantic to hear him lecture, but arrived too late, professed themselves content with the aura of a hall in which he had spoken. Theodore Roosevelt demanded Bergson's presence at breakfast, though he had evidently been able to understand little of his guest's work. The philosopher's books were notoriously difficult, but they sold in tens of thousands.

As a schoolboy, Bergson seems to have been one of those annoying young people who give the impression of being born middle aged, with studious habits, encumbering spectacles, mature good manners, mysterious self-isolation from classmates, and intellectual proclivities that shone, in Bergson's case, from an alarmingly bulging forehead.[21] He was good at every subject. His maths teachers felt betrayed by his preference for philosophy. His mastery of Latin and Greek equipped him, he claimed, to read and think outside the trammels of the language of his day. Like all French professional intellectuals, he had to endure a punishing system of protracted education and professorial apprenticeship in secondary schools before becoming the great celebrity-guru of his age.

English pragmatism influenced him and, even when his thinking became abstruse and metaphysical, he liked to start with hard, scientific evidence. His case, for instance, on behalf of the proposition that mind is a metaphysical entity, different from the brain, began with observations of the persistence of memory in severely brain-damaged patients—victims of industrial accidents and wars. He grounded in experience his confidence in intuition as a source of truth. He often appealed to art as evidence of how perception could transform reality. Not surprisingly, he loved Impressionism, which replaces distinct facts, registered by the eye, with subtle forms, abstracted in the mind. He preferred questions to answers and hated teachers who demanded cut-and-dried solutions.[22] That seems a virtuous eccentricity. Solutions spoil good problems, stripping them of interest.

He thought up the first steps in his theory of change while teaching schoolboys about the Eleatics and about Zeno's paradoxes in particular. He suddenly realized—at least, he represented his insight as the result of a sudden intuition, rather like a religious convert describing a 'Damascus moment'—that, in a passage of time or an episode of change, like Zeno's imaginary races and journeys and arrow-flights, moments are not separable nor successive. They are continuous. We should think of moments as constituting time only in the sense in which points constitute a line. Time, conceived as being made of moments (as if it resembled matter, made of individual atoms) is 'an idea contorted and debased by association with space'.[23]

Bergson preferred to speak of 'duration', which we experience within ourselves through consciousness.[24] The concept is baffling and Bergson's definition of it was opaque: 'the shape taken by the succession of our states of consciousness when our inner self lets itself live, . . . when it abstains from establishing a separation between its present states and the preceding states'.[25] However elusive, Bergson's rethinking of the nature of time was immensely powerful for anyone who understood it. It helped shape the revolution in our understanding of language, pioneered by Fernand Saussure, who in lectures he gave in 1907 proposed that text is a kind of verbal duration in which terms, like moments, are inseparable. Many creative writers got the same sort of idea directly from Bergson. Novels in the 'stream of consciousness'—a term William James coined after reading Bergson—were among the result. If Bergson had not encouraged contemporaries to think of time as a mental construct rather than an absolute, external reality, I doubt whether Einstein's idea of the relativity of time would ever have caught on. Indeed, Bergson anticipated many of the inessential tics of Einstein's thinking, down to his fondness for analogies with trains.

The problem of how to understand time is inextricably part of the problem of how to understand change. No time, no change. No change, no time: only the kind of changeless eternity that religious traditions call 'God'. Bergson gave his clearest statement of this doctrine of change in lectures he gave in French at Oxford in 1911. His purpose was, he said, to rehabilitate (or 'seize back', in his words) change from the Eleatics, who had denied its existence. His method was to invite his audience to discard perceptions that, he admitted, were 'natural'.

'We like,' he said, 'to think of change as a series of states that succeed each other.' When we perceive such a state, we are like travellers in a train who think we have stopped, because another train is passing at the same speed in the opposite direction. The continuity of change seems arrested by a false perception. Bergson insisted, furthermore, in another insight that helped shaped mainstream thinking for much of the twentieth century, that reality and experience are identical. 'There is change,' he said, 'but there are no "things" that change,' just as a melody is independent of the strings that play it or a stave on which it is written. Change exists, but only because we experience it. And experience, Bergson argued, in common with most philosophers up to his day, is a mental process. Our senses transmit it; our brains register it; but it happens elsewhere in a transcendent part of the self that we call 'mind'.

'I admit,' Bergson conceded, 'that we routinely locate ourselves in time conceived as analogous to space. We've no wish to hear the ceaseless hum and buzz of deep life. But that's the level at which real duration lies.... Whether it's inside us or outside us, whether in me or in external objects, it's the continuous changing (*la mobilité*) that is the reality.' People who need to cling to fixed points, he suggested, may find the idea 'vertiginous'. Bergson, however, found it reassuring, because it resolved the paradoxes with which Zeno confounded the world.[26]

In the work generally considered his masterpiece, *L'Évolution créatrice*, Bergson had already characterized and christened the motive force that makes change happen. For Augustine, it was a force external to nature, which he knew as God. For Bergson, it was a force inside nature, which he called *élan vital*. In any case, neither thinker seemed to have added anything practical to the problem as ancient Greeks understood it. We are left with no explanation of change, except to say that it is rationally inexplicable, and has to be accepted, either as the inherent reality of the universe, or the product of a metaphysical source of power.

* * *

Meanwhile, instead of trying to explain change, strenuous thinkers again switched their efforts to the attempt to describe it.

Broadly speaking, two approaches encompassed the field. One assumed that Providence impels change, urging the world, from outside it, towards some divinely ordained consummation; the other started from the assumption that changing systems are powered by an internal dynamic of their own—the 'force of history', for instance, in the case of cultural change, or the progressive exhaustion of energy, such as the laws of thermodynamics envisaged, or a process of ageing, such as living organisms undergo, that, by analogy, might apply to civilizations or to the Earth or to the cosmos.

Rivals in love and philosophy contend comically in one of the funniest novels of all time: Thomas Love Peacock's *Headlong Hall*, published in 1816. One of the principal characters, Mr Foster, insists that 'everything we look on attests the progress of mankind in all the arts of life, and demonstrates their gradual advancement towards a state of unlimited perfection'. His counterpart, Mr Escot, whose pessimism is a sort of caricature of the author's own conservative apprehensions of change, replies, 'Your improvements proceed in a simple ratio, while the factitious wants and unnatural appetites they engender proceed in a compound one; and thus one generation acquires fifty wants, and fifty means of supplying them are invented, which each in its turn engenders two new ones; so that the next generation has a hundred, the next two hundred, the next four hundred, till . . . the whole species must at length be exterminated by its own infinite imbecility and vileness'.[27]

Between them, the two characters express the prevailing schools of thought on cultural change. Mr Foster represented the notion that change is progressive, and that the end of the line is perfection. In the early- and mid-eighteenth-century West it was a widespread idea—indeed, it was the orthodoxy of the age. The idea that, in general, allowing for fluctuations, everything is always—and perhaps necessarily—getting better is so contrary to the experience of most of humankind that it is not surprising that it won general acceptance so late in history. For most of previous time, people had stuck to the evidence and assumed they were living in an era of decline or a world of decay—or of indifferent change, in which history is just one truly damned thing after another.

To make progress credible, someone had to think up a way of comprehending evil that made all the woes of the world seem somehow for the best. This was a long-unfulfilled task of theologians, who never satisfactorily answered the atheists' challenge: 'if God is good, why is there evil?' In the seventeenth-century West, the growth of atheism made the task urgent. 'To justify the ways of God to man' was the objective

Milton set himself. *Paradise Lost* was the result. But it is one thing to be poetically convincing, another to produce a reasoned argument.

In 1710, Gottfried Wilhelm Leibniz did so. He started from everyday experience. Good and evil are inseparable, because each is meaningless without the other. Freedom is good, but includes freedom to do evil; altruism is good only if selfishness is an option. Of all logically conceivable worlds, he submitted, ours has the greatest possible surplus of good over evil.[28] So—in the phrase Voltaire used to lampoon the theory, 'all is for the best in the best of all possible worlds'. In Voltaire's novel of 1759, *Candide*, Leibniz appears in the character of Dr Pangloss, the hero's tutor, whose infuriating optimism is equal to every disaster.

Leibniz wanted to show that God's love is compatible with human suffering. It was not his purpose to endorse progress, and his 'best world' could have been one of static equilibrium, into which an ideal amount of evil was built. But, in alliance with the conviction of human goodness that most thinkers shared in eighteenth-century Europe, it made a secular millennium possible, towards which people could work by using their freedom from divine predestination to adjust the balance, bit by bit, in favour of goodness. The Marquis de Condorcet, for instance, thought he could see 'the human race . . . advancing with a sure step along the path of truth, virtue, and happiness', because political and intellectual revolutions had broken the hold of religion and tyranny on a human spirit 'emancipated from its shackles and released from the empire of fate'.[29]

Ironically, he wrote this endorsement of progress in 1793, under sentence of death from the French Revolutionary authorities. The Revolution and the wars it provoked bloodied optimism with the splashes from the guillotine and streaked the Enlightenment with shadows. The Marquis de Sade, pretending unconvincingly to exercise revolutionary freedom, tortured prostitutes and proved the inexistence of God, to his own satisfaction, by inserting consecrated Hosts into the rectums of his buggery victims. In 1798, Etienne Gaspard displayed a freak light-show in Paris, making monstrous shapes loom at his audience from a screen or flicker eerily, projected onto clouds of smoke. Meanwhile in electrifying demonstrations of the newly discovered wonders of galvanization, real-life precursors of Frankenstein made corpses twitch to thrill audiences.

It was not the 'sleep of reason' that produced monstrosities like these. They were creatures of its most watchful hours: the hideous issue of scientific experiments, tortured by 'crimes committed in the name of liberty'. They were prefigurations of how monstrous modernity could be. The collapse of the Enlightenment brought down the house of reason, exposing human irrationality and violence. All that remained—to Immanuel Kant, looking out at the world from his perch in Königsberg—were 'crooked timbers' with which 'nothing straight' could be made. Progress—the straightest of all lines linking the history of culture—could no longer convince.

Mr Escot's deteriorationism was a satire on the grim thinking of Thomas Malthus—an earnest, rational clergyman, peering with anxious charity into a grave new world of overpopulation tempered by disaster. Prior to Malthus's *Essay on Population* of 1798, no one seems to have thought that there could ever be too many people. On the contrary, the more, the better seemed a reliable principle. More people meant more economic activity, more wealth, more manpower, more strength.

In the second half of the eighteenth century, however, the world experienced an unprecedented population boom. The reasons are ill understood but are surely connected with two developments: a boost in food production thanks to global exploration and trade, which stimulated the exchange of biota; and a reduction in the incidence or virulence of plagues, probably resulting from evolutionary changes in microbes that had formerly targeted humans. Between about 1750 and 1850, the population of China doubled, that of Europe nearly doubled, and that of the Americas doubled and doubled again.

Most contemporaries surveyed the evidence with delight. Malthus, indeed, got the statistics that inspired him from the work of the arch-optimist, Condorcet, who cited rising population as evidence of progress. Malthus refiltered the figures through his own pessimistic vision. He concluded that population was rising so much faster than food production that humankind was bound for disaster. Only 'natural checks'—an apocalyptic array of famine, plague, war, and catastrophe—could keep numbers down to a level at which people could be fed.

Some forms of pessimism persisted throughout the nineteenth century. Thermodynamics inspired the notion that since the universe is an isolated system, it will run out of energy. A persistent philosophical minority scoffed at the ideal of a world consistent with reason or morality. Arthur Schopenhauer, who during the second decade of the century lost faith in reason as a means of identifying reality, became, instead, the spokesman for the primacy of what he called 'will', which leads by 'subterranean passage and secret complicity akin to treachery' to self-knowledge so distinct as to be convincing. His readings in Buddhism added a chilling dimension: the ultimate purpose of the will was the extinction of everything—which, he claimed, was what Buddha meant by nirvana. Schopenhauer was not as pessimistic as most readers thought. He aimed at a kind of mystical ascent towards a state of ecstatic self-realization through the abnegation of the external world; but his work encouraged nihilists to celebrate the violent, destructive, and selfish strands in human nature. G.K. Chesterton's amoral, murderous Swami was a vivid fictional personification. 'I want nothing. I *want* nothing. I want *nothing*,' he declared.[30] The shifts of emphasis indicate the slide from egotism, to autarchy, to annihilation.

Gradually, however, in the nineteenth-century West, as war receded and prosperity accumulated, pessimism largely evaporated. The idea of progress revived. Instead of a golden age of the past—the normal *locus* of utopias in earlier periods—the perfectibilians of the nineteenth century thought the golden age of the world was still to come. Confidence strengthened and fed on the 'march of improvement'— the history of industrialization, the multiplication of wealth and muscle power, and the insecure but encouraging victories of constitutionalism against tyranny. It became possible to believe that human failings could not reverse progress, which evolution programmed into nature. Improvement came to be seen as driven by vast impersonal forces—'laws' of nature, of history, of economics, of biology, of 'blood and iron'.

In the same period, the study of change bifurcated. Cultural and organic change became the provinces of discrete, mutually uncommunicative bodies of specialists, broadly characterizable as 'historians' and 'scientists'. The reasons for this divergence are obscure, but it has been hard to reverse, despite efforts to rebridge the gap by *soi-disant* social scientists and advocates of interdisciplinary studies.

The split occurred in defiance of some of the most stunning intellectual trends of the era. When academic history departments began to be established in nineteenth-century universities, the most tremendously exciting developments were under way in scientific perceptions of the world. In the second third of the nineteenth century, geology exposed the stratigraphy of the Earth, disclosing that the planet was many millions of years older than most people had ever suspected. Every new estimate added millions of years more. At the same time paleoarchaeology demonstrated the sometime existence of creatures very like ourselves, turning up evidence that hominid species had preceded or formerly coexisted with *homo sapiens*—Neanderthals, first, then an increasingly bewildering array of other hominids, whose behaviour might have cast light on our own. Theories of evolution, meanwhile, located human history in vast contexts, comprehending the whole of creation and a long tranche of time.

As these startling revelations accumulated, history departments multiplied in universities and a historical profession took shape. Yet the historians, almost without exception, ignored the science of their times and focussed on a brief period and on almost trivially tiny problems. Two circumstances help to explain this surprising outcome.

First, the rise of the nation-state warped historians' work. States—or public institutions dependent on them—founded or seized most nineteenth-century universities in Europe, and in the United States, where churches and private philanthropists played a big role, institutions of higher education tended to imitate those of Europe, or otherwise to subscribe to the urgent task of nation-building. Indeed, in the USA, the task seemed even more urgent than elsewhere, as huge numbers of immigrants had to be educated or re-educated in common nostrums—stirred into the melting-pot.

Even religious schools had to focus their historical curriculum on the vindication of the state, which regulated them with a power the Church could challenge only feebly, at best. Almost everywhere, in consequence, professional historians became imprisoned in narrowly inward-looking, national curricula. Most of them were literally state functionaries or, directly or indirectly, servants of statist agendas. Ideally, the vigilance of historians, as the guardians of posterity, should have restrained elites and improved government. One can see this ideal embodied in the old chamber of Congress in Washington, DC, where a statue of Clio, the Muse of History, carved in marble by Carlo Franzoni in 1810, dominates the room. In her day, the wheels of Time propelled her chariot, while she sternly surveyed the legislators at work, writing their deeds in the book she held open before her. Unfortunately, however, the power relationship was the reverse of what the statue implied. The consequences of the subordination of history to the purposes of the state were disastrous, because national histories are almost always distorted by the need to defend or dethrone myths.

The second reason for this severance was that universities recruited historians from the ranks of already over-subscribed academic constituencies: lawyers, classicists, and theologians. These were all followers of 'humanistic' disciplines—that is, text-based researches. Classicists might have studied writers, but overwhelmingly they studied writings instead. Lawyers might have studied people's foibles, which might have brought them into alliance with physicians and psychologists; instead, however, the traditions of their profession diverted them into the perusal of laws and the transcripts of cases. Theologians—Christian ones, at least—should perhaps have studied human beings, in whom God is instantiated and Christ incarnate. Their first task, however, as most of them saw it, was to scrutinize the Bible and patristics. History became another branch of 'humane letters', in the academic jargon of the time. Historians regarded everything unwritten as alien. They foreclosed on the study of non-literate times or peoples and became fixated on texts: mainly laws, chronicles, legal records, and charters, at first. At their best, historians tried to make texts intelligible by seeing them in the context of their times, which involved excursions into archaeology, antiquarianism, and philology, but hardly much further into interdisciplinary adventures. The model historian, who dominated the discipline and whom aspirants imitated, was Leopold von Ranke, who prescribed a single method—working with written documents—to establish 'how the past really was'. His emphasis made the grand, empyrean vision of the 'philosophic' historians inaccessible. When François Boucher, Madame de Pompadour's favourite painter, depicted Clio, the muse dwelt in the clouds, surveying the world. Corot's version of the same subject shows a down-to-earth Clio, listlessly rolling her scroll, amid crumbling landscape, indistinct ruins, and a faded, inscrutable inscription.

Because each generation of scholars filters candidates to succeed it, and because established authorities sometimes tend to choose sycophants and imitators, it takes a long time for any academic tradition to alter. In 1959, C.P. Snow, a ferocious advocate of compulsory science in the curriculum, imagined asking humanistically educated people what they understood 'by mass, or acceleration, which is the scientific equivalent of saying, *Can you read?*' Few of them, he opined, 'would have felt that I was speaking the same language. So the great edifice of modern physics goes up, and the majority of the cleverest people in the western world have about as much insight into it as their neolithic ancestors would have had.'[31] The history curriculum I followed at Oxford as an undergraduate in the late 'sixties and early 'seventies was still almost entirely focussed on the rigorous reading of documents. It was a valuable kind of intellectual formation, but I got into trouble for wanting to use this as a basis for departure into other kinds of work, and as a young graduate student I could find no professors to share my interest in environmental history—or 'historical ecology', as we called it then—except Alistair Crombie, the Reader in the History of Science, who was himself a somewhat marginalized member of the faculty.

In practice, in consequence, for most of the nineteenth and twentieth centuries, historians had little or no scientific education and enclosed their discipline within arbitrarily narrow limits. The natural part of human behaviour was studied apart from culture, and vice versa, by different groups of academics, who barely communicated with one another. Efforts to recombine what Snow called the 'two cultures' are the subject of the next chapter.

2

THE FRUSTRATION
OF SCIENCE

The nineteenth-century struggle to restore nature to culture

Annie Oakley was proud of her unveneered honesty. After real life as a star in Buffalo Bill's Wild West Show, she became the rootin', tootin', sharpshootin' tomboy-heroine of Irving Berlin's 1946 musical, *Annie Get Your Gun*. In one of the show's rumbustious solos, she derides 'learning' and advocates 'doin' what comes natur'lly' instead. The rewards for natural behaviour seem, from the lyrics, to be mainly amorous—in the pale moonlight, behind a tree—but also practical in diverse ways, from paying bills to raising a family. Despite her professed lack of education, Annie had grasped two basic assumptions of Western civilization: that nature is different from culture, and that 'learning' transforms the one into the other. What comes naturally is instinctive. Behaviour we have to learn is culture. Annie exaggerated, but her sense of the difference was a kind of common sense.

Eating is natural, in Annie Oakley's sense of the word, and we all do it, irrespective of the culture that surrounds us. But our diversity of culture shows in what we eat, how we cook and dress it, whom we eat it with and where, what technology we wield to get it to our mouths and stomachs, and what code of table manners, if any, we apply. Sex is natural, but whom we admit or prohibit as partners and the rites with which we surround lovemaking are the results of our cultural circumstances. It is in our nature to seek shelter—but our building practices diverge dazzlingly from time to time and place to place. You can tell a lot about people's social milieu from the way they walk or stand or sit, because we learn to modify these instinctive behaviours according to the expectations of society and the instruction and example of our elders. Conflict and peacemaking are natural activities, but the ways in which we do them—the scale and spirit of our violence, the destructiveness and duration of our wars, our reasons for choosing allies and enemies, our motives for submitting or negotiating—belong to the realm of culture. Everyone, by nature, is capable of thinking some of the same thoughts, but culture stifles some and stimulates others. In most cases our individual idiosyncrasies are the results, no doubt, of inborn peculiarities of temperament and taste—but we defer to the society that surrounds us when we select which of them we practise and which we suppress. Most human behaviour is modified by acquired characteristics, stimuli, and constraints, such as tradition, fashion, ideology, mimesis, peer pressure, and law.

Even sleep has a history, with conventions about how and when to do it varying between cultures.[1] In Europe in antiquity and the middle ages, people usually had two nightly sleeps, separated by a period of wakefulness. The Pirahã of Amazonia's Maici valley, according to the brilliant renegade missionary who knows them best, hardly sleep at all. They bid each other farewell by warning 'don't sleep—there are snakes'. They say this, Daniel Everett explains,

> for two reasons. First, they believe that by sleeping less they can 'harden themselves,' a value they all share. Second, they know that danger is all around them in the jungle and that sleeping soundly can leave one defenseless from attack by any of the numerous predators around the village. The Pirahãs laugh and talk a good part of the night. They don't sleep much at one time. Rarely have I heard the village completely quiet at night or noticed someone sleeping for several hours straight.[2]

Gestures and grimaces make the point about the primacy of culture with a kind of dumb eloquence. Those that express emotion genuinely seem instinctive, because they are common to every culture—or nearly so—and are identical or very similar in many animals, especially, as Darwin noted, among primates. The masks of comedy and tragedy, for instance, are recognizable all over the world as stylizations of smiles and sadness. As early as 1839, when he was only beginning to formulate the theory of evolution, Darwin began to think that all our facial expressions are instinctive, after observing the infant behaviour of his first child.[3] Some universally meaningful motions of other parts of the body, perhaps, belong in the same category, such as the involuntary spasms with which we, like other apes, shield our eyes or hide our faces when we do not want our emotions betrayed, or the way we clasp foreheads and rub chins in pensive moods or surprised moments. As evidence of the instinctive ways we register emotion physically Darwin listed, among others, astonishment, signified by dilation of the eyes and raising of the eyebrows; blushing for shame; tensing and clenching in defiance; snarling in anger; pouting in indifference; sneering in contempt; shuddering with fear.

On the other hand, a further repertoire of gesture—especially in areas beyond emotion—seems to be peculiar to some groups of people, who learn bits of it from each other. Margaret Mead was the outstanding pioneer of the relevant research. Nowadays she is chiefly notorious as the good and gullible anthropologist whom her Samoan study-subjects in the 1920s allegedly misled into admiration for and advocacy of extremes of sexual promiscuity they never practised.[4] Mead's book about them helped revolutionize Western sexual behaviour by identifying sex with liberation.[5] But other work she did was more helpful and has endured better. She thought gestures vary as much as spoken language from culture to culture, not necessarily because they are intrinsically different in different circumstances but because they acquire nuances of interpretation in contrasting cultural contexts. She helped to inspire fellow anthropologists to compile a great lexicon of over a quarter of a million non-verbal expressions from around the world—creating an impression of diversity so complex as to defy, though not quite dispel, claims that gestures are universal. Mead's pupil, Ray Birdwhistell, devoted much of his life to compiling the evidence, pointing out, for instance, that whereas an Arab might communicate appreciation of a passing girl's beauty by rubbing his beard, a South Italian will convey the same judgement by pulling the lobe of his right ear, while a North American might make suggestive wiggling motions with his hands or kiss his fingertips.[6]

Even some of the responses we make unthinkingly and that seem to us almost automatic vary from place to place. Not every group identifies nodding with assent or head-shaking with denial. Kissing is nearly universal, but in some cultures nose-rubbing is a preferred way of signalling or initiating intimacy. Shrugging is an almost universal signifier of indifference, but not quite; so it might be cultural or anomalously instinctive. A few years ago HSBC—the banking conglomerate that descends from the old Hongkong and Shanghai Banking Corporation—mounted a publicity campaign to convince potential depositors that its employees possessed critical local knowledge. The advertisements showed gesticulators committing terrible *bêtises* as a result of making one culture's gestures in another culture in which they bore distinctive meanings. A diner in Brazil innocently made a sign that, almost everywhere else, would signify approval, but in Brazil amounts to a warning against the evil eye, or an accusation of cuckoldry. In parts of Greece, according to the same campaign, an open palm signifies repugnance rather than the more usual friendliness or congratulation. Overall, therefore, gesture and grimace confirm the effective dichotomy of nature and culture.

Two years after Annie Oakley sang, the fashionable academic pundit, Alfred Kroeber, pronounced the same principle in language more feeble and less catchy than hers, but with the same insistence on the essential difference between inherited and learned behaviour. 'There are,' he wrote, 'certain properties of culture—such as transmissibility, high variability, cumulativeness, value standards, influence on individuals—which it is difficult to explain or see much significance in, strictly in terms of the organic composition of personalities and individuals.'[7] The way the academic world was arranged bolstered the sense of the distinction. But doubts were already circulating. They have accumulated steadily ever since. Students of culture and biology have exchanged data and thoughts, bringing to light ever-accumulating commonalities that link their spheres. It is now possible to climb up the rickety scaffolding of minute monographs and recondite articles to a lofty, if insecure, level of analysis at which history and natural history are one. The rest of this chapter recounts the nineteenth-century effort to attain that level and restore biology and culture to each other.

*   *   *

Common sense was on both sides of the question. At a deep level, the same sort of intuition that made Annie Oakley separate culture from nature has inspired the reconvergence of history with natural history. As I have already insisted, the distinction between nature and culture is imperfect. We can do nothing inconsistent with our natures; to that extent, all behaviour is natural. Our propensities for teaching and learning are innate—part of the equipment evolution gives us and our genes encode. Since humans depend entirely on their parents or other elders during many years of nurture, ours is a species peculiarly adapted by nature to the transmission of culture.

The relationship, moreover, that binds culture and nature is mutual. They are linked in a kind of strange loop, in which each influences the other. I do not think, for instance, that anyone would hesitate to admit that human behaviour of kinds we classify as cultural modifies some aspects of what we generally regard as the natural world: just about every society we know of has modified the environment it inhabits, if only by winnowing selected species, managing forests and grazing, appropriating shelter, and diverting waterways. Farming fundamentally recrafts the land. Domestication produces new species. Over-exploitation eliminates old ones. Urbanization remodels the natural environment unrecognizably. Medicine extinguishes some pathogens and encourages others. Some diseases are the results of lifestyle. It is hard to imagine the recent explosion in the incidence of asthma and allergies outside modern, urban societies.

Every time human culture strokes or scars the biosphere, new life-forms invade the eco-niches we open up. The 'ecological revolution' of the early modern era swapped biota across oceans and between continents, replacing an æons-old model of evolution, in which each continent evolved distinct plants and creatures, with a new, convergent history—a global environment, in which the same species inhabit comparable climates worldwide. Today, the same life-forms occur, the same crops grow, the same species thrive, the same creatures collaborate and compete, and the same micro-organisms live off them in similar climatic zones all over the planet. To some extent the ecological revolution happened without any input from human behaviour. Weeds colonized niches without help from conscious human agency; pests and pestilence spread in defiance of everything culture did to stop them. But without the initiatives of the explorers, travellers, conquerors, and colonizers who opened the routes other biota traversed, the whole process would never even have started. Nor could it have happened without the agency of planters and breeders who nurtured transmissions, founded gardens of acclimatization, grafted plants, and cross-bred animals.[8] Culture turns gardens into deserts and deserts into gardens. Nowadays, it even has measurably accelerating effects on climate change.

It is not surprising, therefore, that culture can transform aspects of human nature, too. Extreme examples are eugenics and, potentially, genetic modification. Some societies breed humans for what we might call 'unnatural selection'—to suit cultural prejudices in favour of particular body-shapes or pigmentation, or particular levels or types of intelligence. Early in the fourth century BCE, Plato's recommendations for a perfect society included a recipe for constructing it out of perfect individuals. The best citizens should be encouraged to reproduce. The children of the dim and deformed should be exterminated to stop them from breeding. Shelved for over 2,000 years the programme reappeared in nineteenth-century Europe and North America, where racism blamed heritable deficiencies for the supposed inferiority of non-whites, while a form of Darwinism suggested that the presumed advantages of natural selection might be helped along by human action. In 1885, Darwin's cousin Francis Galton proposed that the selective control of fertility and marriage could perfect the human species by excising undesirable mental and moral qualities. By spending 'a twentieth part' of the effort breeders put into improving horses and cattle, he promised to breed 'a galaxy of genius'.

Within a couple of decades, his suggestion became one of the orthodoxies of the age. In early Soviet Russia and parts of the United States during the same period, the right of marriage was officially denied to people officially classed as feeble-minded, criminal, and even (in some cases) alcoholic. By 1926, half the states of the USA compulsorily sterilized some of these people. Nazi Germany brought the eugenic idea to its logical conclusion: the best way to prevent undesirables from breeding was to massacre them. Anyone in a category the state deemed genetically inferior, including Jews, gypsies, and homosexuals, was liable to extermination. Meanwhile Hitler tried to perfect what he thought would be a 'master race' by means of experimental copulation between big, strong, blue-eyed, blond-haired, human guinea pigs.

Nazi excesses made eugenics unpopular for generations, but it was lawful in Sweden to sterilize mental patients as recently as 1975. Eugenic programming has resurfaced recently in some apologetics for abortion on the grounds that it disproportionately kills off the offspring of a criminally inclined, economically feckless underclass.[9] And banks of semen donated by men of allegedly special talent or prowess are widely available to mothers willing to shop for a genetically superior source of insemination. Genetic modification, meanwhile, gives us the opportunity, if we wish, to produce genetically engineered 'designer babies'. The isolation of particular genes associable with various inherited characteristics makes it theoretically possible to filter undesirable variations out of the genetic material that goes into a baby at conception. We can replace natural selection with cultural priorities. Most readers—I hope and trust—will find the prospect repellent. But it could work. Just as eugenics might have helped modify the appearance and enhance the health of populations it produced, so genetic modification might eliminate the genes society condemns as undesirable, and produce populations of conformists.

In any case, an enormous amount of evidence shows that culture shapes human bodies and brains in other, subtler ways, morally neutral or benign.[10] Richard Nisbett and Dov Cohen, who published the results of one of the most famous experiments, at the University of Michigan, in 1996, selected subjects from different parts of the USA and measured their hormonal responses to insults. Southerners responded with much higher releases of cortisol and testosterone than Northerners. The researchers concluded that the peculiar value Southern culture attaches to honour has a physiological effect.[11] It is possible to interpret the data differently, but other, comparable experiments have tended to confirm the conclusion.[12] Some of the ways in which human bodies change over time or from place to place are the results of genetic isolation or relative isolation; some, like variations in pigmentation, originate as adaptations to environmental variations. Some experiences can trigger heritable changes in the relationship between genes, without affecting the structure of DNA: trauma, privation, and smothering mother-love can affect successive generations of humans and rats.[13] Plenty of physical differences are traceable to the impact of culture on human breeding habits.

A compelling illustration of culture reshaping bodies is that among populations that practise dairying lactose intolerance virtually disappears. Those that farm starchy staples develop a so-called 'sickle cell' that adapts their digestions. In India, where strong traditional prejudices discourage interbreeding between castes, measurable genetic differences are among the results.[14] Cannibals in Borneo have alleles that counter the brain-corroding prions that would otherwise madden feeders on human brains.[15] A gene frequent among the Yanomamo of Amazonia, who value war, is almost non-existent among the peace-loving San of the Kalahari, presumably because the two cultures privilege contrasting types of potential parents.[16] The apparent convergence of male and female body shapes during the twentieth century in Europe and North America seems to reflect cultural change—the critique of gender, the elimination of most forms of economic specialization by gender, and the correspondingly revised values people apply in choosing their mates. Women no longer demand physically conspicuous masculinity in potential husbands; men can see the advantage in selecting women physically well qualified for traditionally masculine roles. The extraordinary drop in fertility rates in highly prosperous economies is probably the result mainly of social and economic change (which affect habits of breeding and rates of contraception).

A further, more problematic, possible example of the effect of culture on bodies is brain size. Vulgar error sees big brains as the cause or a cause of the multiplicity and ambition of human achievements. But the simple-minded assumption that bigger is better does not necessarily apply to brains. Beyond a certain threshold the size of our brains makes little or no difference to the potential range of our abilities. There is no determining connexion between brain size and genius: Turgenev had a large brain, but Anatole France had one of the smallest ever measured. Men and women, on average, are equally clever, despite general differences in brain size. Large-brained primates, such as cebus monkeys and apes, outperform other species in tasks that humans generally regard as tests of intelligence, but no known test is unpolluted by human standards.[17] On the whole, the skill with which some apes adapt to human-style intelligence tests is astonishing, when one takes account of brain size and the chasm of understanding that has opened since the disappearance of our last common ancestor 6 million years ago. In categorization tasks, for instance, such as sorting a random assemblage of foods and objects of different shapes, colours, and substances—metal bells, wooden cubes, red grapes, green toys—into two piles, chimpanzees, despite their relatively smaller brains, perform similarly to human children of about 3-and-a-half to 5 years old.[18]

Homo floresiensis—a diminutive species, which the media nicknamed 'hobbit'—emerged from a dig in Indonesia in 2003. Despite having a brain comparable to chimpanzees', *floresiensis* had a tool kit very like that of our own ancestors, whose brains were three times as big, about 40,000 years ago.[19] In a sense, therefore, *homo sapiens* is overencumbered with more brain than we need. Big brains are costly in energy terms—they need a lot of nourishment—and do not seem to deliver proportional advantages. So they could be evolutionary aberrations, with no specific evolutionary function, or they could be the result, rather than a cause, of culture.

One of the most eloquent and unremitting advocates of the primacy of biology thinks the latter. The Oxford Professor of Evolutionary Psychology, Robin Dunbar, is famous for two attractive theories: that we can only know 150 people well, and that language originated as a substitute for grooming when the size of hominid communities crossed a critical threshold. He has also argued that humans' relatively big brains are a consequence of the same cultural change, towards large groups with consequently unwieldy amounts of information to manage.[20] The theory seems to need some reformulation, at least, since small brains, well organized, can handle as much data as big ones.[21] Nevertheless, the theory that brains grew as a consequence of the growth of human groups represents a remarkable concession to the primacy of culture. Over the last ten or fifteen thousand years, moreover, people who live in sedentary societies have shrunk—with somewhat feebler bodies and slightly smaller brains. That those changes in physique and brain-size are the consequence of sedentarism, with corresponding shifts in diet and patterns of labour, as people abandoned the mentally demanding complexities of foraging ways of life, is an irresistible presumption; though we have made no discernible progress in intelligence over that period, we seem to have remained on average, as good or bad as ever at thinking.

The power of culture shapes our bodies and grows our brains. Michael Tomasello, an anthropologist who heads the Max Planck Institute and is a renowned defender of the notion of human uniqueness, thinks that the appearance of distinctive human elements of cognition—and therefore the very emergence of humankind in the evolutionary record—happened too quickly to be the results of unaided biological evolution; they have to be explained by self-driving cultural changes.[22] Peter Richerson and Rob Boyd, in their work (to which we shall return) on environmental science and anthropology at the University of California, Los Angeles, made disinterested efforts to sort cultural from biological influences on behaviour and decided that the categories were indistinguishable at the margins. They have speculated that 'perhaps human nature itself is substantially a product' of culture.[23]

It makes sense, therefore—however paradoxical it seems—both to treat culture and nature as distinct subjects of study and at the same time to search for a level of analysis at which we can see how they interact. The next few pages tell the story of how that search began—unpromisingly, as it turned out, among advocates of biological and environmental determinism.

* * *

Even while the nineteenth-century bifurcation recorded in Chapter 1 above was under way, some thinkers—nearly all of whom were outside or on the margins of academic establishments—were striving for reconciliation. One of the greatest of these pioneers was, for a while, interned in a madhouse. In lectures he began to publish in 1830, when he was struggling with self-diagnosed insanity and the frustrations of a stagnating academic career, Auguste Comte predicted a new synthesis of scientific and humanistic thinking. He called it 'sociology' or 'social science'. He was unsure, however, about how to frame or forge the new discipline he imagined. Active seekers of a synthesis almost always proposed one (or both) of two strategies or programmes: biological and environmental determinism. Logically, exponents argued, if individual behaviour can be predicted from the size or shape of one's head or hands, or one's 'life lines', or one's skin colour, so can culture. If the climate or ecosystem determines what we do, it also determines what we pass on to our children.

Take biological determinism first. It has a long tradition behind it in the West, but Christian prejudice has tended to reject it on the grounds that it is incompatible with the free will God concedes to humans. Until the nineteenth century the contexts in which it flared conspicuously concerned slavery and monstrosity.

Slavery is a hard subject to contemplate without prejudice, because our own culture demonizes it. Most human societies, however, have regarded slavery—or some very similar system of forced labour—as entirely normal and morally unchallengeable. Most practitioners have not bothered to justify it, therefore. In classical Athens, however, Aristotle was aware of the contradiction between enforced servility and the values he espoused—such as the independent worth of every human being and the moral value of happiness. He formulated the world's first justification of slavery: some people, he proposed, are inherently inferior and, for them, the best lot in life is to serve their betters. For instance, Aristotle argued, races inherently inferior to the Greeks could be plundered for slaves; or in wars caused by the resistance of natural inferiors to conquest, captives could be enslaved. In the course of developing the idea, the philosopher also formulated a doctrine of just war: some societies regarded war as normal, or even as an obligation of nature or an act of piety enjoined by the gods. Aristotle, however, regarded war as just if the victims of aggression were inferior people who ought to be ruled by their aggressors. This teaching, though it may sound repugnant to my contemporaries, at least made war a subject of moral scrutiny in the West for ever after, but that would be little consolation to the victims of it.

In practice, Aristotle's doctrine of slavery was ignored for centuries, because slavery was largely unquestioned and masters could admit, without prejudice to their own interests, that their slaves were equal to themselves, except in legal status. In general, slaves in medieval Latin Christendom were regarded like prisoners today: they had forfeited their freedom (and sometimes, implicitly, that of their descendants) in exchange for some benefit conferred by their masters, or by virtue of crimes against natural law, or by taking part in just war on the wrong side, or by surrendering in war in ransom for their lives. Or else they were acquired by purchase on the assumption that their status was already resolved. But Aristotle's argument became important from the sixteenth century onwards, when it supplied the basic moral authority for slavery whenever the justice of the institution was challenged in the

West. As the Scots scholiast John Mair put it, justifying the enslavement of Native Americans in 1513, 'some men are by nature slaves and others by nature free. And it is just . . . and fitting that one man should be master and another obey, for the quality of superiority is also inherent in the natural master.'[24] Because anyone who was a slave had to be classified as inferior, the doctrine stimulated racism, and the victimization of people of particular 'races' as slaves. From the point of view of a slave-owning society, the notion that slavery was biologically encoded had an obvious advantage: it cut costs by enabling masters to breed slaves.

The argument from biological inferiority never monopolized the case for the heritability of slavery, but it tinged most others, especially—in the eighteenth- and nineteenth-century West—the justification from the Bible story of Noah, who uttered a curse on a transgressor's son: 'a servant of servants shall he be to his brethren'. There was no biblical authority for identifying black skin as 'the mark of Cain' but self-interested heuristics made the association anyway.[25]

As much as disputes about slavery, debates about monstrosity inspired biological determinism. Legendary monsters seem—to most people, I suppose—the products of over-active imagination; I suspect, however, that they are really evidence of human imaginative deficiencies—in particular, people's inability to conceive of strangers in the same terms as themselves.[26] It is probably true that in most languages no term for 'human' exists to comprehend those outside the group. There is, as it were, no middle term between brother and other. The word that denotes outsiders is usually close or identical in meaning to 'beast', or 'demon', or some similarly pejorative term. The inclusive doctrine of humanity—our sense of species—is a relatively recent innovation in the way we think of each other.[27]

In medieval Latin Christendom, the debate over monstrosity pitched two views against each other. In the thirteenth century Albertus Magnus was the voice of one side, treating physical deformity—which might in principle include any departure from prejudicially decided norms, such as, say, black skin or woolly hair—as evidence of mental incapacity; or one could follow the orthodoxy of St Augustine, who thought monstrosity was an illusion that merely reflected humans' inability to appreciate the perfections of God's creatures. The question was a serious one, because it affected the scope of salvation. In the great, hierarchically ordered schemes of creation that one can still see, for instance, in the stained glass of the windows of León Cathedral, where images of every order of beings are ranged between earth and sky, only creatures with rational souls were close enough to heaven to leap the gap on death. Humans were just below the angels—near enough to heaven to hope. Brute beasts and vegetative life were too far down the 'chain of being'. But how much space was there in between? And who qualified for the privileges of human status?[28]

Along with the monsters whom anyone might encounter in the routine of life—the dwarfish, the birth-maimed, the occasional enslaved or visiting black person, the physically freakish of all sorts—a crowd of traditional, fictional monsters jostled medieval imaginations. For those that occupied the rung immediately below humankind on the ladder of creation, the general name was *similitudines hominis*—likenesses of man. From classical antiquity the West inherited a long catalogue of monstrous races in this category, listed in the medieval period's most popular and influential encyclopedia of nature, Pliny's text of early in the last quarter of the first century CE, the *Natural History*: Nasamones, who wrapped themselves in the shelter of their enormous ears; Sciapods, each of whom reclined under the shade of his or her single, huge foot; Cynocephali, whose dog-like heads reposed on bodies of otherwise human aspect; and a host of similarly odd creatures, whose existence, though never witnessed, was attested in revered texts, including hairy folk, pygmies, 'anthropophagi and men whose heads do grow beneath their shoulders'. In the twelfth-century carvings that adorn the doors of the monastery Church of Vézelay you can still see them, streaming in procession towards salvation in the outstretched arms of Christ. In eastern Christendom, icons of St Christopher often depicted him as a cynocephalus, confirming not only that monstrous beings could get to heaven but also that they could help the physically normal along the way.

Later in the middle ages, the question of where these liminal beings belonged became urgent as European explorers opened up access to parts of the world where unfamiliar physical types abounded. With every new discovery of strange creatures, Pliny's panorama of creation became more credible. The New World threw up naked people, real-life anthropophagi, and reputed giants and Amazons. In Africa it turned out that there really were pygmies, and people with surprisingly distorted or selectively distended physiques, like the bulbous posteriors ascribed to females of so-called Hottentots. There were also hairy creatures—gorillas and baboons—that some observers took, at first sight, to be degenerate kinds of humans. Did all these monsters qualify for their collateral share of bliss, or should they be relegated to a category of natural inferiority—subject to conquest and enslavement by their betters?

On the whole, Christian revulsion from biological determinism protected specimens of doubtful humanity (but only falteringly, fitfully, stutteringly, and slowly, because Christians, like the adherents of every religion, cannot be relied on to observe in life the principles of faith). Native Americans were the first to benefit. 'All the peoples of humankind are human,' said the Spanish moral reformer, Bartolomé de Las Casas, in the mid-sixteenth century. His pronouncement sounds like a truism, but it was an attempt to express one of the most novel, powerful, and contested ideas of modern times. Still, it took a Papal Bull to convince some people that Native Americans were exempt from indelibly heritable inferiority. Even then, some Protestants denied it, suggesting that there must have been a second creation of a different species or a demonic engendering of deceptively human-like creatures in America.

For it was one thing to assert the disunity of humankind, another to devise a theory that made it credible. The most obvious option was the theory of polygenesis, according to which creatures loosely classed as human had emerged separately, whether by nature's laws or heaven's command. The Calvinist theologian, Isaac de la Peyrère, was the first to advocate this solution, in a work published in 1655. He was not addressing directly the problem of the diversity of humankind but that of the origins of the peoples of the New World in particular. Were they the lost tribes of Israel? Had Noah settled in Brazil, as one early seventeenth-century authority argued? Or had the first settlers come from Asia, according to the theory in which the Spanish Jesuit, José de Acosta, pre-empted the discoveries of modern anthropology? At the time, all these hypotheses seemed equally improbable. La Peyrère suggested that the universal paternity of Adam should be understood metaphorically, making credible the origins-myths that so many native American peoples cherish: that they were sprung 'from their own earth'. The theory was dismissed by no fewer than twelve respondents in its year of publication. It was as contrary to the religious orthodoxy of its day as it was to the Darwinian orthodoxy of a later age. Its periodic revivals were, on the whole, feeble and of limited appeal.

Meanwhile, after long, heartfelt equivocations among anatomists and taxonomists, a dividing line emerged between species to exclude apes from the category of *homo*. The question perplexed seventeenth-century anatomists, who dissected apes in attempts to establish their relationship to humans. It flummoxed Linnaeus, when he devised his scheme for classifying all life-forms in the 1730s: he opted to class apes and humans in different genera, but only after equivocating and before changing his mind. The question was hardly settled until the early nineteenth century, when the scientific consensus finally determined against the human credentials of the last ape to qualify for consideration, the orang-utan. Doubts concerning blacks, Hottentots, pygmies, and Australian aboriginals persisted for at least as long. Advocates of enslaving or massacring them were understandably unwilling to forgo the claim that their bodies condemned these creatures to an inflexibly inferior place in the world.

*   *   *

Nineteenth-century science produced new arguments and uncovered new evidence. Classification of humankind into races was thought to be scientific, by analogy with botanical taxonomy. William Lawrence, whose influential lectures on anatomy were delivered in London in 1817, revived the claim Albertus Magnus had made: 'physical frame and moral and intellectual qualities', as he put it, were mutually dependent. 'The distinction of colour between the white and black races is not more striking than the pre-eminence of the former in moral feelings and in mental endowments.' The Comte de Gobineau died in the same year as Darwin. Relying more on what was then beginning to be called anthropology rather than on biology, he worked out a ranking of races in which 'Aryans' came out on top and blacks at the bottom. 'All is race,' concluded a character in one of Disraeli's novels. 'There is no other truth.' Anthropology, phrenology, craniology, and criminology accumulated vast amounts of data to show that people were the prisoners of their physiques.

Various methods were proposed for linking physical characteristics to behaviour and ranking races accordingly—by pigmentation, hair-type, the shape of noses, blood-types (once the development of serology made this possible), and, above all, cranial measurements. This last method was devised by the late eighteenth-century Leiden anatomist, Pieter Camper, who arranged his collection of skulls 'in regular succession', with 'apes, orangs and negroes' at one end and central Asians and Europeans at the other. To readers and interpreters of Camper's data, there was obviously an underlying agenda: a desire not only to classify races but also to justify disparities of power by ranking them in terms of superiority and inferiority. Hence the emphasis on the shape and dimensions of the skull, which were alleged to affect brain-power.[29]

Degeneracy was another potential theoretical framework for understanding supposed racial inferiority. The popularity of the term among nineteenth-century anthropologists is intelligible in the context of a 'discourse' of degeneracy, employed to explain all sorts of exceptions to progress: criminality, psychiatric pathology, economic dislocations, national decline, and, ultimately, the supposed 'degeneracies' of modern art. In the late nineteenth century, says its chronicler Daniel Pick, degeneracy 'slides over from a description of disease or degradation as such, to become a kind of self-reproducing pathological process—a causal agent in the blood, the body and the race—which engendered a cycle of historical and social decline perhaps finally beyond social determination'.[30]

In 1870, Henry Maudslay, professor of medical jurisprudence at University College, London, united some of the themes of biological determinism and specified some of the effects of physical degeneracy on cultural attainments. When the development of the 'brute brain' within man, he reasoned, 'remains at or below the level of an orang's brain, it may be presumed that it will manifest its most primitive functions ... We may without much difficulty, trace savagery in civilization, as we can trace animalism in savagery; and in the degeneration of insanity, in the *unkinding*, so to say, of human kind.' Among supposedly degenerate groups of humans, the concept of 'gradation' offered an apparent means of measuring degeneracy. The term was coined by Charles White in the 1790s, when he produced an index of 'brutal inferiority to man', which placed monkeys only a little below blacks, and especially the group he called 'Hottentots', whom he ranked 'lowest' among those who were admissibly human. More generally, he found that 'in whatever respect the African differs from the European, the particularity brings him nearer to the ape.'

The habit of classifying life-forms into species, and apostrophizing species as 'higher' and 'lower', invited speculation about who belonged to the highest one. Edward Long had justified slavery in 1774 on the grounds that blacks were distinguished from other peoples—*inter alia*, by a 'narrow intellect' and 'bestial smell'—so as almost to constitute a different species from such humans as himself. Henry Home in the same year went further: humans constituted a genus in which there were numerous different species, of which blacks were an obvious example. According to Samuel Morton of Philadelphia, who died while Darwin was at work on *The Origin of Species*, Native Americans were unrelated to people in the Old World: they had evolved separately in their own hemisphere. The findings *à parti pris* of Josiah

Nott and George Gliddon—that blacks were more like gorillas than full-ranking human beings—appeared a year before Darwin's work was published. In the 1860s, John Hunt, founder of the British Anthropological Society, endorsed the similarity between blacks and apes and attributed cases of high attainment among blacks to exceptional instances of interfertility among separate species—admixtures of white blood (which, he thought, were nonetheless non-viable in the long run). Meanwhile, his sometime associate, John Crawfurd, revived the notion of polygenesis, while explicitly denouncing the view that distinct human species could be ranked on grounds of colour.

At first, the severance of mankind among different species was generally rejected for the obvious reason that humans of all extant kinds are capable of breeding with one another; but the compulsion to find a way of characterizing the diversity of humankind consistently with the prejudices of the times was keenly felt among scientists. Louis Agassiz—the revered pioneer of geology and anthropology in mid-nineteenth-century Harvard—staked a great deal of investment on a research trip to Brazil, where he hoped to prove that people of contrasting colours were distinct species by showing that miscegenation led to infertility. Mating blacks with whites, he thought, was like breeding mules from horses and donkeys.[31] Even Darwin, who repudiated racism and subscribed to the Anti-Slavery Society, thought races were 'sub-species' or potential species: blacks and whites, for example, might eventually become separate species, if kept apart from one another, by analogy with the separation of different species of gibbon, say, or tern, or of closely related felines. To many other scientists of his day, 'human' was a misnomer for races already divided from the human norm by unbridgeable chasms, if they were not actually products of polygenesis—the 'separate creations' that Darwin denied.

* * *

Environmental determinism provided no relief, in practice, to the victims of exploitation and extermination. It provided a superficially attractive explanation for variation in pigmentation—exposure to sunshine made skin dark—or body size: extreme climates favoured smallness. Boswell recorded a conversation in which Samuel Johnson explained why blacks are black: ever-deepening sun-tans had been transmitted to their progeny over many generations. But emphasis on the environment as the cause of differences between populations opened the way to another kind of irrational censure: climate might affect not only the outward appearance but also the inner moral and intellectual qualities of entire communities, condemning inhabitants of the tropics to inveterate laziness or incorrigible stupidity.

The eighteenth-century debate known to historians as 'the Dispute of the New World' vividly illustrates the ambiguities of environmental determinism. Georges-Louis Buffon, one of the foremost naturalists of the mid-eighteenth century, who specialized in the acclimatization of plants from around the world, launched the dispute by claiming that the Americas could be characterized in general as a horrible, corrupting hemisphere, where the extremes of climate, the exhalations of swamps, and the inferiority of the very air debilitated all life forms, restricted the variety of species, and condemned human inhabitants to puny stature, feeble physiques, and backward intellects. Where the Old World had lions and tigers, America had pumas and ocelots; to rival the camel, the best the New World could come up with was the llama; to challenge the elephant for majesty, America had only the tapir.[32]

Buffon formulated these claims in the context of a broad theory of environmental determinism. He thought, for instance, that fierce sun and winds were responsible for varied pigmentation. As with so many *philosophes* of the Enlightenment, anticlericalism underpinned his thinking. He sought to explain the diversity of species in a way that was independent of the Bible, defiant of the Church, and even dismissive of God. He thought—as many scientists do today—that life originated spontaneously and evolved in response to environmental change, which also, *a fortiori*, accounted for humans' variety of aspect and character. Contemporary readers—especially those who shared his secular outlook—found his work persuasive. Voltaire endorsed much of it.

Followers and admirers added to the stock of examples. According to Cornelis de Pauw, Siberians and Canadians shared 'natural melancholy', which 'the gloom of their forests' induced. The Abbé Raynal, who was one of the most influential spokesmen of the Enlightenment and a patron and inspirer of Rousseau, thought America induced degeneracy that incapacitated its people. In all the hemisphere, he opined, there was no civilized race, no individual genius. The congenital laziness of the natives extended to erotic indifference, which evinced an 'organic imperfection' similar to that of pre-pubescents in the rest of the world.[33] Claims of this sort could not survive the accumulation of evidence of what the New World was really like. American partisans responded with counterclaims that the New World, governed by 'new stars', stimulated progress and genius.[34] Thomas Jefferson is said to have disproved the theory that the American environment had stunting effects by towering over his fellow diners at a party in Paris.

The Dispute of the New World ended in the New World's favour; in general, the failure of the tradition Buffon founded probably helps to explain why history and natural history could part company in the nineteenth-century West. Yet environmental determinism survived. Still popular in the early nineteenth century, for instance, was the widely held eighteenth-century theory that Jean Baptiste de Lamarck reformulated in 1809. Summarizing a commonplace of the time (which, for example, as we have seen, Dr Johnson had espoused in the previous generation), Lamarck argued that organisms adapt to their environments and pass on adapted characteristics by means of heredity. Darwin—whose theory of evolution is now recognized to be incompatible, or at least in tension, with Lamarck's—actually endorsed his predecessor's views. In deference to Lamarck, Darwin advised young women to acquire 'manly skills' before starting families. The Lamarckian idea has never quite vanished from the repertoire of scientific explanation, though the arguments of Darwinism have tended to eclipse it. Experimental data do not seem to support it and common observation is against it. You may sit in the sun all your life, but your children will be no darker for it.

Even after Darwin's critique made environment seem less decisive in determining physical characteristics of life-forms, almost everyone who thought about the subject continued to invoke environmental determinism to explain differences of culture. Early in the twentieth century, Ellen Churchill Semple—notable as one of the first women to make a major contribution to environmental science—summarized the tradition: physical geography was 'the physical basis of history, . . . immutable in comparison with the other factor in the problem: shifting, plastic, progressive, retrogressive man'.[35] The superiority of Aryans over others, she argued, for instance, was the result of 'inherited aptitudes' and 'traditional customs' forged by the influence of 'remote ancestral habitats'.[36] In general, she concluded, 'a close correspondence exists between climate and temperament'. Hence northern Europeans are energetic, serious and cautious, whereas sub-tropical dwellers are improvident, easy-going, and emotional, 'all qualities which among the negroes of the equatorial belt degenerate into grave racial faults'.[37]

Most proponents of environmental and biological determinism, in short, based their views on irrational prejudices, false data, and super-annuated thinking. If history and natural history were to be reunited—if culture and nature were to be reintegrated in a single subject of study—at least one new starting-point was needed. In the mid-nineteenth century the world got two.

* * *

The new foundations were the work of two geniuses who, independently but roughly simultaneously, from the 1830s to the 1870s, approached nature and culture from contrasting perspectives, though both thought of themselves as scientists. Both were outsiders, however, in the academic world of their day. Charles Darwin was a scientific *amateur*, whose inherited prosperity enabled him to think independently and work capriciously. Karl Marx, who also inherited wealth but could not manage it profitably, was an indigent journalist, whom exclusion from the establishment liberated for radicalism.

Both were theorists of change—not of change in general, but of changes of particular types: Darwin's theory of evolution described and to some extent explained how life-forms change; Marx's theory of class struggle tried to do the same for history.

According to Marx, every instance of progress is the 'synthesis' of two preceding, conflicting events or tendencies. He based his theory on a method of thinking that German philosophers devised or developed in the first two decades of the nineteenth century: everything is part of something else. So if x is part of y, you have to understand y in order to think coherently about x. You cannot know either without knowing x+y—the 'synthesis' that alone makes perfect sense. This seems unimpressive: a recipe for never being able to think coherently about anything in isolation. As well as 'dialectical', as this method came to be called, Marx's thinking was 'materialist'. Change was economically driven (not, as most of the German exponents of dialectic thought, by 'spirit' or 'ideas'). Political power, for instance, ended up with whoever held the sources of wealth. Under feudalism, land was 'the means of production'; so landowners ruled. Under capitalism, money counted for most; so financiers ran states. Under industrialism, as the British economist David Ricardo had shown, labour added value; so the society of the future would be under the rule of workers. A further, final synthesis remained vaguely delineated in Marx's work: a classless society in which the state would 'wither away', everybody would share wealth equally, and all property would be common.

Apart from this last, perfect consummation, each transition from one type of society to the next, Marx thought, was inevitably violent: the ruling class held on to power while the rising class struggled to wrest it. So he tended to agree with the philosophers of his day who saw violence as conducive to progress. The effect of his idea was therefore generally baneful, helping to inspire revolutionary violence, which sometimes succeeded in changing society, but never seemed to bring the communist utopia into existence.

Surprisingly, perhaps, Marx, who read insatiably in history, economics, and philosophy, took little interest in biology or physiology.

He assumed, however, that all human behaviour starts with instinctive imperatives. In a work he wrote with his patron, Friedrich Engels, in 1846, 'we do not start,' he said,

> from what men say, imagine, or conceive, nor from people as narrated, thought of, imagined, or perceived in order to understand them in flesh and blood. We look at the real lives of people in action, and on the basis of the way they really behave we show how their ideologies reflect their material circumstances. The phantoms that take shape in people's brains are also, inescapably, sublimations of the way they live, which is the product of experience and of objective determinants. In the light of our findings, morality, religion, metaphysics, and ideology of all other kinds, with the thinking that goes along with them, no longer look spontaneous or like products of free choice. They have no history, no dynamic of their own. Rather, as the means of production change, and the material ways in which people interact develop, so, in a direct chain of consequences, their real existence, their thinking, and the issue of their thoughts change. Life is not determined by consciousness, but consciousness by life.[38]

Marx and Engels never succeeded in demonstrating those egregious claims, because they had no way of proving that material circumstances govern thought. It could be the other way round. When Marx read Darwin's work, he recognized it as supplying something his own thought lacked: a scientific basis for the assumption that biological urges drive human behaviour, 'a basis in natural science', as he wrote, 'for the historical class struggle'. Nowadays, most readers detect a profound antipathy between Darwin and Marx: capitalists extol the former as an apostle of a competitive approach to life and vilify the latter as an enemy of enterprise. But they were kindred spirits in some respects, both of whom immersed human life deeply, inextricably in the struggle for survival of all biota where 'nature, red in tooth and claw' tears culture to shreds.

Their characters, however, could hardly be more different. Marx, the prophet of peace, was combative, restless, declamatory, venomous, and relishing of controversy; Darwin, the hierophant of struggle, recoiled from conflict in his personal life and scientific relationships.

He was shy, retiring, deferential, and tentative; though he could treat enemies viciously he preferred to do so secretly, behind their backs.

* * *

Whereas Marx developed his thinking in reaction to the prevailing attitudes of his day, Darwin reflected them. The air of the mid-nineteenth century was thick with comprehensive schemes for classifying the world. George Eliot satirized them in the obsessions of the characters in her novel of 1852, *Middlemarch*, in which one character sought 'the key to all mythologies' and another 'the common basis of all living tissues'. Darwin was part of the second of these projects. Most scientists already believed that life had evolved from, at most, a few primitive forms. What they did not know was 'the mystery of mysteries': how new species arise.

In 1832, on Tierra del Fuego at the southern tip of South America, Darwin encountered 'man in his savage state . . . a foul, naked, snuffling thing with no inkling of the divine', apparently 'bereft of human reason or at least of arts consequent to that reason . . . The difference between savage and civilised man', he added, 'is greater than between a wild and domesticated animal.' Islanders' language 'scarcely deserves to be considered articulate. Captain Cook has compared it to a man clearing his throat, but certainly no European ever cleared his throat with so many hoarse, guttural and clicking sounds.' The specimens encountered later in the voyage, on the western side of the island, were even more bestial, sleeping 'coiled up like animals on the wet ground', condemned by cold and poverty to a life of 'famine, and, as a consequence, cannibalism accompanied by patricide',

stunted in their growth, their hideous faces bedaubed with white paint, their skins filthy and greasy, their hair entangled, their gestures violent and without dignity. Viewing such men, one can hardly make oneself believe they are fellow-creatures and inhabitants of the same world . . . How little can the higher powers of the mind be brought into play! What is there for imagination to picture, for reason to compare, for judgement to decide upon? To knock a limpet from the rock does not even require cunning, that lowest power of the mind. Their skill in some respects may be compared to the instinct of animals; for it is not improved by experience.[39]

The Fuegians taught Darwin two things: that a human is an animal like other animals and that the environment moulds us. The germ of the theory of evolution entered his head as he puzzled over how Fuegians could endure the climate in a state of near-nakedness. 'Nature, by making habit omnipotent and its effects hereditary, has fitted the Fuegian to the climate and productions of his miserable country.' Later in the Galápagos Islands, he observed how small environmental differences cause marked biological mutations to take hold.

When he was back home in England, among game birds, racing pigeons, and farm stock, Darwin realized that nature selects strains, as breeders do. The specimens best adapted to their environments survive to breed and pass on their characteristics. Darwin held the struggle of nature in awe, partly because his own sickly offspring were victims of it. He wrote, in effect, an epitaph for his dying children: the survivors would be more healthy and most able to enjoy life. 'From the war of nature', according to *On the Origin of Species*, which he published in 1859, 'from famine and from death, the production of higher animals directly follows'. Orang-utans, whose influence on humans' self-image has been so pervasive, were a further source of inspiration for Charles Darwin. He liked to visit London Zoo to observe little Jenny, the menagerie's curious specimen of the species. She was, he thought, uncannily like a human child, understanding her keeper's language, wheedling treats and showing off her pretty dress when her keepers presented her to the Duchess of Cambridge. Darwin evidently preferred her to some of the humans he knew.

The narrative of the genealogy of man that Darwin published in 1871 started with marine *animalculi* which he likened to larvae. From these descended fish, 'a very small advance would carry us on to the amphibians . . . but no one can at present say by what line of descent the . . . mammals, birds and reptiles were derived from . . . amphibians and fishes'. Among mammals, placental animals succeeded marsupials.

We may thus ascend to the *Lemuridae*; and the interval is not wide from these to the *Simiadae*. The *Simiadae* then branched off into two great stems, the New World and Old World monkeys; and from the latter, at a remote period, Man, the wonder and glory of the Universe, proceeded. Thus we have given to man a pedigree of prodigious length, but not, it may be said, of noble quality . . . We thus learn than man is descended from a hairy quadruped, furnished with a tail and pointed ears, probably arboreal in its habits.[40]

Gregor Mendel, the kind and gentle Austrian monk whose experiments with peas established the foundation of the science of genetics, died two years after Darwin published the *Origin of Species*. The implications of Mendel's work were not followed up until the end of the century, but, when drawn in, they were abused. With the contributions of Darwin and Gobineau, they helped to complete a supposedly scientific justification of racism. Genetics provided an explanation of how one man could, inherently and necessarily, be inferior to another by virtue of race alone. To the claim that this represented a new departure in the history of human self-perceptions, it might be objected that racism is timeless and universal. What the nineteenth century called 'race' had been covered earlier by terms like 'lineage' and 'purity of blood'. No earlier idea of this kind, however, had the persuasive might of the scientific racism of the first half of the twentieth century; nor the power to cause so much oppression and so many deaths.

* * *

Evolution, meanwhile, opened up new possibilities for reintegrating the study of nature and culture. As Darwin's theories became accepted, other thinkers proposed refinements that later came to be known as 'social Darwinism'—broadly speaking, the idea that societies, like species, evolve or vanish according to whether they adapt successfully in mutual competition in a given environment.

Three probably misleading assumptions underpinned the move to appropriate evolution for the study of society: first, that society is quasi-organic—that it behaves, in some respects, like a beast—and could be said, for instance, to grow from infancy to maturity and senescence; second, that, like plants and animals, society tends to get ever more complex over time (which, though broadly true, is not necessarily the result of any natural law or inevitable dynamic); and finally, that what Darwin called 'the struggle for survival' favours what one of his most influential readers, Herbert Spencer, called 'the survival of the fittest'. Spencer put it like this:

> The forces which are working out the great scheme of human happiness, taking no account of incidental suffering, exterminate such sections of mankind as stand in their way with the same sternness that they exterminate beasts of prey and useless ruminants. Be he human being or be he brute, the hindrance must be got rid of.[41]

Spencer claimed (with conscious mendacity, as his autobiography made clear)[42] to have anticipated Darwin, not to have followed him; but the very disavowal seems to align him with social Darwinism.[43] Well disposed scholars have exempted Spencer from the charge of engendering the doctrine on the grounds that his understanding of biological evolution owed as much to Lamarck as to Darwin. He was a practitioner of compassion and an advocate of peace—but only in acknowledgement of the overwhelming power of the morally indifferent force of nature. He was ideally placed to spark and stimulate the reintegration of history and natural history, because he had little formal academic training and was never encumbered by the need to specialize. He achieved vast influence, perhaps because his confident assertions of the inevitability of progress helped restrain or dispel contemporaries' uncomfortable doubts. He fancied himself as a scientist—his rather exiguous professional training was in engineering—and he ranged in his writings over science, sociology, and philosophy with all the assurance, and all the indiscipline, of an inveterate polymath. He hoped to bring to fruition Auguste Comte's prediction of a synthesis of science and humanism in 'social science'. His aim, he often said—recalling

Comte's search for a science that would 'reorganize' society—was to inform social policy grounded in biological truths.

Instead, he encouraged political leaders and policymakers in dangerous extrapolations from Darwinism, including the idea that conflict is natural, therefore good; that society is well served by the elimination of antisocial or weak specimens; and that 'inferior' races are justly exterminated. Hitler made the last turn in this twisted tradition: 'war is the prerequisite for the natural selection of the strong and the elimination of the weak'.[44] By advocating the unity of creation, Darwin implicitly defended the unity of humankind. But there was no clear dividing line between social Darwinism and the original 'scientific Darwinism'. Darwin was the father of both.

The fact that the theory of evolution has been abused should not obscure the fact that it is true. Natural selection probably does not account for every fact of evolution. Random mutations happen—they are the raw material with which natural selection works, but they occur beyond its reach. Functionless adaptations survive, unsieved by struggle. Mating habits can be capricious and unsubmissive to natural selection's supposed laws. The glaring problem, however, of Darwin's theory was and is where and how to fit culture into it. In the twentieth century, enquirers whose work is the subject of the next chapter proposed solutions.

3

THE GREAT RECONVERGENCE

Restoring biology to history

Half a line from Vergil's *Æneid* confronts the visitor to the main foyer of the London School of Economics. Painted elegantly on the wall that faces the door, proclaiming a motto for the scientific study of society, the words *rerum cognoscere causas* appear. Out of context the phrase sounds like an audacious aspiration: 'to know the causes of things'. For Vergil, it was part of a more modest, pious aphorism, evidently to be fulfilled only rarely: the whole line reads, '*Felix qui potuit rerum cognoscere causas*'—happy is he who is able to learn the causes of things. The LSE's motto, I think, is unrealistically ambitious. Perhaps even Vergil was excessively sanguine.

I can remember encountering his line when I was, I suppose, about 15, reading the *Æneid* for homework and thinking to myself what a good joke of the poet's this was. For Vergil's world resembles the cosmos of chaos theory, where causes are untraceable and effects untrackable. The fates spin away offstage, directing history towards a pre-ordained goal; meanwhile, the random interventions of shifty people and capricious gods keep twisting and snapping the thread. What makes the *Æneid* a good story is that it is impossible to know what is going to happen next. You cannot know the causes of things; therefore you cannot predict their outcome.

Yet this irony of Vergil's has been transformed on the wall of the LSE into a solemn pronouncement that some academics take all too literally. Maybe there are no causes to know, or, at least, maybe much that happens is uncaused. Anyone who thinks that everything is explicable as the result of something else—who sees causation as the 'cement of the universe', making each event adhere closely to the next—may be the victim of an unwarranted assumption. 'Just-so' explanations may be the only true ones. Or put it as Alexander McCall Smith does in one of his canny, quaint novels of life in Edinburgh. A character worries about whether to take the initiative with the man she loves. To her father, a psychiatrist, she puts her suspicion that evolution has equipped men with filters against sexually forthcoming women. He denounces her for 'sociobiological nonsense' and assures her that her inhibitions are culturally induced. We behave as we do, he concludes, for much of the time, 'for no discernible reason'.[1] Or say, as the anthropologist Robert Lowie famously said in 1920, that culture is 'a planless hodgepodge', a thing of shreds and patches.[2]

The disciplines that we class as scientific deal in predictability and there are only two ways of making a successful prediction: you might succeed with an inspired guess; or you might set about your task systematically, assuming that the future is a consequence of the past. Scientists rarely admit to guesswork. By observation and experiment they generally establish an apparent pattern of cause and effect and expect it to be repeated. When Edward Cannan devised the LSE's motto in 1922 he was one of the great cohort of economists, led by Alfred Marshall, who piloted the School away from its early role as a partisan training-ground for moderate socialists, to become an independent institution in which people studied society objectively. In selecting from arts students' favourite text, Cannan was making a bid to proclaim the LSE's curriculum as scientific—picking a path through the complexity of causation to predictable outcomes. Therein lay the happiness of knowing causes.

He was not alone. Almost all scholars in the early twentieth century wanted their disciplines to ape or filch the prestige of science. Even the theological tendency called 'fundamentalism'—which we now think of as being at war with science—started, according to a historian who has open-mindedly studied its origins,[3] as an attempt in the early years of the twentieth century by divines in Princeton and Chicago to root the study of God in incontrovertible facts, in imitation of the methods of the observatory and the lab.

In the course of the new century, science came to set the agenda for the world. While previously scientists had tended to respond to the demands of society, now science drove other kinds of change. The pace of discovery—with dazzling revelations about the cosmos, nature, and humankind—commanded admiration and radiated prestige. Ever larger and costlier scientific establishments in universities and research institutes served their paymasters—governments and big business—or gained enough wealth and independence to set their own objectives and pursue their own programmes. New theories shocked people into revising their images of the world and their place in it.

No wonder every academic department wanted rebaptism in these transforming waters. No wonder every art wanted to be a science. All academic disciplines became highly professionalized and specialized, with their own jargons and long training-programmes designed to exclude outsiders and amateurs. Practitioners of other kinds of learning tended to treat science as a benchmark discipline, the objectivity of which they wished to emulate, but the language and findings of which they could barely comprehend. In these conditions, the reconvergence of nature and culture in academic thinking became possible.

*　*　*

The way, however, was hard and fraught with frustration. Almost as soon as Marx and Darwin seemed to have discovered the means of putting science and culture back together, critics tried to drive them apart, or to keep them in the distinct spheres to which the nineteenth-century curriculum assigned them.

In the early twentieth century, the two disciplines that supplied the most effective critics were sociology and anthropology. This may seem surprising, as in theory sociology matched Comte's dream of an all-embracing discipline that would subject culture to scientific scrutiny; and, as we have seen, anthropology had produced a stream of biological and environmental determinists. The turnaround is best exemplified in the lives and work of three individuals, representatives of the new directions sociology and anthropology took: the sociologists Max Weber and Lester Ward, and the anthropologist Franz Boas.

Weber's education in history and law focussed his attention on the unscientific side of life—the arbitrary, contingent, chaotic mess of experience. He wanted to sort the mess out—to make some sort of sense of it, in which predictable consequences flow from identifiable causes, but neither Marx's nor Spencer's models attracted him. His nurturing under his mother's wing, against his hedonistic father, on the committedly Christian side of his divided household, prejudiced young Max against materialism. His own conviction of the power of thought made him recoil from the idea that instincts could chain it. Weber, who was a bourgeois Evangelical, reacted to trends of his times by extrapolating from his own circumstances—searching for an Evangelical and bourgeois answer to Marxism. Between the lines of his many citations of Marx, Weber's real revulsion emerges. Marx was the great bogey, the dominant, malign intellectual force of the era. Marx said economics determine religion. Weber stood Marxism on its head and said that religion determines economics. Marx said religion was the opium of the workers. Max tried to show that, on the contrary, it stimulated work. It was Max *versus* Marx.

Weber, who was very active in Evangelical politics, wanted to make values, especially religiously inspired values, the cause of everything else—the motor of civilization, in the way that evolution is the motor of organic life. You can see why this sort of thinking is misleading by considering a modern instance. People who say nowadays that Confucianism explains the stagnation of China in the nineteenth century and its rise in the twentieth make the same mistake as Weber. Something so elastic that it can explain everything cannot be exact enough to explain anything. It would be wonderful if people really did behave as their religion teaches. The world would be so much better if Christians practised universal love and Buddhists actively strove for enlightenment. But practically nobody does. Religion is unhappily over-rated as a source of influence in society. Still, Weber's influence helped to convince historians and sociologists that they could continue to study their subjects without having to trouble themselves with scientific knowledge. Culture could be treated—to borrow a term from science—as 'autocatalytic', changing from within, according to a dynamic of its own.

Rather as Weber responded to Marx and his schematic reconstruction of history, Lester Ward, at about the same time, reacted against Spencer and social Darwinism. He knew the struggle for survival too well to like it. In his early teens, he had been a frontier pioneer, travelling by wagon with a family of trail-blazers to settle in Iowa. He fought in the Civil War and sustained three wounds. He defied poverty and worked his way through college. He rated collaboration higher than competition. He denounced *laissez faire*—social Darwinists' standard prescription for improving society. You could transfer to the present, without modification, his denunciation of the effects of the under-regulated business practices of his day. 'Nothing,' he wrote, 'is more obvious to-day than the signal inability of capital and private enterprise to take care of themselves unaided by the state.' He defined the 'paternalism' capitalists decry as 'the claim of the defenseless laborer and artisan to a share in this lavish state protection'. He accused fat-cat bosses of 'besieging legislatures for relief from their own incompetency'.[4] He was a typical liberal in the US sense of the word: he wanted the state to restrain the iniquities and inequalities of capitalism; but he was equally anxious to reclaim human freedom from history as the Left saw it—as the plaything of vast, impersonal forces that dwarf human wills.

Ward did not repudiate science. He claimed to work on 'the highest of all sciences'.[5] He did, however, dismiss as simplistic Spencer's insistence on a close analogy between the ways in which organisms and cultures develop. He rejected biological determinism on the grounds that human physiology changes insignificantly or not at all, while society changes immeasurably. 'The artificial modification of natural phenomena'—the effects, that is, of culture on nature—greatly exceeded any changes biological evolution wrought in society.[6]

History, according to Ward, was 'not a simple extension of natural history' but 'the results of will, ideas, and intelligent aspirations for excellence, and hence conscious and personal'. In some respects, his rejection of the claims of nature was disturbingly uncompromising. He denied that humans are naturally gregarious—on the contrary, he thought that, if anything, humans are mildly antisocial creatures. Therefore he denied that culture is part of nature. Rather, it is a contrivance humans have thought up for themselves: 'purely', as he put it, 'a product of reason'.[7] He was surely wrong on that score, partly because reason is a faculty with which nature equips us, and partly because—as we now know—humans are not the only cultural animals. In general, however, Ward's critique of Spencer was highly effective. It is not hard to envisage the victim, for instance, of this delicious lampoon:

> When a well-clothed philosopher on a bitter winter's night sits in a warm room well lighted for his purpose and writes on paper with pen and ink in the arbitrary characters of a highly developed language the statement that civilization is the result of natural laws, and that man's duty is to let nature alone so that untrammeled it may work out a higher civilization, he simply ignores every circumstance of his existence and deliberately closes his eyes to every fact within the range of his faculties. If man had acted upon his theory there would have been no civilization, and our philosopher would have remained a troglodyte.

Ward concluded in favour of what he called the 'spontaneous development' of culture, the 'improvement of society by society'.

In anthropology, meanwhile, Franz Boas led a similar reaction in favour of the autonomy of culture. Among the supposedly scientific certainties treasured in the late nineteenth-century West was that of the superior evolutionary status of some peoples and some societies: an image of the world sliced and stacked in order of race. This picture suited Western imperialists, who treated it as a justification of their rule over other peoples. But Boas upset it. Like Darwin, he had a formative experience among people Westerners dismissed as primitive. But whereas the Fuegians disgusted Darwin, Boas admired the Inuit. When he worked on Baffin Island in the 1880s he found himself looking up to them and appreciating their practical wisdom and creative imaginations. He turned his perception into a principle of anthropological fieldwork (which also works well as a rule of life): empathy is the heart of understanding. When you work with others, you have to strive to see the world as they do. In consequence, your eye is drawn to the intriguing peculiarities of different cultures. You eschew risky generalizations. Determinism of every kind becomes unconvincing, because no single explanation seems adequate to account for the divergences you observe.

As well as a teacher, who dominated the study of anthropology in North America, Boas was a fieldworker in his youth and, additionally, a museum-keeper in maturity, in touch with the people and artefacts he sought to understand. His pupils had Native American peoples to study within little more than a railway's reach. The habit of fieldwork piled up enormous quantities of data to bury the crudely hierarchical schemes of the nineteenth century. Boas showed that no 'race' is superior to any other in brainpower. He made untenable the notion that societies can be ranked in terms of a developmental model of thought. People, he concluded, think differently in different cultures not because some have superior mental equipment but because all thought reflects the traditions to which it is heir, the society by which it is surrounded, and the environment to which it is exposed. Shortly after the end of the first decade of the twentieth century, he summarized his findings: 'the mental attitude of individuals who . . . develop the beliefs of a tribe is exactly that of the civilized philosopher'.[8] And

> there may be other civilizations, based perhaps on different traditions and on a different equilibrium of emotion and reason, which are of no less value than ours, although it may be impossible for us to appreciate their values without having grown up under their influence. The general theory of valuation of human activities, as developed by anthropological research, teaches us a higher tolerance than the one we now profess.[9]

Each culture shapes itself. There is no universal pattern; therefore there are no universal determinants. The facts fieldwork disclosed, as

Robert Lowie, one of Boas's brilliant students put it, are 'inconsistent with the theory of linear evolution'.

The new anthropology took a long time to spread beyond Boas's students. But it was already influencing British methods in the first decade of the century, and gradually became orthodoxy in the other major centres of anthropological research in France and Germany. Cultural relativism was among the results: the doctrine that cultures cannot be ranked in order of merit but must be judged each on its own terms. This proved problematic: should cannibals be judged on their own terms? Or cultures which license slavery or the subjection of women? Or those which practise infanticide or head-hunting or other abominations? Or even those that condone relatively milder offences against values approved in the West—offences such as the mutilation of criminals, or female circumcision? Cultural relativism had to have limits, but anthropology compelled educated people everywhere to examine their prejudices, to see merit in cultures formerly despised, and to question their own convictions of superiority.

Boas's revolution deprived anthropology of the power of prediction by filleting determinism out of it. Cultural anthropology split from physical anthropology—reinforcing the division of academic life in uncommunicating trenches. Boas's disciples included some of the most tenacious opponents of biological and environmental determinism, including two we have already encountered: Alfred Kroeber and Margaret Mead. Perhaps the most influential anthropological book of all time was Mead's *Coming of Age in Samoa*, published in 1928. The author worked with pubescent girls in a sexually unrepressive society. She claimed to find a world liberated from the inhibitions, hang-ups, anxieties, and neuroses that psychology was busily uncovering in Western cities and suburbs. In the long run, as she rose to the top of her profession, to academic eminence, and social influence, her work helped to feed fashionable educational nostrums: uncompetitive schooling, rod-sparing discipline, cheap contraception. Western educationists could learn from Samoan adolescents in a world without barbarians and 'savages', in which the language of comparison between societies had to be value-free. What had once been called primitive cultures and advanced civilizations came respectively to be labelled 'elementary structures' and 'complex structures'. The long-standing justification for Western imperialism—the 'civilizing mission'—lapsed, because no conquerors could any longer feel enough self-confidence to impose their own standards of civilization on their victims. Mead made naïve mistakes, but she stuck to the lessons she learned from Boas: 'in the central concept of culture,' she wrote, 'as it was developed by Boas and his students, human beings were viewed as dependent neither on instinct nor on genetically transmitted specific capabilities but on learned ways of life that accumulated slowly through endless borrowing, re-adaptation, and innovation.' Culture fought free of biology and asserted its own dynamic. For a moment, it looked as if Boas might have unchained culture from biology forever. 'The ethnologist will do well,' declared Boas's student, Robert H. Lowie, in the lectures he gave as Curator of the New York Museum of Natural Sciences in 1917, 'to postulate the principle, *omnis cultura ex cultura*'—rendering as a Latin aphorism, in effect, Lester Ward's principle of culture as an autonomous system.[10] 'Sociology', affirmed Luther Lee Bernard at the University of Minnesota in 1923, 'is at last shaking itself free from biological dominance'.[11]

While Boas and his pupils were at work, the autonomy of culture got a curious, unintended boost from the psychology of Sigmund Freud. This is surprising, because psychology aimed to explain individual behaviour scientifically, by uncovering universal urges. Crucially, however, by concentrating on universals and individuals, Freud left culture, in a gap between them, to explain itself. He was even more subversive of scientific orthodoxy than Boas, because his discoveries or claims reached beyond the relationships between societies to challenge the notions individuals had about themselves. In particular, the claim that much human motivation is sub-conscious challenged traditional notions about responsibility, identity, personality, conscience, and mentality. In an experiment Freud conducted on himself in 1896, he exposed his own 'Oedipus Complex', as he called it: a supposed, suppressed desire—which he believed to be universally, sub-consciously present in male children—to supplant his father. In succeeding years he developed a technique he called psycho-analysis, designed to make patients aware of their sub-conscious desires: hypnosis or, as Freud preferred, the mnemonic effects of free association, could retrieve repressed feelings and ease nervous symptoms. Patients who rose from his couch walked more freely than before.

Freud seemed able, from the evidence of a few of his patients, to illuminate the human condition. Every child—he claimed to show—experiences before puberty the same phases of sexual development; every adult represses similar fantasies or experiences. Women who only a few years previously would have been dismissed as hysterical malingerers became, in Freud's work, case studies from whose example almost everyone could learn: this made an important, indirect contribution to the re-evaluation of the role of women in society. For some patients psycho-analysis worked, and in his own lifetime Freud was successful in representing his psychology as scientific. His 'science', however, failed to pass the most rigorous tests: when Karl Popper asked how to distinguish someone who does not have an Oedipus complex, the psychoanalytic fraternity had no answer. And despite its pretensions, the study of the sub-conscious tended to make society seem unscientific: if the mental features Freud claimed to discover really did occur, as he thought, at all times in all cultures they were of no help in explaining cultural differences. Ironically, as he only studied directly members of the Western bourgeoisie of his day, it may be that features he represented as universal were themselves the products of cultural divergence.

* * *

Weber, Ward, Boas, and Freud, considered from one aspect, were immersed in the intellectual priorities of their own days: part of an immense project, a loosely connected movement, among radical thinkers to unpick the complacency of nineteenth-century Western thinking. Historians have a habit of tampering with chronology:

treating the twentieth century as starting in 1914, for instance, as if the trenches of the Great War were a crucible for the world. The years preceding the war become, in this tradition, a period of inertia when nothing much happened—a golden afterglow of the Romantic Age, turned blood-red by the real agent of change—the war itself. But even before the war broke out in 1914, when the worlds of thought and feeling were already alive with new hues, a scientific counter-revolution exploded inherited certainties.

When the century opened, the scientific world was in a state of self-questioning, confused by rogue results. In the 1890s, x-rays and electrons were discovered or posited, while puzzling anomalies became observable in the behavior of light. In 1902 a young French mathematician, Henri Poincaré, questioned what had previously been the basic assumption of scientific method: the link between hypothesis and evidence. Any number of hypotheses, he said, could fit the results of experiments. Scientists chose between them by convention—or even according to 'the idiosyncrasies of the individual'.[12] Among examples Poincaré cited were Newton's laws and the traditional notions of space and time. He provided reasons for doubting everything formerly regarded as demonstrable. He likened the physicist to 'an embarrassed theologian,... chained' to contradictory propositions.[13] His books sold in scores of thousands. He became an international celebrity, whose views were widely sought and widely reported. He frequented popular stages, like a celebrity-scientist today, haunting TV chat shows. Unsurprisingly, in consequence, he claimed to be misunderstood. Readers misinterpreted Poincaré to mean that 'scientific fact was created by the scientist' and that 'science consists only of conventions ... Science therefore can teach us nothing of the truth; it can only serve us as a rule of action.'[14] But the history of science is full of fruitful misunderstandings: Poincaré was important for how people read him, not for what he failed to communicate.

Without Poincaré, Einstein would have been unthinkable. The former published his critique of traditional scientific thinking in 1902. Three years later Einstein emerged from the obscurity of his dead-end job in the Swiss Patent Office, like a burrower from a mine, to detonate a terrible charge. Relativity made absurdities credible: twins of different ages, light that is simultaneously waves and particles. Within the next few years physicists split the atom and revealed the dazzling gyrations of the quanta of which all matter is composed. While science subsided to the level of convention, Ferdinand de Saussure raised doubts about the reliability of language to capture facts. In lectures he gave in Geneva in 1907, the influence of which gradually seeped into every educated mind, de Saussure questioned whether words can match reality. He made meaning seem a construct of culture, rather than an objectively verifiable property of the world, and placed language outside the reach of scientific explanation. Common sense crumbled. Notions that had prevailed since the time of Newton turned out to be misleading.[15]

The arts made confusion visible and audible. Painting, which is the mirror of science, held up shattered or distorted images of the world. Primitivism subverted racial hierarchies. Cubism distorted perceptions. After reading about the splitting of the atom, Kandinsky set out to paint 'abstract' pictures that were as removed as possible from anything real. The syncopations of jazz and the new noises of atonal music—released in Schönberg's Vienna in 1908—subverted the harmonies of the past as surely as quantum mechanics began to challenge ideas of order. The period was both a graveyard and a cradle: a graveyard of certainties, the cradle of a civilization of crumbling confidence, in which it would be hard to be sure of anything.

Potentially devastating philosophical malaise eroded confidence in traditional notions about language, reality, and the links between them. By 1914, the *New York Times* averred, 'the spirit of unrest' had 'invaded science'.[16]

* * *

Still, the linear narratives of change that Marx and Darwin had proposed survived and scholars' desire to explain cultural change scientifically kept resurfacing. In part this was because science continued to solve other kinds of problem with enviable ease. Science remoulded life—

sometimes for the worse, but generally with godlike dexterity. Technology hurtled into a new phase. The twentieth century would be an electric age, much as the nineteenth had been an age of steam. In 1901, Marconi broadcast by wireless. In 1903 the Wright brothers took flight. Plastic was invented in 1907. The curiosities of late nineteenth-century inventiveness, such as the telephone, the car, and the typewriter, all became commonplace. Other essentials of technologically fulfilled twentieth-century lives—the atom-smasher, the ferro-concrete skyscraper frame, even the hamburger and Coca-cola—were all in place before the First World War. It began to look as if technology could do anything. In the rest of the century it almost did. Military technology won wars. Industrial technology multiplied food and wealth. Information systems devised in the West revolutionized communications, business, leisure, education, and methods of social and political control. Medicine saved lives.

Partly in consequence of progress in technology practical medicine registered spectacular advances. X-rays and the successor technologies that improved on their readings made the secrets of physiology visible. Doctors could control diseases ever more effectively by imitating the body's natural hormones and adjusting their balance: that story began with the isolation of insulin, which controls diabetes, in 1922. In 1931, penicillin was discovered: the first antibiotic—a killer of micro-organisms that cause disease inside the body. Microbes evolved with stunning rapidity, but on the whole the drugmakers kept pace with them. Preventive medicine made even bigger strides, as inoculation programmes and health education—gradually, over the course of the century—became accessible almost everywhere in the world. Doctors sometimes aggravated bad health by inventing new diseases, medicalizing social problems, and convincing healthy people that they were ill—but these things were evidence of the prestige and power of medical professionals. Despite the annoying way in which new diseases evolved, there seemed no limits to what medical science could do: prolonging life to the point at which it became conceivable to defeat death.

Meanwhile new fields of study transformed human biology, with further consequences for medicine. Beginning in 1908, T.H. Morgan at Columbia University initiated a series of experiments in animal breeding that ultimately demonstrated how some characteristics are inherited by means of the transmission of genes and led, in the second half of the century, to a new form of medicine in which doctors could treat disease directly by manipulating people's genes. After Morgan's famous work with fruit flies—demonstrating how chromosomes are vectors of heredity—no reasonable person could doubt the power of evolution to explain the way living organisms change. Neuroscience, increasingly, appropriated psychology for biology, making enormous progress in mapping the brain, demonstrating the distribution of mental functions, and recording how electrical impulses and releases of proteins occur, as different kinds of thinking, feeling, memorizing, and imagining take place. Even the notion of 'mind' distinct from brain became incredible to some observers. Among them was Charles Hockett, one of the few scholars educated in Boas's tradition—a pupil of Boas's pupils, formed in the kind of fieldwork Boas enjoined—to react unreservedly against the master (we shall meet another, Leslie White, soon: below, p. 160). He turned back to the project of reclassifying culture as a subject of biology. In 1948 he proposed the term 'sociobiology' to denote the kind of science he foresaw.[17] Later developments would make Hockett seem representative and his terminology prescient.

*   *   *

The science that grew most spectacularly in the twentieth century focussed on the environment. The rise of ecology, the study of the interconnectedness of all life and its interdependence with aspects of the physical environment, exposed a vast range of new practical problems arising from human overexploitation of the environment and became a major source of influence on changes in the late twentieth-century world. The context was rampant consumerism in the Western world. While global population roughly quadrupled during the twentieth century, per capita consumption increased almost twenty times over—almost all of it concentrated in the United States and a few other Western countries. As early as the 1920s the Jesuit polymath Pierre Teilhard de Chardin saw the pain of what he called the biosphere, stressed by the demands of humankind. He proposed a synthesis of evolutionary science and theology, which proved too religious for many scientists and too scientific for many theologians. But he had a convincing message: what he called the biosphere was a single, vast, fragile, system, every part of which depended on others.

The effects of the ecological turn were equivocal. On one hand, growing awareness of global environmental problems gave science a new role: to confront previously unidentified dangers from climate change and microbial mutation, which threatened to shrink humans' habitats or decimate them in a new age of plagues. On the other hand, science seemed to be adding to the problems rather than solving them. Every technology scientists devised seemed to spawn adverse consequences. Hydroelectricity supplied energy but leeched moisture and nutrients from soil. Nuclear power improved on fossil fuels but generated intractable waste. The 'Green Revolution' fed millions who might otherwise have starved, but decimated bio-diversity and impoverished poor farmers.

People's awareness gradually increased of the potential exhaustion of the Earth's resources and the havoc arising from the growing volumes of fertilizers, pesticides, and pollutants that poisoned the Earth.[18] Insects lost their weedy habitats. The birds, reptiles, and small mammals that feed off the insects lost their food supply. By the 1960s, the effects were so marked that Rachel Carson, a former United States' government agronomist, published her immensely influential book, *Silent Spring*, in which she predicted an America without birdsong. An ecological movement sprang up and mobilized millions of people, especially in Europe and America, to defend the environment against pollution and overexploitation. 'Pollution, pollution,' sang the satirist Tom Lehrer, warning listeners to beware of two things: 'don't drink the water and don't breathe the air'.

Norman E. Borlaug, the Nobel Prize-winning agronomist who helped to develop fertilizer-friendly crops, denounced 'vicious, hysterical propaganda' against agrochemicals by 'scientific halfwits', but he could not stem the tide of environmentalism at a popular level. Only the resistance of governments and big business could check it. Partly because the environment seemed too important to leave to any one body of experts, environmental studies became an interdisciplinary opportunity. Oxford is usually comfortably padded against shocks from the outside world, but even there, in the early 'seventies, a few of us, led by Alistair Crombie, started a seminar on what we called 'historical ecology', trying to understand humans in relation to the whole of the rest of nature: the climate that surrounds us, the landscape that enfolds us, the species with which we interact, the ecosystems in which we are bound. So although the environment was a zone in which scientists faltered or failed, the effect of the ecological movement was, on the whole, to make students of the humanities yearn to be better informed about science.

Other twentieth-century circumstances also favoured the reconvergence of science with the humanities. In the North American system of higher education undergraduates had to study both. The United States increasingly dominated the world of learning, as wars and relative economic decline undermined the former superiority of German, British, and French universities. By and large, US institutions scooped the prizes, forged the innovations, financed the research, and published the journals. The cleavage of universities into 'two cultures' was still strong at the level of the professorate: indeed, the chasm broadened during the course of the twentieth century, as all disciplines got increasingly specialized, and therefore increasingly introspective, while some interdisciplinary departments split—physical anthropologists, for instance, deserting their cultural colleagues, environmental scientists separating from geographers, and econometricians abandoning practitioners of social studies. Yet at least the US universities bred scientifically literate, numerate humanists.

* * *

Meanwhile, social problems opened up an opportunity for science and a battleground with the arts: first war, which dominated the first half of the century, then postwar anomie, which dominated the rest.

The First World War checked the drift to Boas's views among students of society: his revulsion from nationalism and jingoism was out of sorts with the time; his pacifism and his refusal to endorse the abuse of anthropologists in espionage and propaganda triggered accusations of treachery. His German origins made him an easy target for his enemies. His views remained precariously supreme among anthropologists, but their wider acceptance stalled or ceased.[19] In any case the climate of war favoured investment in technology and gigantic intellectual oversimplification, not subtle thinking or avowedly useless knowledge. War in general, rather than any war in particular, was the main source of re-evaluations of the relationship of culture and evolution.

Alike for those who made a virtue of conflict—who thought it winnowed the weak, or enabled progress, or stimulated heroism and self-sacrifice—and those who knew its vices, it was vital to know why war happened. The problem of whether it was natural or cultural brought the relationship between nature and culture to the foreground of the debate. Everyone responded according to his or her prejudices. Field Marshal Montgomery used to refer enquirers who asked about the causes of conflict to Maeterlinck's *The Life of the Ant*, whereas, according to the free-thinking relativist, Margaret Mead, 'war is an invention, not a biological necessity'.[20]

Ever since classical antiquity, at the latest, the issue had divided learned opinion. According to a notion widely diffused among ancient philosophers, humans are naturally peaceful creatures, who had to be wrenched out of a golden age of universal peace by socially corrupting processes. Equally little evidence supported the opposite view: that humans' natural violence is uncontrollable except by coercive social and political institutions. After watching the death-tolls of the First World War pile up, Freud frankly proposed to fill the evidence gap with speculation, inspired by the recurrence of traumatic themes in dreams and in children's play. A death-wish, he thought, may be embedded in the human psyche and—in conflict with the drive for life, which includes a potentially violent sex-urge—'comes to light in the instinct of aggressiveness'.

The politics of the twentieth century exacerbated the dispute: it suited the Right to extol competition as natural, while the Left wanted to believe that naturally collaborative instincts would shape society.

Some supporters of the view that war is part of the natural order of things attempted to supply the deficiencies of proofs by appealing to analogies with various animals. Indeed, zoologists and ethologists often seem to find it hard to resist the temptation to extrapolate to humans from whatever other species they study. In the case of animals closely related to humans in evolutionary terms, such as chimpanzees and other primates, the method is often fruitful. Konrad Lorenz, however, got his inspiration from studying gulls and geese. His work before and during the Second World War inspired a generation of research into the evolutionary background of violence. He found that the birds he worked with were determinedly and increasingly aggressive in competing for food and sex. He suspected that in humans, too, these instincts would overpower any contrary tendencies. Neither the taint of Lorenz's enthusiasm for Nazism, nor the selectivity of the data he used to support his views of human and non-human animals, could prevent Lorenz from winning a Nobel Prize, or exercising enormous influence, especially when his major work became widely available in English in the 1960s.

Among his admirers, Robert Ardrey, the Chicagoan playwright and pop-anthropologist, focussed the search for the origins of war on 'a force' in evolution 'perhaps older than sex'.[21] He called it 'the territorial imperative'. He was an accomplished popularizer, who helped convince inexpert readers of the African origins of humankind. His intervention in the debate about instinct was less felicitous. He explained war as the indirect outcome of the drive for survival, which demands territory—it is tempting to retranslate Ardrey's use of the word as

Lebensraum—to secure food and water. In the case of humans, Ardrey argued, a long past spent in dependence on hunting as a food-source sharpened and deepened the aggressive instinct. Our reasons, he said, for fighting to defend land are 'no less innate' than those of other animals. He airily dismissed the notion that culture could contribute anything to behaviour independently of nature. One day, he ventured, science would discover that learning and instinct are both 'based on the molecule within the cell'.[22]

At the time, the relatively scanty archaeological record of intercommunal conflict in paleolithic times seemed to support the case for seeing war as an artefact of some cultures. Now, however, evidence of the ubiquity of violence has heaped up, in studies of ape warfare, of war in surviving forager-societies, of psychological aggression and of bloodshed and bone-breaking in Stone-Age archaeology. In some versions of the fate of the Neanderthals, our own ancestors wiped them out. The evidence is insufficient to support this, but the world's earliest known full-scale battle was fought at Jebel Sahaba about 11,000 years ago, in a context where agriculture was in its infancy. The victims included women and children. Many were savaged by multiple wounds. One woman was stabbed twenty-two times. The strategy of massacre is found today among peoples who practise rudimentary agriculture. The Maring of New Guinea, for instance, normally try to wipe out the entire population of an enemy village when they raid it. 'Advanced' societies seem no different in this respect, except that their technologies of massacre tend to be more efficient.

Primatologists have witnessed so much warfare in the wild that many of them assume that our wars are part of a general pattern of behaviour among apes. A team led by the mould-breaking primatologist Jane Goodall, whose fieldwork uncovered numerous previously unknown aspects of chimpanzee behaviour, first saw it in Gombe late in 1974, when a group of chimpanzees sent out a party of eight warriors—including the group's alpha male and one sterile female—against neighbours to the south. The mature males did the killing, while the female provided whoops of encouragement, and a young member of the expedition watched and learned.[23] The primatologists kept up observations of prolonged, generally seasonal raids between the hostile groups. The war lasted four years. Further outbreaks in the same region have occurred periodically. The level of violence is horrific. Encounters take the form of raids from each community into the other's foraging grounds; when they find a lone male some of the invaders pinion him while others, yelling and leaping with frenzy, hurl rocks and batter him insensible, and usually to death, ripping at testicles, limbs, and fingers, crushing bones. The raiders typically abduct females, rather than killing them, but slaughter their young. Because among chimpanzees, as among humans, warbands are staffed almost entirely by males, at Ngogo in Uganda John Mitani of the University of Michigan has reported what looks like chimpanzee imperialism. Over a period of ten years, an exceptionally large group, some 150 strong, has made war a specialized strategy for increasing its resources. Bands of about twenty raiders infiltrate neighbouring territory, advancing in single file, cautiously and silently, picking off enemies one by one. The war ends with the extinction or absorption of the victim group and the annexation of the entire territory.[24] Robert Ardrey's nightmare of humans' ancestral 'killer apes' seems embodied in the tale.

These data do not, however, prove that humans are hard-wired for war. On the contrary, the evidence from chimpanzees puts war into the category of culturally variable behaviour, rather than an inescapable, universal, hard-wired trait. Primatologists in Côte d'Ivoire have watched for war but have not seen it.[25] The archaeological evidence suggests, at least equally, that the scale and degree on which societies organize violence made a huge leap when people started settling in permanent villages and practising tillage.

Talk of an 'aggression gene' makes no better sense than any other reference to straightforward, one-on-one mapping of genes and behaviours. If there were a preponderant violence gene in most modern people's DNA, it could be an effect of a warrior culture, not a cause of it. Not all cultures behave as if they have it, and, as we have seen (above, p. 42), the balance of probabilities is that the San, say, lack the supposed 'aggression' gene found among the Yanomamo because their culture eschews conflict, while the Yanomamo abound in aggression because their society exalts violence. In any case, it is doubtful whether the causes of war are best sought through the quest for an explanation of violence. The evidence from ape violence is impressive, and shows that chimpanzees can organize for bloodshed and battle in small bands, like human gangs of streetfighters and thugs; but it also suggests that violence-genes, if they exist, are not enough to make whole cultures warlike: for war, individual urges to violence have to be controlled by collaborative imperatives. War is, in one sense, more the result of collaborative than competitive tendencies. If one wants a gene to be responsible, it might be better to look for a team sport-gene than a violence-gene: war more resembles games like rugby or hockey than crimes like murder or mugging.

* * *

Though war has proved a disappointing line of enquiry, another, better opportunity arose for relating culture to biology in the context of a broader controversy about the origins of social problems in general. One of the twentieth century's most significant scientific disputes—significant, that is, in its direct impact on people's lives— was the 'nature *versus* nurture' debate. On one side were those who believed that character and capability are largely inherited or otherwise determined, and therefore not adjustable by 'social engineering'. On the other were those who believed in the power of experience and who insisted that culture can therefore affect our moral qualities and achievements. Broadly speaking the conflict again pitched the Left against the Right, with supporters of social radicalism ranged against those reluctant to make things worse by ill-considered attempts at improvement.

The controversy staggered and stalled and ended in stalemate, with an undogmatic consensus that emerged among experts in the 1920s and remained more or less intact for four decades. 'Hereditarians and environmentalists', according to the summary by the historian of the conflict, Hamilton Cravens, 'assumed the interaction of culture and nature . . . reaffirmed man's animal ancestry, his descent from the brutes, and at the same time they explained his social behaviour in cultural terms'.[26] During the late 1960s the debate recrystallized, however, in the pages of rival academic reports. Arthur Jensen, at the University of California—Berkeley, claimed that 80 per cent of intelligence is inherited (and, incidentally, that blacks are genetically inferior to whites).[27] Christopher Jencks and others at Harvard used IQ statistics to argue that aptitude is predominantly learned. The same argument was still raging in the 1990s, when Richard Herrnstein and Charles Murray published *The Bell Curve*, arguing that society has a hereditary 'cognitive elite' and an underclass, in which blacks are disproportionately represented.[28]

The IQ evidence was unconvincing: subjective tests, unreliable results. Developments in genetics, however, fed the anxieties. Genetic research in the latter half of the twentieth century seemed to confirm that more of our makeup is inherited than was previously supposed. In lectures in Dublin in 1944 the Austrian physicist Erwin Schrödinger speculated about what a gene might look like. He predicted that it would resemble a chain of basic units connected like the elements of a code. The nature of DNA as a kind of acid was not yet known, and Schrödinger expected a kind of protein, but the idea he outlined stimulated the search for the 'building blocks' of life.

A few years later, James Watson, a biology student in Chicago, read Schrödinger's paper. When he saw x-ray pictures of DNA, he realized that it would be possible to discover the structure Schrödinger had envisaged. He joined Francis Crick's project at Cambridge University to identify DNA's molecular form. They got a great deal of help (not very generously acknowledged) from a partner laboratory in London, where Rosalind Franklin suspected that DNA had a helical structure. It took a long time for the significance of the results to emerge fully: increasingly, Crick's and Watson's readers realized that genes in individual codes are responsible for some diseases. By analogy, behaviour, perhaps, could be regulated by changing the code. Two fundamental convictions have survived in most people's minds: that individuals make themselves, and that society is worth improving. Still, we find it hard to resist the feeling that genes circumscribe our freedom to equalize the differences between societies and individuals.

Progress in research has been so rapid that it has raised the spectre of a world recrafted, as if by Frankenstein or Dr Moreau, with unforeseeable consequences. People now have the power to make their biggest intervention in evolution yet—selecting 'unnaturally', not according to what is best adapted to the environment but according to what best matches agendas of human devising. 'Designer babies' are already being produced in cases where genetically transmitted diseases can be prevented, and the prospect that some societies will want to engineer human beings along the lines that eugenics prescribed in former times is entirely likely. Morally dubious visionaries are already talking about a world from which disease and deviancy alike have been excised.

Meanwhile, the genetic revolution filled in a gap in Darwin's description of evolution: genes provided what it is tempting to call a missing link in the way evolution works—explaining the means by which traits pass from parent to offspring. It became rationally impossible to doubt that Darwin's account of the origin of species was essentially right. Evolution seemed attractive again as a theory of potentially elastic power that could stretch to cover culture. The decoding of DNA, moreover, profoundly affected human self-perceptions, nudging people towards a materialist understanding of human nature. It has become increasingly hard to find room in human nature for non-material ingredients, such as mind and soul. 'The soul has vanished,' Crick announced.[29] Cognitive scientists subjected the human brain to ever more searching analysis. Neurological research showed that thought is an electrochemical process in which synapses fire and proteins are released. These results made it possible, at least, to claim that everything traditionally classed as a function of mind might take place within the brain.

Artificial intelligence research reinforced this claim—or tried to, with a new version of an old hope or fear: that minds may not even be organic but merely mechanical. Pablo Picasso painted an amorous machine in 1917. Automata were an old topic of romance, but after Karel Čapek introduced what he called robots in a play in 1921, mechanical humanoids featured increasingly as antiheroes of science fiction—the imaginary next stage of evolution, succeeding human-kind as the inheritors of Earth. In the second half of the century, computers proved so dexterous, first in making calculations, then in responding to their environments, that they seemed capable of settling the debate over whether mind and brain were different. The debate was unsatisfactory because people on different sides were really talking about different things: AI proponents were not particularly concerned to build machines with creative, artistic imaginations, or intuitive prop-erties, or with susceptibility to love or hatred—things opponents of the AI concept valued as indicators of a truly human mind. Questions of this kind could only be tested by working on ever more sophisticated robotics, and seeing whether robots with highly complex circuitry developed the cognitive properties humans have.

Progress in AI did, however, influence the debate about culture. Obviously the intelligence machines AI researchers bade for could hardly qualify as 'natural'. Nevertheless, they helped undermine people's confidence in 'mind–body dualism'—the belief that mind operates in ways beyond the scope of the brain. Maybe humans' thinking equipment is not merely mechanical, but if AI's assumptions are right, it must be biological, at best, and not metaphysical. Early in the twenty-first century, some AI exponents shifted focus to bio-logical, rather than mechanical modelling, attracted, in particular, by the impressive brainpower of cuttlefish and octopods, who can manipulate shells to obtain shelter and communicate by radiating colour-coded signals. According to some experiments, they can imitate observed behaviour—which is a prerequisite for culture.

*   *   *

In significance for the debate about the origins of cultural diversity, genetics and AI pale by comparison with the big new source of data in the 1960s and 1970s; the lessons that accrued (as we shall see in the next chapter) from the study of the cultures of non-human primates. It became possible to envisage what the ingenious Harvard entomologist, Edward Wilson, called a 'new synthesis' of nature and culture. Wilson loved his ants. I recall an occasion when my wife jokingly asked his advice on how to cope with an infestation of carpenter ants in our house. 'The important thing is,' Wilson smilingly replied, 'when you feed them honey, which is their favourite food, don't forget to add a little water. It's bad for them to eat too much if you don't dilute it.' In 1995, when an ill-tempered controversy with Harvard colleagues made Wilson think about taking a chair elsewhere, he decided to stay, because 'I could not bear to leave Harvard's ant collection'.[30]

Consciously, I think, Wilson made an implicit contribution to political debate. He favoured nature over nurture in the dispute about the origins of social problems. He found cultural relativism disturbing and looked for arguments in support of the superiority of some societies over others. He helped to create a powerful scientific constituency for the view that differences between societies arise from evolutionary pressures and for the inference that some societies can be ranked accordingly as more evolved than others and therefore, in a sense, as better. He often insisted that biological and environmental constraints do not detract from human freedom, but his texts seemed bound in iron, with little spinal flexibility, and close-printed without space for freedom between the lines. He imagined a visitor from another planet cataloguing humans along with all the other species on Earth and shrinking 'the humanities and social sciences to specialized branches of biology'.[31] Ants and bees were his models for understanding humans, as gulls and geese were Lorenz's. Humans differ from insects, according to Wilson, mainly in being individually competitive, whereas ants and bees are more deeply social: they function for collective advantage.

The comparison led Wilson to his great insight. What he called 'flexibility' or variation between human cultures is, he suggested, the result of individual differences in behaviour 'magnified at the group level' by the multiplicity of interactions. That seems a promising line of thought, since there is, as we shall see, an observable link between the size and numbers of intercommunicating groups, the range of exchange between them, and the cultural diversity they exhibit. Wilson was on less secure ground in supposing that the mechanism that makes cultural change possible is genetic. By the time he wrote his most influential text, *Sociobiology*, in 1975, researchers had already discovered or confidently postulated genes for introversion, neurosis, athleticism, psychosis, and numerous other human variables. So it was theoretically possible, Wilson argued, that evolution 'strongly selected' genes for social flexibility, too, although there was and is no direct evidence.[32]

He also reasoned that lack of competition from other species has meant that humans can occupy a wide range of possible social configurations, just as they can dominate an extraordinary range of physical environments; the argument seems fallacious and the premise false. Humans have colonized most of our habitats in defiance of competitors; and in any case there is no reason, as far as I know, why cultural diversity should not promote human success in competition with rival species. It might well be an advantage, since the more cultures construct means of coping with competitor species, the greater the likelihood that a successful strategy will emerge. Strictly speaking, if cultural diversity were not conducive to the survival of species, it would fail to match the basic criterion of a successful evolutionary adaptation.

Wilson admitted the possibility of 'nongenetic' cultural traits that 'could be arrayed alongside biology'.[33] But these were only the fastest-changing kinds, such as fashions and tastes, which are too volatile to explain genetically. Universal features of culture, such as incest prohibitions, taboos, totemism, magic, religious beliefs, and rituals must, according to Wilson, be genetically encoded. Their emergence would be predictable, even in a society built from scratch in isolation.[34] That may be true, but it still leaves unexplained the practical variety of these features' forms that different societies display.

Working in parallel with Wilson, but independently, the equally ingenious Richard Dawkins produced what, on the face of it, seemed an appealing take on the question the year after *Sociobiology* appeared. Like Wilson, he claimed to believe in human freedom to elude genetic inheritance, but never made it clear how. Unlike Wilson, who was conciliatory in his language about religion, Dawkins was an apostle of atheism. Though he was a zoologist by training and spent a quarter of a century as a zoology tutor at Oxford, he was more gifted as a writer and populist than as a researcher. He produced delightfully eloquent books, becoming a professor not of science but of the 'public understanding' of it, occupying a chair specially created for him.

Whereas Wilson argued that cultures are collections of evolved individuals, whose inherited characteristics determine what happens to human communities, Dawkins claimed that 'units', of which, he said, culture is composed, behave in ways so closely analogous to genes as to conform to evolutionary rules. Biota evolve as genes replicate. Genes, according to the standard figure of speech, are units of information or fragments of code. Dawkins thought culture is composed of similar bits of information, which he called 'memes'. Successful memes replicate spontaneously, using and sometimes abusing their hosts, just as viruses do. They evolve, for instance, by selection of environmentally successful variations or by way of competition among units within culture, just as genes replicate within organisms. Culture spreads like a virus, colonizing minds the way microbes invade bodies.[35]

In outline, there was nothing new about drawing analogies between cultural and genetic change. 'Cultural heredity is analogous to genetic heredity,' wrote an earlier ant-enthusiast, the Chicago zoologist, Alfred Emerson, in 1965.[36] Earlier researchers preceded Dawkins in claiming to be able to split culture into discrete units.[37] Wilson called such units 'culturgens'.[38] But none of Dawkins's predecessors quite anticipated his key innovation: the division of culture into units that were not only discrete but also self-replicating. Emerson, for instance, even endorsed 'the valid division line between social and biological sciences', because he could see no medium, other than ideas transmitted from teacher to learner, for what he called 'social heredity'.[39] The name Dawkins coined for the replicators he postulated was irresistibly cute. Thanks, I think, to his deftness as a wordsmith, the notion was staggeringly successful: to borrow one of the author's own favourite similes, it spread like a virus among his readers and their readers in turn. 'Memes' passed instantly into the realm of popular wisdom. 'Memetics' became an academic sub-discipline.

Yet on close examination the whole notion seems vacuous, not least because there is no evidence for the existence of memes, in the sense of evolved units of culture, or of any mechanism analogous to heredity, by which evolution could select them for transmission to other cultures. Unlike genes, which can be transmitted intact, from one generation to another between bodies that cannot modify them, culture is transformed in the act of transmission, between active brains that sometimes modify it—by misunderstanding it, or consciously revising it, or reacting to it with some new inspiration. So, if culture could be broken up into constituent units, they would not resemble self-mutating replicators so much as mutable representations.[40]

According to Dawkins, a meme is a 'replicating entity' and 'a cultural trait [that] may have evolved in the way that it has, simply because it is advantageous to itself'[41]—not to the people or society who adopt it. It would be inconsistent with Dawkins's concept even to speak of memes being 'adopted' in any sense that implies conscious adoption: rather, they colonize their host societies, somewhat as parasites infest bodies. This is a doubly unsatisfactory doctrine. First, it requires another set of explanations to account for why different traits achieve different levels of social influence: it is easy to accept, for instance, that genes for brown eyes should prevail over those for blue eyes in a body where both are inherited; but the same mechanisms cannot explain why, say, Islam should prevail over Christianity in a society with access to both.[42] Second, in the imaginary world of the meme elements of culture have no way of emerging except by a form of self-replication reminiscent of spontaneous generation: innovations occur by way of random mutation, rather than as a result of human inventiveness.

Even Dawkins finds this an unsustainable way of thinking about culture. He credits Socrates, Leonardo, Copernicus, and Marconi with 'contributions' of 'meme-complexes' commendable for their longevity. He admits, in effect, that human minds originate cultural traits—which is what everyone's experience suggests. If that is so, it is unnecessary to endow memes with a life of their own. Humans think them up in the first place; so humans can adopt them and reject them as they wish.

Indeed, what Dawkins calls cultural traits can all be fairly represented as ideas, because everything else he includes—technologies, techniques, tunes, teachings—does not appear on earth fully formed or leap from culture to culture except, in the first instance, as purely mental facts, communicated between minds. Even in the case of an artefact that arrives by trade or chance in a milieu where it is unfamiliar, and spreads by being copied, it is not effectively transmitted from its culture of origin to its host culture unless and until a recipient conceives an idea of it. At the risk of oversimplification, we might summarize the case against memetics like this: in genetics, mutations arise randomly and spread according to evolutionary laws, whereas in culture, innovations arise consciously and spread capriciously. Unsurprisingly, despite its short-lived vogue, and the passion of some enduring partisans,[43] memetics has become part of the lumber of sociobiology, rejected even by scientists keen to maintain faith in biological models of culture change. In the second edition of their textbook on cultural evolution, the biologist Kevin Laland and the evolutionary psychologist Gillian Brown have simply dropped the chapter on memetics in its entirety.[44] The doyen of British sociology, Walter Runciman, who used his immense influence admirably to try to reconcile sociologists to science, clung to the word 'meme' in the distillation of his life's work, *The Theory of Cultural and Social Selection*, which appeared in 2009. He defined the term, however, more strictly than Dawkins as 'packages of information', leaving 'practices'—which are what culture consists of—out of the category and shifting the explanation for the success of some such packages away from the supposedly inherent self-advantage of the unit to 'the features of the environment which do or not favour the reproduction and diffusion of the memes'.[45] 'Meme' was a term of convenience for Runciman, eluding circumlocution, without the magical, angelic, or demonic nature or function it had in mainstream memetics.

Dawkins was right, I think, to suppose that when culture begins, biology yields the driving seat and culture's own dynamic takes over. He was wrong to think that ensuing changes are properly called 'evolution' and happen in ways closely analogous to changes in organic life.

* * *

In any case, we do not have to rely on speculative vapourizings for a sense of how cultural changes happen. There are plenty of empirical data, which the memetics fanatics overlook, in the field known as diffusion studies, which sociologists, economists, and business students till freely and deeply in their own work, but which has still-unrealized implications for the understanding of cultural change in general. Diffusion students focus on innovation, but all cultural change starts as innovation; so their findings are relevant and, on the whole, they subvert memetics.

The scholar with the best claim to have founded diffusion studies, or at least to have launched the diffusion studies movement, was Everett Rogers, whose 1962 book *Diffusion of Innovations* might have made a good case-study, attracting imitators, generating allied research, and diffusing in its own, right around the world. His starting-point was in agricultural economics, the discipline to which his background as a farmer's boy called him. When he was only 5 years old, Rogers found his father's selective attitudes to new farming technologies puzzling. Dad embraced mechanical innovations, but distrusted hybrid seed corn, which the state of Iowa promoted heavily in the 1930s. Like some of his neighbours, Rogers senior feared sacrificing independence to the experts and committing himself to reliance on the suppliers of new seed, instead of selecting it himself from his previous season's corn. The rest of young Rogers's life was devoted to making sense of his childhood experience.

Successive editions of his *magnum opus*, though tedious to read, do a great job of summarizing his research and that of the followers he inspired. Rogers thought he was engaged in a scientific enterprise. He aimed to expose scientific laws that would predict which innovations would succeed, and how fast people would take them up: the illusion of predictability attracted funds from business and governments and made the diffusion discipline rich and active. Rogers devised mathematical models that are still useful to some forecasters. He devised a standard narrative of the spread of innovation, dividing the process into phases according to the rate of adoption, and produced descriptions of the adopters most likely to emerge at each phase. These were convincing mainly, perhaps, because they were platitudinous: young, educated, large-scale operators would likely be among early adopters, for instance, while the poor and old would bring up the rear. Some of Rogers's nostrums were of the kind you hardly need expensive research to anticipate: if you want to promote innovation, get opinionmakers on your side, appeal to the existing prejudices of the community, advertise.

The most interesting findings of diffusion research, for our present purposes, were of a different kind, demonstrating the prevalence of wild cards in the pack and the importance of serendipity and misunderstanding in making some innovations catch on. Most surprising of all the revelations of diffusion research is the fact that what an innovation is hardly matters to its chances of success. The nature of an innovation—how good or bad it is, how economical, how attractive, how flexible—has far less impact than the cultural context that receives or rejects it. Among Rogers's key examples, one of his most engaging stories was of 'Serendipity in the Discovery of Warfarin'. The research that produced the drug in the 1930s was the result of an investigation into the cause of haemorrhaging in cows; people accepted it, a generation after its discovery, with an extraordinarily counter-intuitive kind of enthusiasm, as the world's most popular rat poison and treatment for human heart disease.[46] Similarly, the video games-player is among the most mysterious success stories in modern marketing, with propensities to amuse and entertain utterly disproportionate to the costs of the games; yet video games displaced traditional competitors of smaller cost and greater power to stimulate, such as the bat and ball or the book. The Nintendo company turned the new technology into a phenomenal world-conqueror by actually suppressing the fact that it was a kind of computer and, until well into the 1990s, inducing most purchasers to forgo most of its functions.[47] According to Everett Rogers, in what sounds like a fictitious case, 'Dr "Chicken" Davis, a US poultry expert' introduced millions of battery chickens into Eastern Nigeria in the 1960s. Despite the project's evident unsuitability, it earned 'handsome profits' and, for Dr Davis, the award of:

> a hero's medal by the President of Nigeria. Two weeks later, a poultry epidemic swept through Eastern Nigeria, killing all the imported birds ... Within a year of 'Chicken' Davis's departure, only an unpleasant memory remained of his work. Not a Western Chicken survived.[48]

Rogers shared a prejudice with evolutionists: the success of an innovation, as of a species, would depend on relative advantage, and among the hard-headed US farmers who were the early subjects of his research 'the economic aspects of relative advantage' counted for a lot. Still, even that cost-sensitive constituency was more prone to value an innovation for promoting physical comfort than for restraining cost. Relative advantage generally proved to be more 'an important part of the message' advertisers spread than of the product itself.[49] In the whirligig of fashion, no one stops to ask whether a shorter hemline is a superior adaptation to the environment. Over and over again, diffusion studies showed that culture is crucial. Women in a Peruvian village resist water-boiling for sanitation because their traditional medicine identify it as a remedy appropriate only for the sick.[50] Typists resist rational keyboard layouts because of traditional investment in the QWERTYUIOP system.[51] Balinese irrigators leave fields fallow because their religious cosmology so commands, not because it makes ecological sense (though, by coincidence, it does).[52] US farmers with elementary scientific education always want to test a product for themselves before adopting it, while counterparts in Colombia will accept an innovation on good authority.[53] The Amish are notorious for resisting consumerism, but Rogers found them 'very innovative in adopting new ideas that fit with their religious and family values', such as sustainability strategies and organic farming techniques.[54] In his story 'How the refrigerator got its hum', Rogers told how the gas-powered 'fridge, which dominated the market until after the First World War, was more economical, more robust, and much quieter than its hum-crazy electric counterpart. But the electricity companies mounted the investment and mobilized the publicity to drive the gas version out of the domestic market in the USA.[55] Some Australian aboriginal peoples refuse to kindle fire, but accept it ready-kindled from neighbouring tribes. The world is full of similar examples of peoples whose cultural prejudices have mandated apparently irrational adhesion to inferior technology or irrational rejection of advantageous innovations: people who have abandoned navigation, or the bow and arrow, or firearms, or blood transfusions.[56]

Caprice and culture also combine to ensure that bad technologies drive out good ones. The snowmobile almost destroyed the economy of the Skolt Sami when it replaced reindeer sleds in the late 1960s.[57] David Edgerton, the renowned historian of science at Imperial College, London, has gathered many fascinating examples in a book that undermines a common form of twentieth-century self-congratulation: the myth that technology has been uniformly progressive in recent times.[58] Some of his most striking examples relate to military technology. The atom bomb, the author argues, was not cost-effective compared with the conventional arms sacrificed to the costs of research. The German V-rockets cost half a billion dollars but were grotesque failures. General Patton longed for cavalry in North Africa and Italy. The contraceptive pill almost drove the condom off the market, but the old technology has proved itself more useful, cheaper, and safer in the long run. From personal knowledge, we can all add at length to the list of examples. In selecting new culture, cultures respond to calculations not of potential advantage so much as of existing coherence.

Like fashions and technical innovations, food taboos illustrate the peculiar intractability of culture to influences from outside itself. All cultures have such taboos: indeed, like incest prohibitions, they might be classed as defining features of human cultures. Typically, enquirers have tried to explain them by seeking some rational, material, scientific motive for preventing the consumption of certain resources. Cicero was first in a long line of theorists to allege economic reasons—where bovines, for instance, are too valuable to eat, elites sacralize them as a conservation measure.[59] But this must be false, since people eat beef in many places where bovines provide vital services in ploughing, transport, and dairying, whereas sacralization greatly diminishes cows' general exploitability. Food bans are not designed primarily to be ecologically adaptive, or to promote biodiversity, or to spare threatened species—though such consequences sometimes ensue. Nor are taboos applied for reasons of health or hygiene—that is a long-discredited bit of silliness—though they may have beneficial effects on practitioners' bodies. There is little or no difference in cleanliness, for instance, between meats Moses categorized as forbidden and those he permitted. The great anthropologist Mary Douglas made the nearest approach to a convincingly systematic justification of the Mosaic rules, arguing that the prohibited creatures are anomalous in their own classes and that integrity, necessary for holiness, is offended by terrestrial creatures that wriggle, or airborne ones with four feet, or those that are cloven-hoofed but non-ruminant, like the pig and the camel.[60] The pretence that health or ecology are at stake vanishes.

It is pointless to seek rational or material explanations for taboos because they are essentially, necessarily super-rational. The lack of any rational purpose for particular taboos makes them socially functional, because they bind those who respect them and brand those who do not. If they had any objective justification—if, for instance, they induced health, or improved nutrition, or protected threatened species—they would not work, because they would appeal as much to outsiders as to those in the group. Permitted foods feed identity, excluded foods define it. In Fiji, no man may eat the plant or creature that is his totem, though a neighbour may eat of it freely. Plants that grow near a shrine or in a graveyard are taboo, but the same plants may be eaten if harvested elsewhere. Bemba women must protect their cooking hearths from practitioners of unpurified sex. Among the Batlokwa of Botswana, pubescent boys may not have honey. Teenage girls are not allowed eggs or fish. New mothers may not eat with their hands.[61]

None of these examples on its own makes culture look like an entirely autonomous system, changing from within itself without input from genetics or environment. But in sum they do suggest, first, that culture has a dynamic of its own, the power of which greatly exceeds that of other sources of change; and, second, that it operates in people's minds: the decision to adopt an innovation or imitate some other community's behaviour is rarely rational, but it is always conscious. Cultural traits do not replicate like genes—people accept or reject them according to criteria of their own—criteria that have nothing to do with the merits of the innovations, or their potential for survival, or for enhancing the survival of the group.

Neither sociobiology nor memetics succeeded in their day in explaining culture satisfactorily. They operated, however, in a uniquely favourable context—not just because the prestige of science in the twentieth-century world disposed people generally to seek or accept professedly scientific explanations for everything, but also because, over the last half century or so, gradually, increasingly, the effort to understand culture has benefited from a previously unknown source of new information. All earlier enquiries proceeded *a priori*, with no evidence to go on except human culture itself and no standards of comparison, because of the conviction that humans are a uniquely cultural species. Now, however, we can do better. We are not alone. We know that there are—and in the deep past have been—other cultures 'out there' and that we have an opportunity, unavailable to our predecessors, to learn about ourselves from them. My own first lesson in the comparative invocation of non-human cultures came—though I did not appreciate it at the time—when I was 5 years old. It is now time to summon up the memory.

4

THE CHIMPANZEES' TEA PARTY

The discovery of non-human cultures

M^{ost} readers are probably not old enough to remember it; but it
is one of my most vivid childhood memories. When I was little,
I lived with grandparents near the London Zoo where, every after-
noon, the chimpanzees' keepers laid out a tea party for them. Trestle
tables, spread with white or gingham cloths, bore pots of tea, jugs of
milk, plates of sandwiches, and cakes. The result was chaos. The
chimps spilt the tea, smeared the jam, clambered over the table, and
used the cakes as inefficiently wielded missiles, while we children and
most of the adults present stood around laughing.

I am penitent at the recollection of my politically incorrect conduct—
a rank offence against the chimps' dignity. Now, however, I suspect the
joke was on us and that, if the chimps had sleeves, they would be
laughing down them. Desmond Morris, the charismatic zookeeper,
suspected that they deliberately hammed up their performance to please
the crowd. But the reason for my present discomfort runs deeper than
that. Why did we humans find the chimps' antics entertaining? Most
of us onlookers were children, and glimpsed, perhaps, some affinity
between the apes and our own former, undomesticated, infant selves,
who had not yet learned to observe table manners. Perhaps we admired
or envied their freedom to be babyish. But the chimps were ridiculous
chiefly, as I recall, because they were victims of a deeper dilemma: to us
children they were like us, but without the opportunity, without the
necessary nature, to grow up in the same way. Like clowns imitating the

lion-tamer or a clod-hopper aspiring to balletics and tripping over his feet, they were attempting something beyond them. Though I should not have put it this way when I was 5 years old, I think the reason we humans found them amusing was that we assumed that our species was uniquely cultural, and that other animals were simply incapable of understanding that a meal could be for more than eating. A human tea party is an opportunity for practising decorum, respecting order, subscribing to cultural norms. Ideas of that sort—according to the assumptions of my childhood—were simply inaccessible to any other creatures.

When I became a man I put away childish things. We now know that chimpanzees do have culture. They even have foodways that vary from group to group. Humans would look as risible at a food-distribution event among hunting chimps as the chimps did at a human-style tea party. Chimpanzees, moreover, are only one among an increasing number of species to exhibit cultural behaviour to observers who look for it. To me, the discovery that there are lots of cultural animals is the most significant new science of my lifetime, eclipsing the exploration of space, the Moon landings, the decoding of the human genome, and the suppression of many diseases, because it transforms our sense of who we are. We are not alone. The behaviours that our forefathers thought made them special turn out to be routine—or, at least, potentially accessible to other animals. Meanwhile, many observations and experiments have cast doubt on belief that humans have unique cognitive properties. For example, as we shall see, non-human apes prove to be self-aware, and show sensibilities hard to distinguish in practice from the senses of morality and transcendence formerly thought to be human peculiarities.

By the end of the twentieth century, ethicists were taking the evidence into account, campaigning for 'ape rights' or for the redefinition of the moral community to embrace great apes. That seems premature, since we have not yet created a moral community that includes all humans, except in frustrated liberal imaginations; it also seems illogical, since it would be almost as 'speciesist'—and equally so in principle—to include five species as to admit one, while excluding others. The proper basis for a moral community, I think, is to include all who seek admission to it.[1]

Even if it were true that peculiar elements of culture could be used to define humankind, it would not necessarily justify us in hiving our species off from the rest of creation in a special category of our own. In some ways, the culture test has served its advocates as a secular substitute for a religious test—an attempt to find an exclusive criterion of humankind without appealing to the soul or to differentiation by divine intervention. But the attempt has failed because, in any case, non-human animals really do have culture.

* * *

The discovery of non-human culture began among observers of macaque monkeys on the island of Koshima by Japanese zoologists in the 1950s, shortly after I began to attend the chimpanzees' tea party. Scientists actually saw a monkey genius—a young female whom her human observers named Imo—introduce two behavioural innovations, which other monkeys copied until they became universal in the group. Imo was less than 2 years old. But she displayed amazingly precocious talents as an innovator and teacher. Her tribe loved to eat freshly cleaned sweet potatoes, scraping the dirt off with their hands. But Imo found out how to wash the vegetables by rinsing them in a stream. She passed the knowledge on, first to her mother and then, gradually, to other relatives, who taught others in turn until most of the tribe had mastered the idea. Eventually, only a few old males failed to adopt the practice. Meanwhile, the sea, rather than the stream, became the favoured location for it.

To this day, the monkeys of Imo's tribe wash their sweet potatoes before eating them, and teach their youngsters to do the same, even if you give them ready-washed specimens off a supermarket shelf. So the custom seems not only to have been transmitted by learning but also to have survived its usefulness—becoming 'pure' culture, like the perpetuation of a rite (although the possibility remains that, by transference to the sea, the practice has acquired a new function, as a means of salting the tubers in brine).

In 1956, Imo made another breakthrough. The monkeys enjoyed wheat that human benefactors scattered for them on the beach. They had trouble, however, separating it from clinging sand. Imo dropped the grains in water. Because the sand was heavier than the cereal, it sank while Imo scooped up the wheat. Again, she taught the practice to the tribe.[2] She excited the scientific world because she helped to prove that humans are not the only species with behaviours that become routines or rituals, practised not necessarily or solely because they are materially useful but because they are traditional or conventional. Since Imo's feats, observers have noticed other innovations emerge and spread in groups of Japanese macaques. At Nagano the monkeys bathe in hot springs. At Arashiyama they play with stones.[3]

Almost before the scientific world had taken stock of the sweet potato-washing revolution among the macaques, studies of chimpanzees switched the focus of interest in non-human culture. The brilliant fieldworker Jane Goodall first got into trouble with the scientific establishment when she was a young researcher in the 1960s, because she did for chimps what any good anthropological student would do with his or her subjects: she sympathized with them. She called them by names instead of following the prevailing convention and using numbers. She referred to each chimp by the personal pronouns that matched his or her sex, instead of calling all of them, 'it'.[4] Happily, because she had no scientific training, she was unprejudiced by ethologists' tribal assumptions. When her professors at Cambridge told her she had 'done everything wrong. Everything', she appealed to higher authority: her dog, Rusty. 'You cannot share your life,' she says, 'in a meaningful way with any kind of animal with a reasonably well-developed brain and not realize that animals have personalities.'[5] Under the impact of the evidence Jane Goodall accumulated, primatologists came to realize that, albeit to a much smaller extent than human beings, chimpanzees have all or almost all the features of culture that were formerly thought to be peculiarly human, including language, war, food-distribution conventions, and political habits.[6]

The critical evidence is of two kinds: not just actual observations of learning processes, such as the macaques of Koshima had demonstrated, but also variations in behaviour from tribe to tribe, place to place, and time to time. Divergent behaviour is *prima facie* evidence of culture (though not of course conclusive in itself) because genetics alone cannot explain it, save in exceptional instances. Generally, genes are not that different, in a single species, from place to place. Huge divergences often happen, moreover, in identical or very similar physical and climatic settings, where environmental influences cannot account for the differences.

In 1999, a group of leading primatologists sifted the studies available up to that time and found that at least thirty-nine widespread procedures varied significantly between chimpanzee groups—including probing and pounding for food, exchanging gestures of comfort or grooming, and using leaves to clean bodies or treat wounds.[7] Research since then has added a further impressive activity to the list: whether in captivity or in the wild, chimps make slightly but significantly different calls to alert each other to danger or food.[8] In Tanzania, different groups of chimpanzees have developed different practices— one is tempted to say 'different rites'—of mutual grooming. Different chimpanzee communities have different technologies; some hunt quite intensively, while others do not.[9] All chimpanzees in Tanzania, when they groom, eat each other's lice; but at Gombe, they first carefully make a pile of leaves and place the louse on top of it, whereas at Mahale they fold the parasite in a single leaf as if making a sandwich, and in the Tai forest they squash the flea on a forearm. These procedures seem to have some social function, as other chimps gather to watch them.[10] Toshisada Nishida, a veteran hero of the study of animal culture, who has devoted a lifetime to the chimpanzees of Mahale, has gathered a great lexicon of twelve peculiar features of the way they behave, most of which he finds inexplicable by reference to ecological influences. The distinctive elements in Mahale culture include sweeping ants from hollow branches to give youngsters a chance to feed on the pupae; licking rocks and old fruit trees; teaching offspring to accept unpalatable but therapeutic herbs; drumming on the metal walls of the primatologists' huts; and the most famous oddity of Mahale—clasping hands during grooming.[11]

The varieties of behaviour on display in different groups of chimps are matched among other primates by evidence of cultural divergence among communities of a single species. In Ethiopia, baboon societies in the highlands include tightly controlled harems herded by individual males, whereas the baboons of the savanna contract much looser relationships of 'serial monogamy'; the respective environments are different, but not different enough to explain the differences in behaviour. In Gabon, gorillas in Lopé eat mound-building termites but not weaver ants; neighbours at Belinga eat weaver ants but scorn the termites. Different groups of primates of a single species have their own ways of dealing with peculiarities in their environments: using leaves as cushions, for instance, where ground is very moist, or strewing sticks as a form of matting to protect themselves from thorns.

Recently established landmark cases include those of orang-utans and capuchin monkeys. In January 2003, for instance, press reports revealed good 'news for orang-utans'. According to *Science* magazine, they are 'almost human'. This is a resonant claim, because of the key part orangs have played in the history of human self-re-evaluation. Jenny inspired Darwin (above, p. 60), who, in turn, was perhaps impressed by the works of James Stewart, Lord Monboddo, the late eighteenth-century advocate of the humanity of orang-utans. Monboddo's agenda was secularist—the typical agenda of the Enlightenment: he wanted to prove that language is a product of culture, not a miracle God implanted in human minds; so he strained credulity by seeking a creature at once supposedly human and speechless. In a novel of 1818 by the comic genius, Thomas Love Peacock, the hero is an orang-utan who, possessing 'every rational faculty except speech', acquires a reputation as 'a profound but cautious thinker' and is rewarded with a baronetcy and election as a Member of Parliament. It is delightful to find *Science* magazine in the twenty-first century vindicating Monboddo against Peacock's satire.

In some communities, orang-utans 'use napkins when eating' and 'kiss each other good night'. In some they 'use leaves for gloves when handling prickly vegetation', while others 'wield leafy branches as parasols to protect them from the sun'. Like human societies, orang-utan groups develop distinctive ways of behaving towards each other. The orang-utans of Borneo and Sumatra resemble *homo ludens*—social humans whose interactions include play. Their games vary from place to place. In Borneo the orang-utans play by knocking over dead trees, bestride them as they fall and leap off just before impact. This game, however, is unknown to the orang-utans of Sumatra.[12] Orangs at Suaq Bambling in Sumatra make unique spluttering noises when building nests and use sticks to comb some favourite fruits out of the mass of hairy foliage that encases them.[13]

From a purely primatological perspective—even before one considers the implications for the study of man—this is a remarkable revelation, because orang-utans, who forage alone, have traditionally been classed as 'unsocial apes'. The solitary wanderings of adult males—who typically spend less than 10 per cent of the time in company—have always impressed observers and have inspired a lyrical myth of lovelorn loneliness, or as eighteenth-century European writers commonly said, 'melancholy'. Though, in understandable ignorance of the differences between great apes, Rousseau sometimes called them 'gorillas' and even muddled them up in his mind with chimpanzees, he obviously had romantic accounts of orang-utans in mind when he described the pre-social condition of 'these truly natural men whose race', as if arrested at a primitive stage of development, 'never had occasion to develop its latent faculties'.[14] For Rousseau, who was casual and promiscuous in his own mating habits, the fact that orang-utan males and females come together briefly to breed was evidently appealing. Yet the societies of orang-utans, like human societies, do have peculiar conventions and, albeit to a modest extent by human standards, they do become different from one another. In these respects, the creatures justify the name they are known by, which their Malay neighbours gave them uncounted years ago. It means 'man of the woods'.

Capuchin monkeys are, in some ways, an even more remarkable recent addition to the list of cultural animals. In Costa Rica they learn a game that involves passing bits of each other's hair from mouth to mouth, apparently with the aim of seeing how long they can make the sample last before all the hairs have fallen to the ground.[15] They prefer to associate with human experimenters who imitate their behaviour—demonstrating a link between socialization and learning.[16] In captivity and in the wild, capuchins seem to prefer to conform to food gathering strategies demonstrated by the alpha male or by a majority of other members of the group, even when they discover equally good alternatives of their own.[17] Studies of other monkeys yield similar results,[18] but the capuchin evidence is exceptionally copious and has implications for the antiquity of culture. Capuchins split from the branch of evolution that produced *homo sapiens* about 30 million years ago. This raises the presumption that culture may have a history behind it so long that it dwarfs human beings and makes us seem pretty ordinary among the products of evolution.

Reticence among academics in acknowledging the force of the evidence for non-human culture reflects professional prejudices. Some philosophers and theologians have heavy investments in traditional evaluations of human uniqueness. Some students of language are reluctant to admit that a variety of animals might have it. Cultural anthropologists, zoologists, and primatologists, however, who are the professionals with the most relevant experience, are almost united in recognizing that all primates—not just humans—evince cultural behaviour.[19]

*   *   *

For understanding humans, I rely on comparisons with other primates, especially apes, and above all on chimpanzees, for obvious reasons: they most resemble us; among surviving species they are closest to us in evolutionary terms; and studies of them abound. Studies of other social animals, however, show impressively similar results, suggesting that not only is culture peculiarly human merely as a matter of degree, but also that it is by no means peculiarly primate or peculiarly simian, except in the same sense. Nowadays research is focussed on examples of what looks like cultural behaviour in dolphins, elephants, marsupials, and even songbirds, bears, musk oxen, caribou, hares, rats, bats, octopods, crows, and pigeons.[20] In some of these cases the evidence is inconclusive, or equivocal, or relates to potentialities for cultural rather than actual cultural behaviour. Rats and rabbits, for instance, can pick up foraging habits as a result of scenting the residue of new food-sources on each other's fur; this is 'learning' only in a rather different sense from what we find in primates. Some birds do innovate in song and imitate each others' innovations, but we should hesitate to call them cultural on the basis of a single apparently cultural activity. Sea otters crack mollusc shells on rocks in California, but not in Alaska; but this is, as far as we know, their only mutual idiosyncrasy. Some fish copy each others' feeding habits.[21] Claims of culturally embedded learning have been advanced on behalf of meerkats on the ground that female pups, who spend relatively more time than their male counterparts with adults, respond to alarm calls faster than males.[22] The argument clearly exceeds the evidence.

On the other hand, the case for culture among dolphins is almost irresistibly strong. Like humans, they spend a relatively long period— between three and six years—under their mothers' tutelage with plenty of opportunity to learn acquired behaviour; so in principle they are likely candidates for culture. Divergent behaviour among groups of bottle-nosed dolphins is well documented. Among those of Laguna, Brazil, observers have recorded a unique hunting strategy in place, among generation after generation, for over a hundred and fifty years: the dolphins collaborate with human fishermen, ushering prey towards the nets in order to be able to plunder the catch with relative ease. In Shark Bay, Australia, dolphins employ two hunting strategies unknown elsewhere—protecting their noses with sponges when diving, and herding prey close to the shoreline. Students of the behaviour of killer whales and sperm whales have been impressed by the fact that they have 'dialects'—an admittedly small range, typically encompassing between about seven and thirty items of meaningful vocalization—peculiar to particular groups. In Argentina, killer whales raid beaches to capture seals; mothers rush the beaches with their young offspring even when there are no seals around—which looks like an instance of teaching. Communities of whales in different locations also have their own hunting strategies and, off Vancouver Island, when groups from the same community meet they line up facing each other and remain still for between ten and thirty seconds before mingling. An anthropologist observing similarly peculiar behaviour in a human community would not hesitate to call it a ritual.[23]

Evidence is piling up that elephants, too, are cultural animals. Humans have long expressed an affinity with elephants because of the eerie sense of something like reverence that they, like us, seem to evince for their sick, dying, and dead: feeding them, moving them, covering them with foliage, guarding them from predators, revisiting their bones. Their longevity and the protracted interactions between generations that are normal in elephant societies create plenty of opportunities to teach and learn. Mothers teach young calves to socialize and to forage. Other activities, though not decisive in themselves, raise presumptions about the cultural nature of elephant societies. When they set off on a foraging trail, members of a herd negotiate with each other before making a collective decision about which direction to take. The social context of the way elephants learn seems obvious, because when unprepared individuals take to the wild, they often respond to other elephants with puzzlement or aggression.[24] So far, however, the published studies show relatively little evidence of behaviour diverging between groups of elephants, compared with unquestionably cultural creatures.[25]

As examples of culture multiply, I expect we shall come to divide cultural animals into two classes, according to the kind of learning that turns behaviour into custom: learning by imitation alone, and learning by conscious teaching. Like other primates and dolphins, humans exhibit both, and both are probably essential for fast rates of cultural change. Imitation alone tends to produce societies of conformists, who resist change. Teaching increases the opportunities for varieties of behaviour to take root, and gives rogue innovators chances to spread their ideas. A few laboratory experiments—only a few have been attempted—on how humans adopt cultural changes suggest this. Conformists predominate: most people will imitate what most other people do, whether the choice is between crops to plant or arrowheads to hunt with. But successful innovators inspire waves of imitators.[26]

*   *   *

Self-ascribed members of our own species should not be reluctant to acknowledge that other species have culture: we know, after all, from paleoarchaeology, that our *homo sapiens* ancestors coexisted for thousands of years with other cultural hominids, and that literally hundreds of thousands of years of previous archaeological records embed the evidence of what look like cultural practices among predecessor species.

The most challenging discoveries have come from the graves of Neanderthals. Save for an accident of evolution, this species might still be around to challenge our human sense of our uniqueness. If one were to meet a Neanderthal in the street, one might experience the same sense of kinship—of instant recognition across differences of aspect and problems of communication—typical of encounters between enlightened modern humans from different races or cultures.

Neanderthals looked rather like us and behaved rather as ancestors of our own species did. To judge from specimens excavated so far, they had, if anything, bigger brains than *homo sapiens*, comparable minds, and highly similar forms of culture. A Neanderthal family is buried together at La Ferrassie: two adults of different sexes are curled into the foetal position characteristic of Neanderthal burials all over what are now Europe and the Near East. Nearby, three children of between 3 and 5 years old and a new-born baby lie with flint tools and fragments of animal bones. The remains of an undeveloped foetus, extracted from the womb, is interred with the same dignity as the other family members, albeit without the tools. Other Neanderthal burials have more valuable grave goods: a pair of ibex horns accompanied one youth in death, a sprinkling of ochre was strewn on another. At Shanidar, in what is now Iraq, an old man—who had survived in the care of his community for many years after the loss of the use of an arm, severe disablement to both legs, and blindness in one eye—lies with traces of flowers and medicinal herbs.

All these cases—and many others of what look like ritual Neanderthal burials—have been challenged by sceptical scholars: explained away as the results of accident or fraud. The survival of aged and crippled Neanderthals, objectors say, means nothing: a famous monkey called Mozu survived to an advanced age in the Shiga Heights, despite being abominably crippled, without much help from her tribe;[27] floods 'must' or 'might' have carried the remains to apparent burial sites. Lions or hyenas dragged away corpses, complete with the beds they lay on. The sleeping Neanderthal in Shanidar 'must have' buried himself by accident by dislodging the cave ceiling.[28] What look like floral offerings must have been blown to their resting-place by a chance breeze.[29] At the other extreme, credulity has drawn irresponsible inferences from this evidence, crediting Neanderthals with a broad concept of humanity, a belief in the immortality of the soul, a system of social welfare, a gerontocracy, a political system of philosopher-rule. They may have had such things: but the burials are not evidence of them.

So what do the Neanderthal burials prove? Mere burial is evidence only of material concerns: to deter scavengers, to mask the odour of putrescence. But ritual burial is evidence of an idea: indeed of two ideas—of life and death. We still find it hard to define them and in particular cases—such as impenetrable comas and the misery of the moribund on life-support—to say exactly where the difference between them lies. But the conceptual distinction we make between life and death goes back to when people began to mark it by rites differentiating the dead. The first celebrations of death hallowed life. They constitute the first evidence of a more than merely instinctive valuing of life: a conviction that life is worthy of reverence, which has remained the basis of all human moral action ever since. They were part—perhaps the most eloquent part—of the common culture Neanderthals shared with *homo sapiens*; some of the present survivors of *homo sapiens*, however, seem unwilling to accept that. The tenacity with which some scientists strive to confine the Neanderthals to a 'lower' order of creation is so virulent, so committed, so obstinate, so indifferent to facts, that it is unintelligible except as part of a partisan programme with an ideological agenda. It is strikingly, frighteningly reminiscent of racists' efforts to exclude blacks or pygmies or Hottentots or aboriginals from the human community.

The claim, for instance, that Neanderthals were physically incapable of language has now been disproved by the discovery of a fragment of a Neanderthal larynx at Kebara in what is now Israel: the sounds of Neanderthal vocalizations would have been different from ours, but they were capable of a range fully adequate to produce language in a sense analogous to that of human speech.[30] Students in my classroom can hardly believe that the debate about Neanderthal language should ever have been conducted at such a superficial level: the assumption that some merely physical impediment would be sufficient to frustrate the development of language displays a fundamental ignorance of what language is. It would mean that the symbolic forms of expression used in sign language would not qualify; or that Morse code, which uses only one sound, was incapable of expressing the same range of meanings as—say—English. Obviously, anyone prepared to concede to Neanderthals a level and form of intelligence comparable with our own would suppose them capable of devising a language consistent with the limitations and opportunities of their vocal tracts.

Equally unconvincing is the claim that Neanderthals were inexpert hunters—'opportunists', like hunting chimpanzees, who exploit prey in their immediate environs—whereas *homo sapiens* is a prescient planner, who tracks his victims, plots their movements, and links them to the passage of the seasons and the state of the ecosytem.[31] This distinction seems unlikely to be valid, as hominids of various

kinds had all the cognitive apparatus necessary for planned hunting—
to say nothing of appropriate technology, represented by cunningly
flaked flints and spear-throwers—long before the evolution of the
Neanderthals, whose material culture was, in other respects, so
impressive for its time. More generally, the Neanderthals' detractors
say that their extinction was the result of failure to adapt: but the
species colonized Europe as far as 52° North—a habitat that was
extreme even in the interglacial area when the Neanderthals pene-
trated it. Their subsequent retreat from those latitudes, as the Ice Age
encroached, and their replacement by our ancestors, is better explained
by the rhythms of the Ice Age—climate change that outstripped the
responses even of these highly adaptable creatures—than by any doctrine of their inherent inferiority.

It is also commonly said that the Neanderthals were self-excluded
from humankind by their lack of art. It is true that they left little art
that has survived; but the same is true of our own ancestors until a
date not long before that of the Neanderthal extinction. In any case,
there is one Neanderthal site in Europe—the Cave of the Reindeer at
Arcy-sur-Cure—where the remains of necklaces of beads and ivory
have been found. Denigrators of the Neanderthals ascribe these to the
influence of (or commerce with) *homo sapiens* but must at least admit
that it shows the Neanderthals could share, if not originate, culture
that, according to earlier orthodoxy, was peculiarly the product of our
own ancestors. This find is also rich in red ochre—a substance usually
associated with body-painting and the only evidence of this otherwise
highly perishable form of early art.[32]

Those who want to exclude Neanderthals from the human community altogether, or relegate them to an inferior class of humankind,
argue that their capacities were inferior, their culture underdeveloped,
their intelligence limited, their rational faculties defective, and that
their potential for interbreeding with properly human primates was
vitiated by unbridgeable incompatibilities. Neanderthals' extinction is
often treated as evidence of their inferiority but they lasted in all for
300,000 years: much longer than *homo sapiens* has managed so far or,

on present showing, looks like managing. Though sceptics have displayed ape-like agility in challenging the evidence there is too much of it to discount. It proves, in combination, that there have been species morally indistinguishable from those we now choose to recognize as human beings. Other finds take the history of hominid culture back to a barely imaginable past, hundreds of thousands of years before the advent of *homo sapiens*.

*   *   *

Take the case of a form of behaviour with good cultural credentials: cannibalism. We have trained ourselves to recoil from cannibalism and to see it as treason against our species: a form of sub-human savagery. The evidence, however, suggests the opposite: cannibalism is typically—you might almost say peculiarly—human and cultural. Human bones, snapped and sucked, lie under the stones of every civilization. No other mammals practise cannibalism so regularly or on such a large scale as we do: indeed, all others tend to avoid it except in extreme circumstances—which suggests that it did not come 'naturally' to our ancestors: they had to think about it. Chimpanzees are the only non-human apes known to eat individuals of their own species, but they do so only in aberrant frenzies, in war or in response to females who break local mating rules.[33] Otherwise, chimpanzees treat cannibals as strange deviants, rather as we do in human societies that have set cannibalism aside—to judge from the way most chimpanzees responded when Jane Goodall witnessed a case in Gombe in 1976, when a mother and daughter made a habit of catching and eating other chimps' babies.[34]

Evidence assembled by modern anthropology shows that human cannibals have sophisticated agendas. Sometimes they eat people for bodily nourishment, to survive famine or top up protein-deficient diets. Overwhelmingly, however, most cases have concerned more reflective aims, moral or mental, aesthetic or social: self-transformation, the appropriation of power, the ritualization of the eater's relationship with the eaten. For the Papuan Orokaiva, until the 1960s it was a way of 'capturing spirits' in compensation for lost warriors. The Hua of New Guinea ate their dead to conserve *Nu*—the vital fluids they believe to be non-renewable in nature. The Gimi women of the same highlands consumed their dead menfolk to guarantee the renewal of their fertility, and to encompass masculinity—as they do again when they bear male children. Such cases have multiple parallels all over the world. Normally, where it is normal, cannibalism occurs in war, as an act symbolizing dominance of the defeated. Or human meat is the gods' food and cannibalism a form of divine communion.

Cannibalism therefore could be a better criterion for representing the 'essence' of human distinctiveness than any of those traditionally vaunted and exploded: tool use, art, language, self-awareness, altruism, and all the rest. At least, we can say with confidence that where we find cannibalism we find culture. But in the archaeological record, evidence of cannibalism precedes the evolution of *homo sapiens* by hundreds of thousands of years—indeed, by a period at least four times as long as the entire span of the existence so far of our own species.

Some of the earliest evidence lies among the detritus of a cannibal feast eaten about 800,000 years ago in a cave in Atapuerca, Spain, at which the eaters split bones of individuals of their own species to extract the marrow. There was more to the feast than physical nourishment. These cannibals were intellectuals. They broke into the spinal cords of their victims to extract the brains.

It would be idle to speculate about what the hominids of Atapuerca thought they were doing when they ate dead specimens of their own species; but it is consistent with just about everything we know about the nature of cannibalism to assume that it was not just a survival-expedient nor an act of hunger or gluttony, but a considered act of ritual, underlain by an idea: an attempt to achieve an effect imagined and immeasurable. If the hominids of Atapuerca were like later cannibals—and devised their cannibal ritual to affect themselves, to enhance their powers or change their natures—they were launching a bold adventure in thought. Not later than about half a millennium after the first cannibal meal at the site, the dwellers began another ritual: stacking the bones of their dead. Though continuing excavation may yield more data, we cannot say for certain, in the present state of the evidence, whether the Atapuerca creatures belonged in the same line of evolution as *homo sapiens*. Once we admit the antiquity of culture, and its presence in a diversity of extinct hominids, we have to surrender our surprise at finding it in other primates and in increasing numbers of other species.

*   *   *

The claim that *homo sapiens* is the only cultural creature was the last in a long series of discarded human attempts at distinguishing themselves from the rest of creation. Reviewing these abandoned pretensions helps demonstrate the limits of human privilege. The great advocate of 'neo-Darwinian sociology', Walter Runciman (above, pp. 92–3), might have been expected, like other enthusiasts for evolutionary accounts of culture, to respond positively to evidence of human commonalities with other animals, but he remained stubbornly attached to faith in human uniqueness; 'no primatologist', he wrote, in rebuttal of evidence that non-human primates have a faculty resembling human consciousness, 'is concerned with a conflict between "their" account of their behaviour and "ours"'.[35] But I do not think many primatologists would really disavow such concern: it is lack of data, rather than lack of interest, that limits the literature. Chimpanzees in captivity who have learned sign-language or key-board-communication are often willing to answer questions such as, 'what are you doing?' or 'what are you painting?' even though their answers seem inscrutable or oblique. In any case, in measurable ways non-human apes evince human-style self-awareness, recognizing themselves in mirrors, displaying guilt, embarrassment, exculpation, and evasion. 'Cooperative hunting and nepotistic food-sharing, Machiavellian social tactics, infanticide, sex for bonding rather than reproduction and intergroup warfare', according to a recent primatologist's list, are among behaviours, formerly thought to be uniquely human, now known to occur among chimpanzees.[36]

One of the commonest false assertions is that humans are uniquely tool-using or tool-making animals. Tool use, indeed, is the headline item in the discarded check-list of humanhood. In the forest of Bossou in Guinea, apes in the wild use much the same technology to crack nuts as humans inhabiting the same environment do: two stones— one as an anvil, the other as a hammer; meanwhile, high in the trees, chimpanzees use leaf-stalks to drill into palm-tree pith for nutritious fibre and sap. In the Tai forest in Côte d'Ivoire, chimpanzees wield ten-kilogram stones in a similar way to crack the armour-like carapace of the panda nut, often shaping a small twig to extract the most inaccessible kernels when the main job is done. This is clearly not an innate skill: on the contrary, it takes a young chimp, on average, three years to learn the basic technique, which requires a good deal of delicacy, and five years to master it with real proficiency.

Jane Goodall showed how even in the wild, without human instruction, some chimpanzees actually manufacture tools—shaping branches to break into termites' nests or chewing leaves to make sponges. Since she made her observations at Gombe, apes at Mahale have introduced similar practices, including making leaves into sponges and spoons, and taught them to their tribes.[37] Of course, no ape makes tools even remotely as complex as those manufactured by hominid ancestors of modern humans hundreds of thousands of years ago: the world's reputedly 'smartest ape', the bonobo Kanzi, who lives with some of the world's top scientists on a university campus in Atlanta, learned to knap flints for cutting the string with which sweet-packets were bound; but he could never master the particular technique used by *homo habilis*. Still, apes make the tools they need for their own purposes: the difference between them and us is a matter of enormous degree, but still only of degree.[38]

A further claim of the same type is that only humans have art. The first thing to be said about this is that maybe not all humans do. In 1909, when Walter Grainge White studied the Mawken or *oran laut*— the destitute 'sea people' of the Bay of Bengal, who had been driven to take refuge on the ocean from earthbound enemies—the deficiency of art was one of the things that most puzzled him. Apart from mats woven patternless, with apparently single-minded concentration on practical utility, they had nothing—no tools carved with patterns or images, no daubings, no dyed garments, not even music or dance. When he asked them why, they replied that they had abandoned them in their 'time of sadness'.[39] This surely does not mean that these people were incapable of art; rather, they chose not to make symbols or images or evocations of things not present. Can the apparent absence of what we recognize as art among non-human animals be of the same sort? Even between human cultures, the differences in the way art is understood and shaped are enormous: we look at each other's works and ask 'is it art?' So there should in principle be no reason why we should not look at the behaviour of other species and ask the same question unprejudicially.

Art is the realization of what is imagined, for even a relatively uncontrived photograph or one of Marcel Duchamp's *objets trouvé*—like the famous lavatory that became, for him, a work of art when he bought it from a builders' merchant's—is changed by appropriation by the artist. We can be sure that many non-human animals have powers of imagination that may not be as prolific or manifold as humans' but which must be sufficiently developed to locate food and shelter, read the weather, and anticipate predators and rivals. So potentially, at least, such animals are artists. Chimpanzees typically love to paint and, if given paints and brushes, need little help to start using them. They clearly understand the idea of art: though, even under human instruction, they do not produce what an adult human's eye normally recognizes as representational art, they do sometimes label their pictures in sign-language, saying 'this apple' or 'this bird' and so on.[40] We do not demand of human artists that they should represent the world as the rest of us see it. Since it would be silly to expect beings of another species to see reality as we do, we should not be surprised if they represent it differently, nor unwilling to classify those representations as artistic. Works by Congo, the most prolific chimp painter, have sold for scores of thousands of dollars at auction.[41]

Chimpanzees make awestruck responses to unfamiliar scenes or artefacts. When Walter Runciman dismisses this awe as fundamentally unlike that of 'Henry Adams in front of Chartres Cathedral' he does so, I suspect, on the basis of assumptions, which come cheaply, not evidence, which is unobtainable.[42] In at least one respect, some non-human apes—even without training—do manifest a symbolic imagination similar to our own: it is commonly and correctly said that apes never adorn themselves in the wild with the kind of *bijouterie* favoured by humans—we can look at rats' teeth, say, and see them as items of adornment or social status or magic power, to be drilled and strung and slung around our necks, whereas other apes see only what is immediately, palpably there. However, at the Yerkes National Primate Research Center in Atlanta, female bonobos sometimes put dead rats or cockroaches on their heads and keep them there all day, deriving apparent gratification from the fact. The parallel with behatted human ladies at Ascot is hard to resist. The transformation of dead vermin into items of *haute couture* is not, after all, unintelligible even in human terms, as any wearer of squirrel skin or fox fur will be obliged to admit. To see a dead cockroach and re-imagine it as headgear requires a mind capable of inventive transformations. According to a report from the 1930s, when playing fighting games the male chimp 'likes to bedeck his body with all sorts of things, especially, strings, vines, and rags that dangle and swing in the air as he moves about'.[43]

Even critics who discount the products of chimp aesthetics as art have to admit that if art is a uniquely human achievement, it seems, at least, to be within the potential of some other animals. The use of fire is another technique in the same category. With this secret, according to King Louie in a movie version of *The Jungle Book*, 'an ape like me can learn to be human'. But without ceasing to be apes they can learn to light cigarettes or strike flame to release the odour of incense and even to keep a kindled fire alight. Some humans do not do much better. Some traditional peoples of Australia will not kindle fire but have to borrow it from neighbouring cultures—but whether because of ignorance of the technique or some sacred fastidiousness has never been clarified. The primatological fieldworker Anne Russon reported a case of an orang-utan, re-introduced to the wild after captivity, who worked at fire-making by juxtaposing glowing embers with dry wood, 'blowing and fanning glowing embers with a saucepan lid', and appropriating kerosene to add to the hearth.[44] The *Jungle Book* fantasy of the ape who wants to seize the secret of fire in order to be able to compete with humans turns out to be true. Many animals are attracted to the embers of naturally occurring fires, where they sift for roasted seeds and insects made edible by burning. This behaviour is observable among chimpanzees in the wild and suggests a context for the origins of cooking: to a creature of imagination and dexterity, some of the features of burnt-out woodland, such as the piles of ash and the partly burned trunks of fallen trees might have appeared as natural ovens, smouldering with manageable heat, in which tough-husked seeds or rough-skinned pulses, unchewable legumes and cartilaginous flesh could be processed.

Yet these considerations may miss the really interesting fact about fire: for it is not only a technology for controlling the environment, and for cooking parts of it, but also a source of socially generative power that, in human history, has created a focus—'focus' literally means hearth—for socially defining rites. The most agglutinative of these rites—those which bind us most tightly to each other—involve the communal cooking and sharing of food. Even without cooking, some chimpanzees seem to have developed or to be developing similar rites. In the Tai forest chimpanzees hunt communally, with some members of the tribe driving prey—small colobus monkeys—towards specialized killers.[45] In Gombe, hunters often seize infant or new-born monkeys, not because the prey is easier to take—on the contrary, it is harder to fight off defenders while stealing an infant than to challenge an adult directly—but because the young specimens are useful as gifts to seal social bonds: the captors fling them to young followers as rewards or encouragement, or barter them with females in exchange for sex. In all known cases of hunting by chimpanzees, they distribute the prey, piece by piece, among members of the tribe in a hierarchical order that differs, along with other aspects of culture, from tribe to tribe. Some groups value dominance order; others prefer to reward hunting prowess; others favour fertile females.[46] The way some chimpanzee communities share hunted food, even though it is distributed raw, resembles a ritual: the gestures with which food is begged and the order in which it is shared are different from those observed when meals consist of gathered foods.

It resembles a ritual. Could it really be a ritual? Perhaps the most remarkable case of all social behaviour among chimpanzees is that of the 'rain dance' Jane Goodall first observed in 1971. There have been many subsequent sightings. At the approach of heavy rain, male chimpanzees gather to sway and stamp in a concerted fashion or charge as if in defiance of the rain. When it occurs among groups in zoos or labs, the rain dance makes keepers joke about whether the chimps' intention is to welcome the rain or ward it off. It looks like a deliberate attempt at a magical practice—evidence of a sense of transcendence or of the power of prayer, such as has often been attributed to animals in anthropomorphic folklore. It is hard to accept such an explanation, but equally hard to think of a better one.

The accessibility of art and fire-use to non-human animals is unsurprising, once one accepts that they can use tools, since all these activities are technological applications. What about the claim that a unique moral sense distinguishes humans? It is hard to speak scientifically about morals because, in a strict sense, scientifically explicable morality is a contradiction in terms. Goodness is not really goodness if it confers an evolutionary advantage or some other computable benefit: for it then becomes a form of selfishness. Compassion becomes externalized fear; generosity becomes an investment in feedback; sympathy becomes a collaborative strategy; love becomes—as Diderot put it—'pleasurable throbbing in a pair of intestines'. To be truly altruistic or truly selfless or self-sacrificial, a moral act must be beyond explanation.

Therefore we have to confine ourselves to the most rudimentary kind of science: putting explanation aside and relying on mere observation. All we can do is scrutinize the behaviour of non-human animals for evidence of the same kinds of act that we deem moral in our own species. If we again look, for example, at chimpanzees, we see sympathy and empathy, friendship and disinterested deference, reciprocity and the obligations that come with it, acts of reconciliation and consolation, and even of self-sacrifice all in abundance. Chimps succour orphans. They guard their dead, cover them with leaves, grieve when they leave them, and shoo youngsters away from the places where cadavers lie. The claim that chimpanzees might have something identifiable as moral sense or show 'concern for unrelated group members' seemed to Walter Runciman dismissible without argument.[47] But though he was right about much else, he was wrong, in this respect, about the facts. Primatological fieldwork reports are full of accounts of fights between two chimpanzees, after which some of the other members of the community will approach the victim and make the standard gesture of consolation by putting an arm around him or her. Nadie Coates, the Russian primatologist, found she could never successfully use threats or treats to circumvent her pet chimp's recalcitrance, but if she feigned pain he would always return to her to console her, with a look on his face that she interpreted as compassion. Washoe, a chimpanzee of the Yerkes Center who, as we shall see, became famous for her prowess in mastering human language, once saved a fellow chimp from drowning and appeared to look reproachfully at human bystanders who had failed to help.

Whether 'animal' morality is human or human morality 'merely animal', how to distinguish the two must be acknowledged as a problem. It seems a fair conclusion to say that—as far as knowledge we can reasonably class as scientific goes—the differences between our species and others are probably of an order comparable with those that separate non-human species from each other, neither much greater nor much less. Humans are unique, but not with any unique sort of uniqueness.

*   *   *

One of the strongest and most widespread assertions about human uniqueness is that only humans have language: that it is, as the great nineteenth-century linguist Max Müller said, 'our Rubicon, and no brute will dare to cross it'.[48] Of course, whether language should be regarded as a matter of culture or as an 'instinct' and, if the latter, whether evolution produced it (or whether it is some special property inexplicable in evolutionary terms) are themselves matters of intense debate. It is a question of perennial interest to philosophers but, until recently, seemed beyond scientific investigation: the only possible experiments involved isolating children to see 'what language' they came to speak among themselves: though such experiments were occasionally reported in ancient and medieval literature they were extremely rare, because they demanded despotic intervention to get them going; and—though they might have demonstrated, as does the 'private language' sometimes shared by twins before they communicate more widely, that language is in some sense probably innate—they were generally inconclusive: Frederick II's, for instance, in thirteenth-century Sicily, failed, as a chronicler reported, because 'all the children died'. Now computer programmers have claimed to be able to model the effects of the imitative transmission of sounds over thousands of generations into something 'that looks a lot like language'.[49] If the technique is reliable it raises a presumption that language is the outcome of learning and does not need any more biological input than you find in a computer.

In the meantime, however, during the 1950s a promising phase of the enquiry started off in a different direction, when Noam Chomsky pondered the fact that the differences between languages appear superficial compared with the 'deep structures'—or D-structures, as he later preferred to call them, the parts of speech, the relationships between terms which we call grammar and syntax—that are common to all of them. Chomsky inferred a link between the structures of language and brain: we learn languages fast because their structure is already part of the way we think. He became impressed at how children learn speech: quickly and easily, without having to be taught—'from positive evidence only', as he put it, with no need of correction, 'and they appear to know the facts without relevant experience in a wide array of complex cases'.[50] They can even combine words in ways they have never actually heard. We now know that non-human apes who learn human language can do the same.

Chomsky's ideas were revolutionary when he proposed them, because the orthodoxies of the time suggested that either heredity or nurture or both explained everything in human behaviour: there was no room for an explanation of any other kind. The way Chomsky saw it, at least at first, was that this 'language instinct' or 'language faculty' was untouchable by evolution, and therefore perhaps unproduced by it—which really would put humans in a category specially privileged in nature. He has since proposed that other kinds of knowledge may turn out to resemble language in these respects: that our 'mental constitution' explains how we acquire all sorts of science. Experience, perhaps, is less important in learning than we thought or, at least, does not have an exclusive role. It does not mediate knowledge directly to our minds, but triggers capacities latent in the structures of our mental faculties, like an interrogation by Socrates. Neither experience nor heredity—if Chomsky is right—make us the whole of what we are.

At first, Chomsky's claims seem to endorse claims of human uniqueness. We do not know for certain of any other animals with such an advantage; we can be reasonably certain that many species have nothing like it. Chomsky, however, was quick to repudiate conclusions favourable to humans' self-image as the climax of creation. On the contrary, our language prowess, on which we tend to congratulate ourselves as a species, and which some people even claim as a uniquely human achievement, is simply another peculiar skill, like the peculiar skills of other creatures—the speed of cheetahs, for instance, or the ruminating of cows, or the bat's radar, or the spider's ability to extrude a web.

It is the richness and specificity of instinct of animals [Chomsky says] that accounts for their remarkable achievements in some domains and lack of ability in others, so the argument runs, whereas humans, lacking such . . . instinctual structure, are free to think, speak and discover . . . Both the logic of the problem and what we are now coming to understand suggest that this is not the correct way to identify the position of humans in the world.[51]

Recently, however, recoiling, it seems, in disgust from primatologists' claims on behalf of chimpanzee masters of human language, Chomsky has contrived an argument in defence of human exclusivity by asserting that part of the innate structures only humans possess is a 'narrow faculty of language' that 'includes the capacity for recursion', manifest in a sense of 'recursive forms', such as embedded relative clauses.[52] To understand the notion of recursion, one might recall the popular song by the Canadian folk-artist, Alan Mills, about the old lady who died after swallowing a horse to catch a goat that she swallowed to catch a dog that she swallowed to catch a cat that she swallowed to catch a bird that she swallowed to catch a spider that she swallowed to catch a fly that she swallowed for unknown reasons. My paraphrase could, I think, be split into a series of one-sentence clauses without losing any of the effect of recursion. In any case, Chomsky's assertion is unproven and other linguists have challenged it.[53] It seems unhelpful, anyway, to foreclose on debate by defining terms prejudicially—but that is the current strategy of deniers that powers of language can exist among non-humans.

Even deeper than the problem of how language arose is that of what it is for. Vulgarly, people assume that it began for purposes of communication, but that may not be so. It is, in any case, not well designed to communicate, as all our misunderstandings proclaim. It is at least equally likely that language arose in self-expression—in the private ululations of grief, pain, and fear, the exhalations of pleasure, the whoops of joy or triumph—and got adapted for communication between individuals once they succeeded, as it were, in communicating each with himself and establishing a code of sound and gesture for every passion. Still, it must be acknowledged that communication by symbolic utterance or gesture—however it arose—has not just become part of culture, but the most important ingredient of it, at least among humans, since we use it to teach and learn everything else that is cultural. Apart from demonstration and imitation it is the only means of transmission we have; and it can be used to convey undemonstrable abstractions of thought. Obviously, creatures that have it can do more, culturally speaking, than those that do not: equipped with language, we can articulate more innovations, represent them more accurately, spread them more widely, and even—by misunderstanding each other—trigger further divergences in behaviour. So if language were uniquely human, it would help to explain some of the other peculiarities of our species.

Unless, however, the disposition to language is a special power of the mind, beyond explanation, it must in principle be accessible to more than one species; indeed, our ignorance of the methods non-human species use to express themselves and to communicate makes assertions of human uniqueness in this respect unconvincing. Alternatively, if only humans have language, how might such a situation have come about? No explanation which bypasses evolution can be convincing. And, in search of an evolutionary explanation, the most obvious route lies through the study of the non-human animals most like us. A look at non-human ape-networking nowadays suggests what might have happened.

Non-human ape communities are small by human standards. They tend to disperse. Chimpanzee communities rarely congregate in a single place at one time, while those of bonobos are fluid because females cross community boundaries to mate with perfect ease. Foraging, hunting, and fighting are all activities in which most apes engage in small groups, rather than fully collective activities in which whole communities unite. The bigger the communities, or the bigger the groups assigned to particular tasks, the more time individuals need to spend networking or cultivating their working relationships. If this has to be done by grooming, the sacrifice of time can simply become too demanding, taking too long, curtailing time for other activities. Species like ours—physically unadept and relatively weak by comparison with many predators—have always had to find strength in numbers and security in collaboration. Robin Dunbar, the leading specialist in the field, reckons that bands of the size normal for hominids a million years ago would have spent 42 per cent of their time on grooming—more than twice that normal for other primates—if they had not devised an alternative socialization technique.

This, perhaps, is how our hominid ancestors might have diverged from our primate cousins and acquired language on the way: speech arose as an alternative to grooming. The growth of the group created the need for ways of networking that were elastic, inclusive, and time-saving. Humans have language because they need it.

Non-human apes, by this reasoning, do not need language and therefore ought not to have it. Yet, in a sense, they do. Chimpanzees associate particular sounds with types and locations of food. They adjust their recruitment screams to deceive enemies. Gibbons follow rules when emitting their song-like signals of alarm.[54] Language, of course, is a kind of symbol system, in which words or signs encode the realities they represent, and so far, despite a lot of evidence in favour of the proposition, it has been impossible to devise an experiment capable of proving absolutely that animal responses to sounds are the results of the mastery of symbols, rather than mere environmentally induced reflexes.[55] To some extent, the distinction may be false: many human gestures and utterances are both symbolic and responsive to environmental stimuli: think of our expletives, curses, and codes for summoning help, or advertising danger, or signifying pleasure and pain. So when animals display consistent responses they may also, in principle, be wielding symbols.[56] If it were true that humans are unique in having language, broader presumptions would follow about our possible uniqueness as symbol-makers—ritualizing life, associating actions and objects with significance that transcends their palpable effects. But since chimpanzees and other non-human primates do understand, wield, and invent human symbols with some fluency, we seem to be confronting, at best, another difference of degree.

It is true that apes do not seem—to human observers, at least—to have systems of communication capable of attaining the range of human speech; but they communicate for their own purposes, sparingly using vocalizations within the range permitted by their relatively poorly adapted speech organs, supplemented by gesture and grimace. Most communication even among humans is non-verbal and therefore does not depend on the specialized larynx and vocal tract, which makes human vocalizations uniquely human. Much of the human repertoire of grimace and gesture is part of a communication system common to primates. Just about all primatologists who have worked closely with great apes acknowledge that they are greatly superior to humans in their skill at non-verbal communication, reading signals in each other's eyes: a mischievous commentator might liken this to the 'thought-communication' that popular science fiction has often imagined as a higher evolutionary recourse than the mere language with which we humans are crudely equipped today.

There therefore seems little mystery in the fact that human-style language is not part of apes' repertoire of social skills in their own homes. Among humans, however, they learn to exchange language with human companions with startling fluency, using conventional sign language or symbolic code-languages punched from computer-style keyboards or touched on signboards. In suitably contrived environments, they acquire it by imitation from humans, without recourse to Pavlovian training; and when they know it, they use it to themselves and among themselves. Apes have brains that seem well suited to develop human-style language, with areas analogous to Broca's and Wernicke's—the areas most involved in the processing and production of human speech. Indeed, chimps have proved better, on the whole, at learning human language than human researchers have proved in mastering ape communication—an outcome predicted by Montaigne who thought 'they may as well esteem us beasts as we them'.[57] No real-life Dr Dolittle has come to light. R.L. Garner, the eccentric autodidact who published *The Speech of Monkeys* in 1892, claimed to have practised on capuchin and rhesus monkeys in American zoos before initiating conversations with apes in the wild in the Congo. One of his declared objectives was to facilitate trade with gorillas.[58] Unless Garner told the truth, the only human to achieve impressive proficiency in ape communication was Dian Fossey. She made startling progress in exploring the way the mountain 'gorillas in the mist' of Rwanda communicate vocally. She learnt to make the sounds that signify peace, friendliness, reassurance, and consolation by breathing stertorously, sucking or blowing through nostrils or teeth in ways that do not sound like speech to a human ear, but that seem to make sense to a gorilla. Her learning experience was cut short by her murder by poachers in 1985. Even Fossey was less adept in learning how apes communicate than apes typically are in mastering human language.

*   *   *

One of the all-time outstanding chimp linguists was Washoe, the first non-human ape trained in the sign language of the deaf and dumb, for which chimps' hands are well adapted, rather than in human speech, which their mouths and throats do not suit. She demonstrated her talents first as a pet, then as a laboratory specimen, in the 1960s and 1970s. She invented her own terms for objects the names of which she did not know by combining terms in her lexicon ('rock berry' for brazil nut was the first name she coined) and even taught some language to a chimp newly recruited to her lab—a facility that has since become common among apes engaged in learning human language. She strung words together in sequences obviously designed to enhance meaning. When the sceptical ethologist Christopher Marler visited her he was astonished to see her sign 'gimme key open door' in order to be able to get at the garage where her toys were stored. He yielded to 'the impression that a primordial syntax is emerging'.[59] No ape has made much progress in mastering the complexities of syntax that seem to come so easily to most human language-learners, though some certainly seem able to distinguish shades of meaning conferred by varying word-order—as do dolphins—and many ape subjects respond to complex strings of terms and formulate others of their own.[60] Many language-learning apes—notably, Sue Savage-Rumbaugh's impressive bonobo pupil Kanzi—routinely combine pairs of terms to establish grammatical relationships between them.[61] It is doubtful, in any case, whether syntactical dexterity should be considered a distinguishing peculiarity of ours, or merely a difference of degree.

Any doubt about whether chimps 'really' understood the signs they learned to use, and composed strings of them in awareness of the rules of basic syntax, ought to have been dispersed by the personal tragedy that clouded Washoe's last wretched years of life in captivity. Her sick baby died and was never returned to her arms: from then on, whenever her carer approached her cage Washoe made the same signs: 'bring baby, bring baby'. Investigations of chimpanzees' ability to count revealed that they have no difficulty in associating Arabic numerals with the numbers they represent—which is surely an instance of remarkable symbolic awareness.[62]

Meanwhile, Maurice Temerlin raised a chimp called Lucy to 'grow up human'. Lucy chatted using American Sign Language with the level at least of a 2-year-old human child, turning the pages of a magazine and interjecting such comments as 'that dog' and 'that blue' at appropriate points. She would take visitors by the hand, stroll with them in the garden, and point out birds and plants with all the pride of a home-owner, signing their names as she went. When her pet kitten died, after a period of touching grief, she came across a picture of herself and her pet in a magazine. She stared at it for a long time, frequently signing 'Lucy's cat'.[63] Sarah, a chimpanzee whom at the same time David Premack in Missouri was training in the use of counters to cue objects, showed that she understood the nature of symbols: she responded similarly both to the objects in question and to the tokens that stood for them—equally, for instance, to an apple and to the blue triangle that represented an apple in Premack's system.[64]

Nevertheless, some linguists have tenaciously resisted the notion that language is accessible without a human mind; but resistance has become untenable—marked by dogma and the myopia of the wise monkey or the ostrich. The performance—if that word is not too demeaning to use—of Kanzi, Sue Savage-Rumbaugh's famous bonobo pupil in Atlanta, is decisive. We have met her as the bonobo genius who could knap flints. She can also build and light a fire. Apparently spontaneously, in infancy, she picked up the rudiments of using a keyboard to communicate: at the time, Professor Savage-Rumbaugh was trying, unsuccesfully, to teach Kanzi's mother, but the youngster showed an aptitude the older bonobo could not rival.[65]

Experiments with gorillas and orang-utans suggest that they can achieve comparable mastery of human language. Chantek, the orang-utan of Atlanta Zoo, who is gifted in the use of sign language, has learned hundreds of words and used some of them to say that he wanted to use the money he earned—performing tasks set by his keepers, like a teenager working his way through college—to buy a bathing pool.[66] Francine Paterson plausibly claimed to have taught Koko, a gorilla in captivity in California, to use about 1,000 terms in American Sign Language.

Apes' knowledge of human language or, at least, their ability to deploy it, may be circumscribed by insuperable limits. The most eloquent so far is Panbanisha, a bonobo who lives in Iowa and can use a keyboard of 400 icons to demand, *inter alia*, iced coffee in hot weather. She commands a lexicon of hundreds—and, passively, thousands—of words, and has taught many of them to her child. She could copy icons in chalk. Even if no successor breaks her record, it is better than most non-native learners of English can manage, and seems impressive enough across the chasm of millions of years of evolution that separates them from us. What is remarkable, however, about her attainments and those of other language-trained non-human apes are not the limits but the amazing extent of their range. That animals separated from us by 6 million years of evolution should understand us so well and communicate with us so copiously is objectively astonishing. 'If they're so smart,' sceptics typically respond, 'why haven't they developed in the wild a language as expressive or as supple as those they learn from humans?' The question is obviously absurd. In the wild they have methods of self-expression and communication suitable to their own needs. They only need human-style language when they consort with humans; and they pick it up with—relatively speaking—impressive fluency.

Even if the concept of human language were genuinely alien to apes, it would perhaps be more helpful to test its intelligibility to animals who do have vocal structures adapted to make human-style sounds. There is an old debate about whether the vocalizations of birds resemble human language: some investigators have explored this problem among birds capable of imitating speech. The most famous case in history was related by John Locke in *An Essay Concerning Human Understanding*. He told of how Prince Maurice of Nassau, one of the most committed and munificent patrons of seventeenth-century science, conducted a remarkable conversation while in Brazil as governor of the Dutch conquests there. Giving apparently direct answers to direct questions, a parrot told the prince that he (the parrot) hailed from Maranhão, belonged to a Portuguese, and kept chickens. The authenticity of the story has been doubted, on the grounds that Maurice relied on translators as intermediaries in the exchange; but many parrot owners have supported it anecdotally with experiences of their own. Now the ornithologist Irene Pepperberg has claimed to have settled Locke's doubts and resolved the long-debated question of whether talking parrots 'understand' what they say: hers answer simple questions with unfailing accuracy and even sometimes, when confronted with unfamiliar objects, apply familiar rules to formulate names.[67] Are her experiments credible to specialists in related fields? The debate goes on, but most of the evidence does seem to be accumulating on one side of it.

Other species-specific communication systems seem analogous to human language, even though they resemble it only very remotely: the dolphin's whistling, the 'dance' of bees, the colour code of cephalopods, and the 'squeaking of ants' that, according to the claims of a recent researcher, is an intelligible code, among ant-interlocutors. The animals people work with are often better at distinguishing the sounds made by human voices than—say—Westerners are in detecting the distinctions of pitch by which meaning is conferred in Chinese.

In suitably modest degree, the story of Dr Dolittle could come true, but Dolittle is himself likely to be a non-human animal. The best available conclusion in our present state of knowledge is that there are many species with forms of communication specific to themselves and it is unclear why language—even if it is in some sense a peculiarly human resource—should be treated as a basis for classifying the species that uses it apart from all others.[68]

Even patient readers, if they have got this far, may demand an answer to the question 'so is language cultural or not?' The honest answer is that we do not know; but, in any species, differences in symbolic communications systems between communities are almost certainly cultural. Anyone who thinks well of existing arguments in favour of evolutionary explanations of language need only read the coruscating demolition-job by the clear-headed South African linguist, Rudolf Botha[69]—though it is possible, of course, that better arguments may be devised in the future (and Botha is confident of doing so). The conspicuous problem that arises when we compare human languages with those of other species is the same as for any other area of culture: why are humans so much more dazzlingly diverse? By most counts, the tally of extant human languages in the world is between five and six thousand. No other species we know of needs more than one, with some variations that linguists are usually happy to call 'dialects'. Similarly, we have thousands of religions, cuisines, modes of dress, coiffures, types of drilling technology, and so on. The problem for the study of culture is not so much 'why do we have symbolic communication?' as 'why do we have so many varieties of it?'

For historians like me, the discovery of non-human cultures has not been threatening, but exciting and enlightening. Only by comparing humans with other cultural animals can we see what, if anything, is special about ourselves. We can now see the human past in a new perspective and, in consequence, see more of it more clearly than before. In most cultures, for most of the past, historians had unconvincingly simple story-lines. They saw the past as a cycle of endless repetitions, or as 'time's arrow', hurtling straight towards some glorious end or catastrophic dissolution, or as progress, or providence, or decay. Now we can see it in three dimensions, as a story of cultural divergence—a true story that has dominated most of the past 100,000 years, and that makes humans intelligible against the background of the whole history of cultural behaviour.[70] While other animals' cultures remained confined in narrow ranges, ours multiplied. That is our human story. Our big human question is 'why?' Grasping the problem aright depends on getting the basic facts right: seeing how little divergence there really is among non-human cultures, and how much among our own.

* * *

Cultural divergence, which is an index of the scale and rate of cultural change, is always very small in non-human species, compared with the immense diversity of human cultures. It is remarkable that there are any cultural differences at all between communities of particular species of apes and monkeys, but they oscillate within a narrow band.

We do know, however, of some instances of cultural change in primate societies—of non-human societies with 'histories' of change. Politics is a conspicuous strand of culture for the present purpose. Human societies have a dazzling range of political forms. To cite only the ways in which we choose our topmost elites, we sometimes share the method that is almost universal among other primates: we submit to the rule of the boss, the toughest strong-arm, assisted by the cronies he selects to share his power. Presumably, at some point in the past of early *homo sapiens* or our hominid predecessors, all our ancestors' communities were ruled in this way. Gradually, however, human political cultures have multiplied. We sometimes choose our leaders by heredity, privileging a particular dynasty, and in some cases we refine our choice of ruler by defining the heir to power more strictly, perhaps as the firstborn son of the incumbent. Sometimes we opt for charismatic leadership, favouring the shaman or the prophet or seer or visionary or magus or priest or wizard or holy man. Sometimes we invest individuals with the right to nominate their successors, or we shift the prerogative to a third party; sometimes we erect intermediary elites to choose the ruler. Sometimes we have monarchs, sometimes dictators, sometimes assemblies, sometimes matriarchies, sometimes theocracies. Sometimes our rulers have fixed terms of lengths that differ from culture to culture. Sometimes they are enthroned for life. Sometimes we choose them by lot. Sometimes we even elect them democratically.

No other animal is as various. Non-human apes have, so far, shown little political inventiveness compared with us. They do, however, have a modest range of political diversity. Some of the most challenging recent discoveries have brought animal politics to light. Frans de Waal, one of the world's most productive primatologists, extolled the machiavellian skills of some of the alpha apes he studied, as they forged alliances, undermined rivals, seized power, and kept competitors in check.[71] Typically, however, an alpha triumphs. He wins supremacy by defeating his predecessor in combat. He rules by force, with subordinate helpers or sometimes in gangs. Sometimes, individual alphas develop their own techniques for supplementing the fights and displays of aggression with which they enforce authority. Yeroen, for instance, who ruled the chimpanzees of Arnhem Zoo in the early- to mid-1970s, made himself look bigger than he really was by walking heavily and inflating his posture—rather in the silly way George W. Bush used to do as US president, extending his elbows as he walked, as if to occupy more space, in a fashion his British admirer, Prime Minister Tony Blair, imitated with even sillier effect.[72]

Other chimps treat the alpha with signs of deference, which might include submissive grunts, deep bows, and the kissing of feet. De Waal succeeded—genuinely, brilliantly—in writing chimpanzee history: a record of shifts of power; but it was almost entirely a story of coups, in which one chimp or group of chimps displaced another without changing the political system. The early editions of his book in the early 1980s related 'one damned thing after another'. The author even chose to suppress some varieties of behaviour so as not to seem to press the parallel between chimp and human politics too far. In a recent re-edition he has confessed, for instance, that he omitted the case of a chimp 'elder statesman', whom he likened to Dick Cheney or Ted Kennedy, 'over the hill' but 'gaining tremendous power' by exploiting younger contenders' rivalries. He also added a picturesque detail: chimps competing for female support by tickling babies, like human politicos at a photo-op.[73]

A spectacular innovation in chimpanzee politics occurred in Gombe in 1964, when a small and physically rather feeble chimpanzee, whom the primatologists called Mike, lost patience with the rule of existing alpha male, Goliath. Mike turned out to be a sort of David. He made up for his relative weakness by technical skill. He raided a primatologists' camp for large tins, which he used as cymbals, clashing them as he challenged Goliath and the gang, and crashing through the forest, making a fearsome racket. He strewed tins across the pathways used by the leaders in what seems to have been a conscious attempt to intimidate them: he persisted until he bamboozled his enemies into surrendering power. This incident constituted, as far as I know, the first known case of a political revolution in the chimpanzee world—where not just the leadership, but the method of selecting the leader changed. Mike gained power and held it for six years without ever attacking another chimpanzee. When the primatologists denied him access to cans he used anything else he could lay his hands on—boxes, chairs, tables, tripods. When they managed to keep all their gear from him, Mike improvised with suitably selected branches. His adaptation of a novel technology to wrest and keep authority was—in chimp terms—a stroke of genius. It gave him a status that, if reproduced in human terms, we might very well call charismatic, since on one occasion he faced down an attack from five allied rivals, even though he was alone and manifestly outgunned. He retained his position as alpha into old age, when his teeth were worn and he could not have fought back against a pretender. He almost initiated a new political tradition: Jane Goodall saw Figan, a young admirer of Mike's, practising imitation of his technique.[74]

Even baboons can revolutionize their political systems. In Kenya in 1986 the gang of toughs that ruled a group of about ninety baboons raided a contaminated rubbish dump for food. They all died. The less aggressive survivors had to extemporize a new way of running their community. The group adopted a much looser power structure, and taught male 'immigrants' from other tribes to adopt collaborative approaches to power: shared activities and much mutual grooming replaced force as the main way of gaining authority and attracting mates. The hierarchy, in the words of the primatologists who wrote up the reports, was more 'relaxed' than previously, with low-ranking males evincing little of the stress typical in the past. Females shared high status. The process genuinely represented the forging of a new political culture, as baboon males always migrate on achieving maturity; by the mid-1990s none of the males in the group had been there a decade before. A decade later, these behavioural patterns persisted. Males leave their natal troops at adolescence; by the mid-1990s, no males remained who had resided in the troop a decade before.[75] These occasional or slow and selective changes in the ways apes organize politically are, of course, of a different order of magnitude from the 'revolutions' that have repeatedly convulsed some human groups in the last 10,000 years or so; and most non-human animal societies are remarkable for their virtually or utterly unchanging trajectories. 'Chimpanzee archaeology'—literally, the excavation of sites chimps formerly inhabited—is in its infancy, and its practitioners still tend to focus as much on what they hope it can tell about humans as on what it says about other apes; so far, it has confirmed that chimpanzees have shaped stones by using them as tools for more than 4,000 years and one day it may yield enough data for us to measure changes in the technologies of non-human primates over long periods.[76]

The general picture of relatively slow non-human change and relatively fast human change over the last few thousand years is unlikely to need modification. Explaining the peculiar pace of change in human culture is the task of the next chapter.

* * *

Non-human animals—I hope readers will now be willing to agree—have culture in the normal, common sense. The inference people often make from that fact, once they can be induced to accept it, is that 'we are like them' and that because we have traditionally explained animal behaviour as the outcome of evolution, we should do the same with our own. Students of 'human ecology' and 'human ethology' commonly do just that, describing people's activities as if they arose not in our minds, but in our environments; or as if they were not shaped in our imaginations and effected through our wills but imposed by evolution and encoded in our genes: or as if every widespread behaviour were naturally selected to be 'optimal', whereas every historian knows that human societies are intriguingly susceptible to self-destructive innovations. As the authors remark in a self-critical textbook on evolutionist approaches to human behaviour, that 'human beings may not be behaving optimally' is a conclusion 'that human behavioral ecologists are reluctant to draw'.[77] The unjustified assumption that evolution governs non-human primates' behaviour inspires the invalid inference that the same constraints imprison human culture, too—an inference that vitiates the strenuous work on primate precedents for and analogues of human behavior accumulated since the 1950s by followers of Sherwood Washburn, who was, as far as I know, the first anthropologist to appreciate the potential impact of the discovery of macaque culture.[78] I once giggled at a cartoon—I suppose it must have been in *The New Yorker*, but I cannot remember for sure—that showed a cocktail-party hostess introducing two big, martini-toting guests. One was human, the other a chimpanzee. 'I guess you two have a lot to talk about,' the hostess gushed. 'You have 98 per cent of your DNA in common.' The absurdity of the gag draws our attention to the way similarities occlude differences, and to the limitations of the power of genes: they are probably not the whole of what makes us the way we are.

The split between sciences and the humanities still imposes mutual incomprehension among students from different traditions of learning. One of the most effective penetrators of disciplinary barriers, William McGrew of Cambridge University, has pointed out that most primatologists cannot think beyond Darwinianism in trying to understand culture, while anthropologists are often inhibited from taking aboard the lessons of science because their formation is in the study of human societies. 'This,' McGrew says, 'is a recipe for misunderstanding.'[79] Some scientists have a frankly anti-humanist agenda, and go to absurd lengths to fillet freedom out of the human psyche, reducing everything we do to ecological constraints and evolutionary urges. A tell-tale strategy is to define culture so widely that all distinctions disappear: even slime-moulds, by some accounts, might attain it, and, in a work with no detectable irony, the 'social amoeba' might behave altruistically.[80] John Tyler Bonner, the distinguished Princeton biologist, traced the evolutionary prerequisites of culture back to a faculty he called motility, 'already full-blown in the lowest bacteria', some of which behave socially because they feed in swarms.[81] The search for the common biological background of cultural creatures is legitimate, but there seems little point in identifying features all or virtually all animals share as potentially leading to culture: one might as well say that life is the ultimate prerequisite. The procedure reminds me of Bertrand Russell's quip about how, to a dedicated Darwinian, there is no logical halt along the human–animal continuum short of 'votes for oysters'. Even the capacity to learn, which is widely shared among animals, does not account even for the emergence of culture—though the two occurrences are obviously related; as Darwin pointed out, creatures of different species can learn from each other, and form temporary associations, often of an affectionate nature, without forming cultures or even societies. The cases he noted were of dogs imitating cats with whom they shared households—using their licked paws to wash their faces.[82] One might add the vulpine habits of wolf-children, or the chattiness of caged parrots.

It is more interesting and more useful to stand the usual inferences on their head. If we (humans) are 'like them' (other animals) it is equally true that other animals are 'like us'. They have wills, individuality, inventiveness, the capacity to discover new techniques, to launch new behaviours, and to teach them to each other or acquire them by imitation. Maybe we should re-examine out traditional reliance on appeals to 'instinct' to explain what non-human creatures do, rather than assuming that every new discovery that aligns us with the rest of creation represents a stage in human derogation to enslavement to nature. It is time, in the next chapter, to identify the limits of evolution.

5

THE LIMITS OF EVOLUTION

Why evolutionary theory fails to match historical reality

When painting a still life, Paul Cézanne used to switch between vantage points, sometimes overnight, sometimes during a single painting session. He was seeking momentary sensations, fleeting perceptions to combine in a single composition. When you see his version of a bowl of apples, for instance, the visible curves of the rim of the bowl look as if they can never meet. Cézanne painted strangely distended melons, because he wanted to capture the way the fruit seems to change shape from different angles. In his assemblages of odds and ends, the distortions of vision, as each object assumes its own perspective, are sometimes baffling, sometimes maddening, always intriguing. He painted the same subjects over and over again, because with every fresh look you see something new, and every retrospect leaves you dissatisfied with the obvious imperfections of partial vision.

The past is like a painting by Cézanne—or like a sculpture in the round, the reality of which no single viewpoint can disclose. I do not say so to occlude reality or subvert truth. On the contrary, I think objective reality (by which I mean, at least, what looks the same by agreement among all honest observers) lies somewhere out there, remote and hard of access—at the summation, perhaps of all possible subjective perspectives. Whenever we shift position, we get another glimpse; then, like Cézanne, we return to our canvas and try to fit it in with all the rest. Clio is a muse we spy bathing between leaves. Each time we dodge and slip in and out of different points of view, a little more is revealed.

We have, for example, to incorporate the perspectives of protagonists and victims when we try to reconstruct a crime. We need the testimony of lots of witnesses to reproduce the flicker and glimmer of events. To understand societies, we need to know what it feels like to live in them for participants at every level of power and wealth. To understand cultures, we need to set them in context and know what their neighbours thought of them. To understand humankind, we have to broaden our vision to comprehend other species. To grasp a core we peel away at outer layers. But the past is ungraspable: we see it best when we add context, just as the bull's eye makes a clearer target when the outer rings define it and draw in the eye.

The most spectacular and objective point of view I can imagine is that of the creature I call 'the galactic observer', looking down on our history across an immense distance of time and space. From the cosmic crow's nest, the whole planet is visible and, as in the thought-experiments by St Augustine and Borges that we met in Chapter 1, the look-out views all its past conspectually. What would history look like to the galactic observer?

I suspect the galactic observer might need prompting even to mention such a puny and, so far, short-lived species as humankind. Wheat, or foxes, or protozoa, or viruses might seem more interesting: all, from a biological point of view, have features as conspicuous as those of humans—vast environmental reach, stunning adaptability, remarkable duration. But the observer would surely notice how we differ from other species in our hectic, kaleidoscopic experience of culture: the fact that we have more of it, of more various kinds, than any other creature. I think a look-out in the cosmic crow's nest would summarize our story in a single word: divergence.

Some people think the big narrative, which encompasses just about the whole of history, is of progress or providence or increasing complexity, or cyclical change or dialectical conflict or some other, irreversible, cosmic trend. The galactic observer, however, would surely notice a subtler but more compelling tale: how the limited, stable culture of *homo sapiens*, at our species' first appearance in the archaeological record, scattered and multiplied thousands or scores of thousands of times to cover the tremendous range of divergent ways of life with which we now surprise each other and infest every inhabitable environment on the planet.

Nowadays, some convergence has set in: we exchange culture globally in what we sometimes call 'globalization'. The same food is available, the same music heard, the same religions practised, the same technologies applied, and the same games played all over the world. We even have a 'world language'—a strange dialect of English, which everyone, except the English, who persist with their own, idiosyncratic version of the lingo, is expected to understand at international gatherings. Meanwhile, some traditions, languages, religions, foodstuffs are becoming extinct. But divergence remains dominant. Even if we were to attain the common global culture of visionary dreams and nightmares, this probably would not make the world uniform. It would not displace all the local variations but coat them with an extra layer. It would not unravel the strands in the fabric of the world, but add one more thread.

If we were to see any animals other than ourselves behaving so strangely, with such a wide range of activities and thoughts, we should seek an explanation in evolution or the environment or some combination of the two. As we have seen, students who approach the subject from the scientific tradition—especially some practitioners who call themselves zoologists, ethologists, biologists, behavioural ecologists, and even some evolutionary psychologists—make that very assumption and seek to apply to human behaviour the same methods of explanation that have characterized our traditional attempts to understand other animals.

They succumb to an understandable temptation. The theory of evolution works well for some kinds of change—the transformations of life-forms by the replication of random genetic mutations. We can apply it successfully to some forms of behaviour, including some human behaviour. We feed and breed and sleep, for instance, and weep and scratch and retch and stand on our feet and band together at the urging of biological necessity, with faculties evolved to help us survive. So there are reasonable grounds—on the face of it—to try to explain all behaviour in the same way. When the effort fails, however, it is irrational to persist in it.

Different kinds of behaviour may require different explanations. That may sound like a truism, but the resolute philosopher of science, John Dupré, has had to struggle, generally unsuccessfully, to try to convince advocates who want to ascribe everything we do to our biological inheritance. He accuses them of 'taxonomic paralysis' and 'essentialism'—thinking that because a species has universal characteristics, the creatures in it cannot also have peculiar ones, except as manifestations of their essential commonality. 'It is open to us,' he declares, 'to conclude from the centrality of culture to human ethology, and the great variability of culture, that for most purposes, *Homo Sapiens* is much too broad and coarse a category for understanding human beings.' In cultural terms it might be more helpful to think of humans as composing many species of culture, rather than as constituting a single biological species.[1]

In any case, the theory of evolution itself includes the acknowledgement that biological systems are subject to random changes—changes, that is, inexplicable in terms of the rest of the theory. That acknowledgement should alert us to the possibility that evolutionary explanations have other limitations. Talk of the 'death of Darwinism', as Mark Twain said of rumours of his own death, is greatly exaggerated,[2] but the trend of research on evolution in recent decades has highlighted random mutations at the expense of natural selection and collaborative traits ahead of competitive ones. The distinguished but combative Harvard zoologist Richard Lewontin found a characteristically trenchant way of making this point, denouncing opponents for adherence to unmodified insistence that selectivity explains everything, and speaking of 'a quaking marsh of unsupported claims about the genetic determination of everything from altruism to xenophobia. Dawkins's vulgarizations,' he adds, of Darwinism speak of nothing in evolution but an inexorable ascendancy of genes that are selectively superior, while the entire body of technical advance in experimental and theoretical evolutionary genetics of the last fifty years has moved in the direction of emphasizing non-selective forces in evolution.[3]

As well as random causes, biological change includes functionless consequences or 'spandrels' in the jargon Stephen Jay Gould coined in joint work with Richard Lewontin: by-products of naturally selected changes.

So without violating the theory of evolution we can propose that cultural change is different: it may resemble evolution's anomalous and unpredictable elements, rather than the rule-driven, inexorable triumph of competitive selection. Evolution can probably explain satisfactorily the way merely social creatures, like ants and bees, behave, but it may not work unaided for fully cultural creatures, like chimpanzees; or cetaceans, perhaps; or us.

It is hard, however, to guide warring parties to a middle way in a minefield, or to make arbitration audible above the rattle of guns. The battle between advocates and opponents of evolutionary explanations of culture has become part of wider culture-wars between mutually deaf ideologies of left against right, and reductionism against religion. Neither conflict is rational. There is no reason for God and Darwin to be rival deities—except in minds clouded by passion. You can adapt evolution to suit the political left as well as the right. But once snipers have dug their foxholes they do not lift their heads above the dirt except to shoot.

Professional rivalries, I suspect, exacerbate the nastiness. Instead of consulting each other, as fellow academics should, ahead of publication, and heeding each other's recommendations, some of the most furious contenders in the debates have exchanged unfriendly fire from rival turrets around Harvard Yard. Richard Lewontin has devoted much of his maturity to pointing out that evolution need not explain everything. He denounced his colleague, Edward Wilson, who at the height of their conflict occupied a room in the same building, just below his adversary's, for devising a theory of human nature that allows its followers to argue that xeno-phobia, hierarchy and competition are the 'natural' state of human societies. Thus, by implication, if inequality and violence are 'natural' to human nature, then the fault does not after all lie with our social arrangements and institutions but with our genes.[4]

Lewontin and his supporters indict scientific schematizers for strong constructive tendencies towards political conservatism and West-centred cultural prejudice.[5] Opponents respond with accusations that Lewontin has allowed his socialist ideals to warp his academic judgement. Edward Wilson accused him of orchestrating 'attacks on science from the political extreme left' and pursuing 'a political agenda unencumbered by science'.[6]

I should not intervene in tribal squabbles. But readers (I know I have some, because they write to me) can confirm that I am politically eclectic and indifferent to ideology. So I can feel at ease in no man's land, defy the cross-fire, and admit the truth: some arguments on the side of evolutionary explanations of culture are helpful, but they are not sufficient; cultures are collections of evolved individuals, whose inherited characteristics condition or limit what happens in history, but do not explain it.

* * *

We can see the limits of evolution, and approach a broader, better way of understanding why cultures change, by looking at the evolutionary explanations currently on the table. It is worth keeping an eye open for five common fallacies or abuses or misuses of language: first, that if non-human animals have culture their behaviour must be explicable in purely evolutionary terms; second, that a society or culture can be studied as if it were any group or population; third, that 'social learning' is the essence of culture; fourth, that what is social must also be cultural; and finally that evolution, to be true, must explain everything.

None of those assumptions is valid. The first is easy to dismiss: if we accept that there is no 'essential' difference between species, and that humans are animals among animals, we should not expect human and non-human cultures to change in essentially different ways; the assumption that humans can exceed the limits of evolution and that other creatures cannot is just another form of human arrogance.

As for the second fallacy—that cultures and populations are effectively interchangeable units of study—we should accept that groups are definable in terms of any common feature the observer cares to ascribe to them. Populations are coherent objects of study because they share a common location; societies, on the other hand, are intelligible only in terms of the relationships that bind them, while cultures have the further defining property of sharing and transmitting learned behaviour. Ants and bees are social, because they live in teeming, closely collaborative communities; but, as far as we know, they are not cultural, because little or nothing of what they do has to be acquired by learning. So while it is reasonable to look for evolved characteristics to explain why humans, too, are social, it does not follow that the reasons behind our cultural variety must be sought in the same way.

In any case, to elide culture and social learning—the root of the third and fourth fatal fallacies—is illegitimate. In culture, innovations usually start with individual learning, such as Imo teaching her mother how to wash nuts (above, pp. 102–3). They spread through the rest of the group. There may be instances where learning processes are institutionalized: typically, for instance, we humans use schools to accelerate our young people's acquisition of vicarious experience; but even in such settings, individual relationships are always critical to the transmission of learning. There may be innovations that arise from collective efforts at disinterested thinking or practical problem-solving, but these only become cultural if a lot of individual decisions to learn, adopt, or imitate them ensue. Michael Tomasello—an advocate of the usefulness of the concept of cultural evolution who heads one of the most prestigious institutes devoted to studying culture in evolutionary terms, has a neat way of expressing what separates cultural from social transmission. In the former, when 'modifications by one individual or group of individuals' spread, they 'stay in place until some future individual or individuals make further modifications'.[7] Social learning, strictly speaking, encompasses a much wider range of experience, including instances of collective adaptation to environmental change, and instinctively imitative responses to new behaviour (cf. above, p. 139).

What about the final fallacy: that evolution is only true if it explains everything? Evolution really does happen, and is the best means we have for explaining biological change. Some irrational people have taken against it, mistakenly thinking that it is a theory inimical to God or incompatible with spirituality and a sense of transcendence. But to respond intransigently, by insisting on applying evolutionary language where it does not belong, is equally irrational. If some of the activities we call behaviours are of different kinds, it is reasonable to look for various kinds of explanation for them.

A really wary weather eye will also be alert for the abuse of the word 'evolve' as a pompous synonym for 'change'. To be useful, a word must have its own, proper meaning. If we use 'evolution' slackly, we obscure the truth: that some change is mere change, while other change is genuinely evolutionary. Evolution differs from mere change by obeying or largely conforming to laws; by having a consistent or at least prevalent direction; by following a broadly predictable course; by responding to a single, coherent set of causes; and, in the strict, Darwinian sense (which we need not insist on but should always have in mind) evolution happens because competitive advantage privileges some changes over others. It is not enough to say, with the sociologist Marion Blute, that 'descent with modification is a fact ... about the sociocultural world';[8] it is not even a fact: it is a metaphor. Cultures and cultural behaviours do not 'descend' from one another as creatures or species do. Their nests are full of cuckoos and creations *ex novo*. When Blute says 'culture, quite literally, evolves',[9] her slack language discloses unclear thinking. You cannot have degrees of literalness. Evolution, like descent, is a metaphor: the question is whether it is a useful metaphor in the context of culture. That question cannot fairly be pre-empted by misrepresenting a figure of speech as a fact.

*   *   *

The next few pages cover the merits and defects of how academics currently attempt to apply evolutionary explanations to cultural change. Apart from memetics, which we can set aside as valueless (above, pp. 90–3), and other approaches we have already dealt with (above, pp. 87–93, 138–40), the theories belong, for convenience, under seven headings: genetic determinism; cultural selection; evolutionary game theory; environmental determinism; evolutionary psychology; 'Big History'; and 'dual inheritance theory' or 'gene-culture co-evolution'. As we go through them one by one, we shall see that they are all of some help, or at least of some potential help, in explaining the origins of culture, or universal features of culture, or of some, particular changes; but they do not provide adequate explanations, even in combination, of how and why cultures change, or adequate descriptions of the range and reach of cultural divergence.

It is fair to point out, nonetheless, that theoretically dodgy assumptions do not necessarily invalidate work based on those assumptions. Some enormously valuable empirical data from archaeological projects all over the world have emerged from work done on the assumption that cultures or even particular cultural behaviours descend from one another like species—in the appropriate jargon, they are 'phylogenetic' or 'hierarchically related by descent'. I do not think the assumption is valid; the professional consensus favours it only when applied to languages (which most people do regard, perhaps misleadingly, as emerging from one another like branches from trees and twigs from branches); and even some of the most distinguished upholders of evolutionary archaeology are candid in admitting that tree-like diagrams give only a very approximate and imperfect notion of the relationships between their findings.[10]

Among evolutionist versions of cultural change, the first and most basic theory is simple: genes determine culture. As we have seen (above, pp. 77–90) this is an unpromising proposition. A conspicuous fact makes it inherently improbable: though humans have incomparably the widest range of cultures among primates, we also have perceptibly the tiniest range of variation in DNA.[11] That does not mean that genes have no power to help mould culture. There are cases of genetic or, in some sense, biological differences that correspond with different cultures, though it is hard to say what the balance is between the results of environmentally induced selection, such as, presumably, influences resistance to malaria in sub-Saharan African populations, or of constraints that arise from cultural bias, such as those that favour lactose tolerance in dairying cultures.[12]

Some evidence has accumulated in data of the origins of sex roles.[13] Similar proportions of younger brothers tend to be gay, for instance, in different cultural environments; no one knows why, but the presumption is worth considering that women who have successive male babies may develop a hormonal response that conditions their offspring. Left-handed men are also significantly more likely to be gay than their right-handed counterparts. Work on this subject is vulnerable to bias, as the arguments in favour of the proposition that homosexuality is inborn, rather than learned, have become a liberal cause as well as a matter of scientific enquiry; and there is no justification for reducing the results to a headline, such as 'Genes Make You Gay'. But the evidence is strong enough to warrant saying that both biology and culture influence sexual preferences.

Some researchers are still scouring data for missing links between genes and culture. Bruce T. Lahn, now of the University of Chicago, tells visitors to his website that his interest in genetics began when he was a child in China, envious of Western prosperity, and curious to know why societies differ. His interests, however, have switched to focus on commonalities that 'make us human'. He has become famous for raising the possibility that Neanderthals and *homo sapiens* may have interbred. The claim, though imperfectly supported in the present, sketchy state of the draft Neanderthal genome, looks increasingly convincing as evidence accumulates.[14] In any case, it is surely well intentioned and intelligible as part of an ethical effort to broaden the reach of our moral community by making us feel fraternal towards extinct hominids. Notoriously on the other hand, in 2005 Lahn's work in tracing genes that affect brain size (and perhaps function) in some populations of Eurasian origin raised presumptions about the possible cerebral deficiencies of people from sub-Saharan Africa. Racist inferences proved misleading, and would in any case have no necessary implications for explaining cultural differences. And Lahn and his colleagues were too hasty to ascribe a straightforward geographical distribution to the genetic material they studied. Later investigations, however, linked the same genes to the distribution of peoples with tonal languages, such as Chinese and Yoruba.[15]

So we should hesitate to rule out the possibility that some cultural differences do match differences in the incidence of genes. Matches may be coincidental and the problem of cause and effect remains: cultures, as we have seen (above, pp. 39–45), select genes. And the total difference genetics makes to cultures may be small, at best. But to dismiss the science as irrelevant would be doctrinaire.[16] Sociobiologists who continue to look for the gene, or at least for the combination of genes 'for' this or that ingredient of culture, are not necessarily wasting their time or their patrons' money (though I would neither invest nor recommend investing). If we were, say, to find a polka gene among Austrians and Hungarians or a tango gene in Finns and Argentines, it would be of enormous interest; but it would not necessarily mean that all cultural differences were explicable along similar lines.

It is also worth considering the claim that cultures evolve as Darwin thought species do—by selection of environmentally successful variations while they compete among themselves for survival.[17] We can, at least, admit weaker claims: that culture in general seems to be an evolutionarily useful adaptation for some species, and that, for cultural species, there are benefits in social and collaborative traits, even if specific cultural variations do not yield to the same kind of explanation. As Binghamton biologist David Sloan Wilson puts it, 'altruistic groups beat selfish groups'. Anti-social individuals do not form functional societies, as anyone who has worked in an Oxford college will know from probably bitter experience. As long as we bear in mind the danger of the fallacies to which we are already alert, it should therefore be worth pursuing the evolutionary background of human gregariousness and sociability.

Some research along these lines, however, seems naive. Evolved characteristics may help to make some creatures social; that does not necessarily mean that those creatures are cultural. Evolution may have programmed those sirens of sociobiology—ants and bees—for instance, to be conformist and self-sacrificial; but we humans need other, more elusive characteristics to conform in our diversity of ways and practise our varied range of self-sacrifice. Wilson's proposal, for instance, that evolution can explain religion as a collaborative strategy for making a society altruistic has attracted a lot of funding and generated a lot of research; but no convincing results have ensued, because 'religion' is too wide and vague a category to study coherently. Even people who regard themselves as religious disagree about what it is. Religions concerned with the control and mastery of nature do not fit into the same framework of analysis as those focussed on submission to a transcendent being or justification in another world. There is nothing in common between the religions of cardinals and cargo-cultists that suggests they might have shared origins. Even if there were an evolutionary advantage common to everything we call religion, we should still want to know about the origins of the particularities that shatter it into dissimilar fragments. Jesuits, pantheists, animists, shamans, and enthusiasts who invent religions of their own cannot properly be understood except in terms of their differences.

* * *

In any case, cultures do not really behave like species, in evolutionary terms, because they do not typically make adaptations that conform to the laws of evolution. One of Darwin's most important insights was that when species adapt, the adaptations that conduce to the survival of the species get passed from generation to generation.

Mutations that actively impede survival disappear or become dormant. David Sloan Wilson's philosophical collaborator, Elliott Sober of the University of Wisconsin, Madison, is a spokesman for the theory of evolution, which he has defended valiantly against some of its wilder critics. His definition of an adaptation comes packaged with the cautious and cumbrous language of professional philosophy, but makes the word's meaning in the Darwinian lexicon absolutely clear: 'characteristic c,' he writes,

> is an adaptation for doing task t in a population if and only if members of the population now have c because, ancestrally, there was selection for having c and c conferred a fitness advantage because it performed task t.[18]

For culture to conform to an evolutionary model, therefore, cultures must adapt in the same way, transmitting innovative behaviours that favour the supreme task—the survival of the societies concerned. But that is not what cultural creatures do. On the contrary, if the study of history teaches us anything, it is that we are engaged in a march of folly, along a way picked across ruins. Many of the practices we adopt most frequently and enthusiastically tend to be destructive.

Some obvious examples are activities that involve high costs and relatively low returns in terms of social utility. Writing history books does little to make societies sustainable, and as historians are often subversive critics of present practices the consequences can impair the chances of survival of communities who come to know their past too well. Their self-defining, nourishing myths are unlikely to survive intact. Yet all literate societies license historiography. Art, music, ritual, ideology, myth, humour, and story-telling form a list of similarly impractical yet equally widely espoused behaviours, listed by the cognitive psychologist Geoffrey Miller in an attempt to invoke sexual selection to explain their popularity.[19] As a dabbler in all the practices listed, I wish I could attest to their sexual attractiveness. But they seem, in common experience, relatively ineffective as sexual selectors—to say nothing of extreme instances of socially dysfunctional or at best marginally useful behaviours, such as self-mutilation, castration, celibacy, and disguise. In any case sexual selection does not operate independently of the laws of evolution in general: to support the theory of evolution it has to favour traits advantageous for the survival of the species.

Further examples abound. War is perhaps the most glaring case of widely adopted dysfunctional behaviours. Almost every human society has had recourse to it, and sooner or later it has done for all of them (as it may yet do for us, when we unleash mutually assured destruction on each other). Population-boosting behaviours, which almost every human community has sought without restraint, often end in Malthusian nightmares. Recently, we have begun to see the destructive power of population control, which, in combination with life-prolonging technologies that gratify privileged individuals and classes but do little for society as a whole, has given some modern communities unsustainably warped demographics: a top-heavy cohort of the elderly and infirm. Highly industrialized and post-industrial societies develop—to judge on the evidence available so far—a fatal tendency to limit population below replacement levels. Foodways, food-garnering techniques, water-exploitation methods, production-boosting techniques, and practices such as city-building that strain the resources on which societies depend, are part of the story of the decline and fall of many peoples. Yet few communities have resisted the temptation to try them out. Broadly speaking, the more they innovate, the shorter-lived they are.

That is why every ambitious and innovative civilization of the past is one with Nineveh and Tyre, while truly successful societies—those blessed with long-sustained and unbreakable durability—tend to be the most resistant to cultural innovations. You find them in isolated deserts and forests, keeping up their ancestors' way of life and defying the push and pull of the world outside. When Robert Louis Stevenson lived in the South Seas, he puzzled over the contrast between the dying societies he observed—literally dying, as populations stopped breeding—and others that continued to prosper in apparently identical environments. He realized that the lethal pathogens were cultural. Wherever indigenous people succumbed to the temptation to imitate the vectors of Western values—the businessmen, imperialists, and missionaries—and forfeited traditions of their own, they lost their reason to keep going. 'Where there have been the fewest changes, important or unimportant, salutary or hurtful, there the race survives. Where there have been most, . . . there it perishes.'[20] The same observation holds true for most of the world, so far, for most of the time.

Perhaps the most surprising and counter-intuitive example of the destructiveness of widely espoused cultural change is farming. In modern industrial society, we have a lot of bucolic, romantic notions about the closeness of farming to nature; but it is harder to think of a more unnatural practice than recrafting the landscape, plants, and animals in the service of humans. Farming is really a form of 'unnatural selection'—using speciation and hybridization to bring new species into the food chain, instead of relying on natural selection to provide the plants and animals we eat, as our forebears did until about 10,000 years ago. Since then, almost every society that has had the opportunity has embraced tillage of the soil as a means of getting food. The effects have in almost every case been disastrous. Typically, societies that adopt agriculture expose themselves to ecological catastrophes, because they become dependent on a single staple food, or a small range of such foods. Their populations show signs of malnutrition and the increased incidence of disease—which tends to be especially virulent if they also keep animals for food: the flocks become reservoirs of infection, eco-niches in which deadly microbes evolve. They need more labour and have less leisure than foraging folk. Because they cannot easily move to a new location, they put themselves at the mercy of environmental change. They become more vulnerable to attack from nomads. Because their territory is too precious to be shared, and neighbours' land too alluring to be ignored, agrarian communities become committed to war. The need to organize labour and warehouse stocks inflicts tyrannous governments, coercive laws, privileged elites, and burdensome police measures on hard-pressed people—which in turn causes revolutionary upheavals that often destroy the system, if war or disease or starvation or environmental collapse do not strike first.[21]

Are non-human cultures equally prone to replicate self-destructive behaviour? We have too little data to say so for certain and, in any case, the rate of change in non-human cultures is so slow that we cannot hope for many testable examples. But I suspect that the temptation to behave dysfunctionally is a widespread aberration that marks cultural systems as deeply different from biological ones. Chimpanzees in Bossou, for instance, pound palm kernels to extract the goodness. It destroys the palm.[22] This behaviour resembles that of human cultures that hunt their prey to extinction, or plunder their own water, or exhaust their sources of fuel.

It is tempting to try to adumbrate a general theory of cultural change as typically or preponderantly dysfunctional: but that is not part of my purpose and I do not claim that the evidence is sufficient for it. Rather, I hope readers will agree that there are enough cases of dysfunctional adaptations in the history of culture to make us sceptical of competitive advantage as the motor-force of such changes. Evolutionarily successful genes do not undermine the chances of survival of the species in which they are selected. Commonly, however, widely adopted cultural practices subvert the cultures that adopt them. In one sense, *homo sapiens* is a successful species, in that it competes successfully with most other species in shared environments and has colonized most of the planet—or at least most of the land surface. But so far it has not been around for long enough to qualify for unconditional success. Most of the cultures that have emerged in human history have been manifestly unsuccessful: they may have flourished briefly, but they have perished quickly. Those that have endured have been least susceptible to innovation.

The self-destructive itch does not necessarily make it impossible to argue that evolution governs cultural change: evolutionary game theory has an answer to the objection. Players adopt strategies that lead to their own destruction, because they make a calculation—that often turns out to be wrong—about how to get a competitive advantage. Arms races and the space race provide examples familiar to anyone whose life overlapped with much of the twentieth century.

So does every madcap over-investment in limited resources: it is better, in the minds of the exploiters, to exhaust the resources hurriedly than to leave them for others. But this argument—based on unobjectionable facts—introduces a further element into our picture of how cultures change: the calculation of short-term advantage demands mind or, at least, in material language, brain—something neither genes nor the impersonal forces of evolution have. To play games you have already to have culture.

*   *   *

Most often, perhaps, cultures make self-destructive adjustments in their relationships with their environments—over-exploiting resources or exposing themselves to disease. Environment always clings to culture, conditioning people's responses, limiting their potential, stimulating their inventiveness. It seems reasonable to suppose that in the early stages of cultural divergence environment drove innovation, as human communities left their homelands to traverse or colonize unfamiliar habitats. There is, however, no predictable correspondence between culture and environment.[23] Years ago, when I worked as a Professor of Environmental History in the University of London, I attempted a big thought-experiment, trying to envisage what the history of the world would look like if one approached it environmentally, biome by biome, rather than—as historians traditionally do—civilization by civilization, or region by region, or country by country. One of the most striking results was that, where human communities occupy identical or nearly identical environments, they respond in dazzlingly different ways, devising contrasting solutions to common problems of coping with the same resources, climate, topography, hydrography, diseases, and soil.[24]

In the wastes of the Saharan Fezzan, the ancient Garamantes built cities and underground canals, whereas the Dawada clung to surface oases and fed on the plankton they dredged from the water. In medieval Greenland, Norse colonists attempted a daring and ultimately unsuccessful project to modify the environment for farming, whereas the Thule practised traditional foraging. In Mesoamerican seasonal rain forests, city Maya and forest Maya led contrasting, mutually baffling ways of life. These examples can be multiplied almost indefinitely from the lessons of modern life. Farmers of German descent in Freiburg, Pennsylvania, operate different inheritance patterns from Yankee neighbours on identical soil in an identical environment a few miles away. In the Upper Amazon, the Jívaro protect their traditional way of life by keeping outsiders at bay with ferocious violence, while the Nukak avoid conflict by minimizing contact. In adjoining quarters of every big, modern, Western city you can find people transposing ways of life from distant environments almost without modification, and pass, say, from Little China to Little Italy across the width of a single street. Political frontiers, flanked by contrasting institutions and customs, cut through otherwise uniform deserts, forests, valleys, and ridges all over the world. This does not mean that cultures are uninfluenced by their physical surroundings and the eco-systems of which they form part. On the contrary, there are plenty of examples of such influence on record.[25] But there is no reason to privilege environment as the supreme determinant. As we have seen, culture and environment interact with mutually transforming effects.[26]

Still, it is likely that, 100,000 years ago or so, when the whole of *homo sapiens* occupied a small, environmentally consistent area, our ancestors shared a single culture, or a range of cultural difference, no greater than that we find among chimpanzees or other primates today. So, according to the theory of evolution, we embarked on our history as a cultural species with mental and physical characteristics appropriate to the east African savanna. The ways of life our ancestors devised in those days were constructed with those characteristics.

Evolutionary psychology applies this insight (certainly reasonable, probably valid) to the subsequent history of culture, explaining much of what we do as the lingering effect of long-ago evolution. Our strategies for storing food, for instance, may vary from culture to culture, but they all arise from the fact that we have bodies ill-adapted to a wide range of foodstuffs. Our tendency to over-eat is a consequence of the insecurities of our scavenging and foraging ancestors. Our inclination to fatness is a relic of the evolution of bodies adapted to store energy sources under our skin. Our ball games are various, but they all originate in the evolved mind-set of a species dependent on missile power to make up for its lack of other kinds of physical prowess in the face of predators and prey. Our development of communication tools and elaborate collaborative strategies is the result of having to form relatively large communities compared with those of competitor species. The forms of incest prohibited in some societies are quite different from those proscribed in others—but all societies have them because we are hard-wired to extend our social relationships beyond our kin. Evolutionary psychology enshrines a reliable principle: we can only do what evolution has equipped us for. It helps to explain features of culture that all cultures share. As we shall see, it has to play a critical part in explaining why we have culture at all. But, except in the minds of irrational devotees, who engage in amazing mental gyrations in order to make everything conform to their theory, evolutionary psychology cannot explain the rich variety of culture. It can explain, perhaps, similarities in diet from St Paul to Sapporo, but not why you find lutefisk in the former and sashimi in the latter.

* * *

On one hand, insistence that culture operates according to Darwinian laws that govern the struggle for survival, and on the other genetic and environmental determinism, here are strong—perhaps extreme—forms of faith in evolution. There are also weak forms—weak, that is, not intellectually but in terms of the degree of commitment to evolution as a universal explanation. Their proponents embrace evolution as analogy, arguing that culture does evolve, but in a way analogous to—rather than identical with—that of organic life. Like life, according to this tradition of thought, lifeways change in a consistent direction, and diversity and complexity are both on the signposts—even if, occasionally the path goes back on itself for a while, or troughs or ditches impinge on it.[27] 'Progress', as the great advocate of an organic notion of culture, Herbert Spencer, put it, 'essentially consists in the transformation of the homogeneous into the heterogeneous'.[28]

I am not sure that the observations on which this formulation rests are accurate. Some biota have got more complex and more diverse at intervals, punctuated by reversals and æons of stagnation, over the last 4 billion years; so has culture—over the last 30 million years by my calculation (above, p. 107), or however long you like—but not consistently. Life-forms seem to obey the Biblical command to multiply, while cultures diverge—but the stories of both processes are stained and splattered with the debris of extinctions. Some changes are progressive, but others leave a lot of things worse or simply unaffected. In almost every period archaeologists and historians can detect evidence of societies that exhibited unprecedented size and complexity in their days—but they usually collapsed and gave way to smaller, simpler successors. Chaos punctuates complexity. Entropy stalks whatever we think of as order.

Still, for the sake of argument, it may be helpful to accept for a moment the assertion that history is bound on a course 'into the heterogeneous' and towards the ever more complex. The most impressive work in the effort to identify such an overall trajectory among all the details of history has focussed on the history of energy consumption, in contributions, for instance, from the school of historians (some of whom are also scientists) who practise what they call 'Big History'.[29] At the heart of the Big History project is a valid observation, sometimes known as White's Law: the more energy a system consumes, the bigger and more complex it tends to be. Leslie White was a renegade pupil of Franz Boas. In the 1950s, at the University of Michigan, he devoted his work to repudiating cultural relativism, and restoring the notion that some societies are more advanced than others by objective standards. He wanted to fillet contingency out of history and make the future predictable. He shared a common US prejudice: admiration of the machine, and a consumerist scale of values that now—in an ecologically anxious age—seems dangerously profligate: the more energy you use up, the better.[30]

White's way of putting it was 'culture evolves as the amount of energy harnessed per capita per year is increased, or as the efficiency of the instrumental means of putting the energy to work is increased'.[31] The formulation is too schematic and inflexible, but White had a point. Plants and creatures really do require more energy to sustain them, the bigger and more active they are. So do social systems. To put it another way: a system will be stable when the energy that passes through it is just sufficient to sustain it; if there is insufficient energy, the system will shrink or collapse; surplus energy makes it possible for the system to change and grow. The quest for energy, more precisely than—in Darwinian language—'the struggle to survive', has driven biological evolution. Maybe we can say the same of cultural evolution. History—according to this way of thinking—is a story of people seeking to harness ever-greater flows of energy.

Big History is an admirable and ingenious attempt to make sense of humans in the context of the whole of nature. Lust for enhanced energy-sources is genuinely a prominent theme of the past and (unhappily) will probably remain so for the future. It helps us understand why humans and some other cultural creatures use tools; why they change the range of their diets and try to develop new sources of food; why humans use fire, and fossil fuels, and mechanical technologies; why they are willing to risk nuclear immolation, or occlude the atmosphere with carbon poison, or the planet with waste. It does not, however, explain the variability of the forms of culture. Changes in energy consumption are themselves cultural changes that reflect the shifting values and priorities of the societies that make them. In biology, energy flows are causes of other kinds of change; in history, they are results.

* * *

One more description of cultural change as evolutionary is worth considering: dual inheritance theory (so-called because it acknowledges that, metaphorically speaking, cultures are heirs to both genetic and non-genetic legacies), is an attempt to produce a synthesis that recognizes cultural change as different from but interdependent with biological evolution.[32] There is a sense in which this is an unquestionable proposition because, as we have seen (above, p. 42), culture affects genes; and without some creatures sharing a genetic predisposition in favour of sociability there would be no such thing as culture in the first place. But despite the prevalence of the terms 'evolution' and 'co-evolution' in the literature, the drift of the work generated in the tradition has been to expose the limitations of evolutionary models for understanding how cultures change.

For instance, to explain forms of culture that do not yield to evolutionary explanation, the term 'cultural drift' has become popular in dual inheritance work. Users of the term differ about what it means, but the common element of most usage is that some cultural changes occur randomly and are imitated capriciously.[33] What is random is not evolved (though it may contribute to evolution). Evolution—it is worth repeating—is not mere change: at least, it has to be change in a particular direction; in Darwinian terms, it has to be change favourable to the survival of the organism or society or gene concerned. To call it 'a process of change' is mere weaselism.[34] Change can be process-less. Random changes happen by means of misunderstandings, errors, deceit, delusion, and chance encounters with other cultures. I detect no process here, only the muddle of minds and the glorious chaos of cultures.

No one can either endorse or dismiss dual inheritance theory without paying tribute to the work of the brilliant collaborators in anthropology and genetics, Peter Richerson and Rob Boyd, whom we have already met (above, p. 44) pointing out how societies exert cultural preferences that affect genetic inheritance. Pioneering methods inspired them, first broached at Stanford more than thirty years ago, when M.W. Feldman and Luigi Cavalli-Sforza sought to quantify culture in an attempt to find 'a theory of cultural change'[35] and 'laid the . . . theoretical foundations' of co-evolution.[36] Like the pioneers, Boyd and Richerson want to be able to model cultural change mathematically, and to keep evolutionary language in their descriptions. Unlike Feldman and Cavalli-Sforza, they also want to go on believing that at some level culture changes in a 'Darwinian' way. But their work is full of examples of the autonomy of culture. 'There are', they say, 'important, persistent differences between human groups that are created by culturally transmitted ideas, not differences in the physical, or biotic environment.'[37] For them, cultural evolution means the accumulation of learning across generations, rather as Darwin saw biological adaptations arising from the accumulation of small variations; but even if this is the case (and as we shall see it only describes a small part of how cultures change) the analogy with Darwin's theory is very weak: for him—for the whole evolutionist tradition—it is not so much the claim that variations accumulate that makes them evolutionary as the process of selection. Richerson and Boyd rehabilitate the 'decisions, choices, and preferences of individuals',[38] which are not of course independent of evolution but constitute a further category that transcends its limits. They want a synthesis of history and biology, but have not got beyond doing a good job of surveying both fields from a rather uncomfortable perch on top of the narrow fence between them.

They accumulate plenty of cases that suggest that evolution cannot explain cultural variation. But they have two answers to the claim. First, they see it as possible for the same evolutionary impulses to have a range of contrasting effects. But how could that be, except by way of environmental differences, which, as we have seen, do not generally correspond to differences of culture? Evolution does generate divergence among species or, in technical language, 'the production of multiple phenotypes from a single genotype'[39] but this almost always happens in response to identifiable environmental changes. Second, Richerson and Boyd point out that, like biological evolution, cultural change throws up maladaptations—widely replicated but functionless or dysfunctional traits that selection fails to excise—and that these account for a lot of cultural divergence. But, as we have seen, most culture is of this kind, resembling, therefore, at best, a phenomenon marginal to mainstream evolution. Human culture is like Swift's 'Fair Nymph Going to Bed'. When you strip off the frills and furbelows, paint and powder, little is left to necessity. Culture, as our species practises it, resembles a Perpendicular church, or Victorian décor, or a *ballo in maschera*, or a rococo frame, or a Mozartian extravaganza with 'too many notes'. Most of it is useless ornament and masquerade that humans add for sheer joy or in unrestrained fancy. It is impossible to account for culture without acknowledging its lithe, magical shifts of colour and shape.

*　*　*

There is a further, pretty nearly fundamental objection that, as far as I am aware, no apologists for evolution have ever faced frankly or fully (though they have sometimes acknowledged or dismissed it) when dealing with the mutability of culture: if culture does evolve, it is logically impossible for it to do so on Darwinian lines. The way it changes more closely resembles the model of biological evolution suggested by Darwin's predecessor, Jean-Baptiste Lamarck, who died ten years before the voyage of the *Beagle*. Lamarck was a protégé of the Comte de Buffon, whom we have met (above, p. 54) as an environmental determinist. In the tradition of his patron, Lamarck sought laws for nature to follow, and environmental influences to explain the apparent self-transformations of species. He was one of the freethinkers in whom the Enlightenment abounded and part of his motivation was to picture a world that makes sense without God. In what he called 'philosophical zoology' he summed up the combined fruits of his own observations, traditional scientific commonplaces, and folklore, proposing that 'the distinctive features individual specimens acquire through the influence of their environments pass by reproduction to the generation that ensues'. Tunnels make moles blind, and they pass blindness to their heirs; giraffes crane their necks to get at remote leaves and their offspring inherit accordingly. All species, Lamarck thought—including humans—adjust their pigmentation according to their exposure to light and transmit their colours to their progeny.[40] 'The blacksmith', as Peter Medawar once joked, 'who is usually called up to testify on these occasions, gets mightily strong arms from forging; somehow this affects the cells that manufacture his spermatozoa, so that his children start life specially well able to develop strong arms.'[41]

Darwin accepted Lamarck's views: he even advised working girls to marry and breed before they acquired rough hands or ravaged complexions, in case they should pass these unattractive features on to their offspring. But Darwin's discovery of natural selection eliminated the need for Lamarck's theory. Except in marginal cases, the evidence that evolutionary research uncovered until well into the twentieth century was against Lamarck. Modern Darwinianism—neo-Darwinianism, as advocates sometimes call it—excludes the heritability of acquired characteristics or (in response to the discovery of some exceptional instances) confines this to a very minor role in evolution. But culture is all about the inheritance of acquired behaviour: indeed, it is definable as such. In biology, the heritable mutations are not acquired: they are already present in the genes, awaiting selection in propitious circumstances. In culture, creatures add new behaviour to their repertoires and teach it or demonstrate it to each other. Culture cannot evolve in modern biologists' sense of the word.[42] The blacksmith might get strong, skilful sons, but only because he teaches them his trade. 'A man', as Medawar said, 'can ... influence posterity by other than genetic means.'[43]

* * *

The effort to invoke biology to explain history has failed because it is basically ill conceived. History, to quote a collaboration between an eminent scientist and an eminent historian, is 'too generally messy' for scientific treatment.[44] Societies do not change by transmission and inheritance, but by acquisition and acculturation. History seems unDarwinian precisely because it is a story of the survival of the unfittest. The societies we class as least evolved, least complex, least developed, with fewest parts, last longest—while elaborate civilizations become playgrounds and photo-ops for romancers amid ruins. Culture is just too different from organic life to invite the same kind of explanation. Cells are self-organizing systems that adapt to survive and resist permeation by hostile intrusions from outside. Cultures, by contrast, are built for chaos and as prone to self-destruction as to survival.

History is not an extension of biology. I do not want, however, to advocate a version of either that excludes the other, because evolution has given us the bodies and brains we work with. We ignore it at our peril if our aim is to understand human behaviour. I think we can get beyond the limits of evolution, and elude the demarcation disputes of historians and biologists, by taking a fresh look at how human cultures differ from those of other cultural animals.

The difference, we know (above, pp. 122, 126, 134) is a difference of degree. But in some respects it is a very big difference: the extent and variety of communication, the rapidity and acceleration of change, the range of divergence, the assortment of behaviour, the fertility of innovation, the multiplication of technologies, the proliferation and conflict of ideas, the richness of symbols, the abundance of creativity, the array of art and music and fun, the vagaries of fashion. If we engage in more possibilities of all these kinds than other cultural animals, it is in part, I want to suggest, because we can envisage more such possibilities. We have teeming minds—if I am allowed that word—full of notions of unrealized worlds that we labour to create. We have a peculiar propensity to see or infer or intuit potentialities that are not present to our senses. These properties of the way humans think are worth investigating, not only because no other animal rivals them but also because artificial intelligence research has, so far, been unable to reproduce them on a human scale. I intend to argue that they generate culture and are responsible, in appropriate conditions, for the accelerations of cultural change.

We need next, therefore, to seek the origins of imagination. It may seem paradoxical, but to understand imagination, we have to begin with memory.

6

THE IMAGINATIVE ANIMAL

Uncovering the dynamism of culture

In the background of one of Salvador Dalí's most famous paintings, an indistinct ocean fades into a vague sky. The work is 'The Persistence of Memory'—but the name is an instance of the artist's ironic sense of humour, because every image in the composition illustrates the evanescence, weakness, wobbles, and waywardness of our powers of recall. The vanishing ocean erodes a neighbouring cliff. A tree withers. Sands shift. Gigantic clocks and watches buckle, melt, and sag with the passage of time. They corrode or house corrupting, devouring bugs and parasites. In the middle of the canvas, a watch mutates into one of Bosch's monstrous fantasies. This seems apt: memories do become monsters.

It is astonishing to me how little interest historians take in the cognitive science of memory, because so many of the sources on which we rely pass through the medium of remembrance before they get to us. Some of us are aware that memories are socially or culturally constructed. Some of us ask our students to read the work of Maurice Halbwachs on social or so-called collective memory and reflect on his maxim that 'the past is not preserved but is reconstructed on the basis of the present.'[1] Yet the problems of memory go much further than that: to the roots of individual recollections, on which social memory depends and of which most historical sources are composed. We know very little about individual memory except that it is usually bad. There has been an enormous amount of work in recent years by psychologists, anthropologists, but above all by neuro-physiologists, which combines to undermine our faith in memory even further.

In the work of a psychologist such as Alan Baddeley, it resembles a trick-mechanism for evading awkward facts, as much as a trap for capturing them.[2] We practise convenient oblivion. We retrieve memories through rosy filters. The memory is the massage. Among anthropologists, in work well represented by a paper by Jack Goody and Ian Watt,[3] it is now a maxim that in non-literate cultures orally transmitted memories are not fossilized, word for word, in bardic retrieval-systems. Perpetual retelling substantially recreates, re-invents them. Memory is wired to be warped. It is not a highway for time travel: the past to which it takes you never really happened quite in the way you think. Recall is a siren call.

Surprisingly, perhaps, this is just what one would expect from the results of experimental work in recent years by cognitive scientists working with literate subjects. Memories are 'recorded' or registered in an environment of hectic neural activity, in which synapses fire and proteins are generated: in the judgement of the leading authority, Daniel Schacter, it is practically impossible to suppose that memories are recorded unchanged:

> Memories are never exact replicas of external reality. Psychophysical studies and electrical recordings from the brain have shown that incoming sensory information is not received passively...In this sense all memories are 'created' rather than simply 'received'. No memory or mental image exactly replicates the constellation of nerve impulses associated with the initial sensation. Past experience, encoded in the strength of synaptic connections throughout the activated neural networks, modifies the incoming information.[4]

This is, for historians, equivalent to the uncertainty principle for physicists. The environment in which memories are retrieved introduces more levels of uncertainty, while often at the same time deluding the memorist into 'a conviction of accuracy which the empirical data does not support'.[5] So memory is always removed from reality, though, for reasons we still do not know, it works better in some cases than others. Unless and until we understand how differences between good and bad memory arise, caution and scepticism are our best recourse.

Despite the glaring deficiencies of human memory, we seem glibly to assume that we must be better at remembering than other animals are. According to a long-standing shibboleth, humans are our planet's only time travellers: only we can remember and therefore situate ourselves in the dynamic of time—revisiting the past, envisioning the future. Obviously animals have to be able to remember objective facts; otherwise they could never return to their caches or nests or retrieve their routes, but most academic experts have endorsed the belief that human memories are of a different order, because self-consciousness enhances them.[6] Most people still share Robert Burns's opinion of his 'wee, sleekit, tim'rous, cowering' mouse, whom, he thought, 'the present only toucheth', as if the little creature were arrested in time, aware only of the immediate.[7]

The distinction between brute memories, isolated in the present, and human memories, comprehending time, now seems false. Western scrub-jays can remember not just what food they hide but also where and when it was hidden. Experimenters with rats have emulated the success of those who work with jays. Rats, who can find their way around mazes the complexity of which would leave me lost, return unerringly to the places where they formerly encountered food. They also pass tests designed to tell whether they can remember the order in which they encounter smells.[8] Clive Wynne, an elegant advocate for believing in non-human minds, who is well known for imagining what it would be like to be a bat, summarizes some of the relevant experiments:

In the laboratory, pigeons can remember which out of hundreds of arbitrary visual patterns will be followed by food, and their memories show little sign of degradation months after the initial experiment. Pigeons also remember what their neighborhood looks like, so that they can find their own loft as they return from homing flights. Honeybees remember which parts of a maze contain food. Chimpanzees in the wild can remember where they left the good heavy stones that make excellent anvils for bashing nuts open. Chimpanzees in the laboratory can remember the correct order to press a series of numerals on a computer screen in order to obtain a food treat. Vampire bats can remember who has given them a blood donation in the past and use that information in deciding whether to respond to a petitioner who is begging for a little blood.[9]

It would be reasonable to object that although we class all these instances as memory, they may represent phenomena best understood as of different types. People who want to belittle non-human memory might insist that many of the non-human animals' responses more resemble conditioned reflexes or reactions to stimuli than recollections retrieved from a permanent store. But, apart from prejudice, we have no good grounds for making such a distinction. St Augustine thought that a horse could remember a path when he was following it, but could not recall it back in his stall. But even St Augustine cannot really have known that: he was making an assumption on the basis of dogma: God could not, in his view, have deigned to give horses minds resembling those of His chosen species. Deniers of non-human animal memory today make pretty much the same mistake.

Experiments with chimpanzees and gorillas provide material directly comparable with human experience. Panzee, an exceptionally adept, symbol-toting, female chimpanzee at Georgia State University, presented the head of her lab, Charles Menzel, with a unique opportunity for research into the memory of a non-human animal with whom it is possible to converse: Panzee communicates using cards or keyboard. While she watched, the research team hid dozens of kiwi fruits, pineapples, and toys—including rubber snakes, balloons, and paper. Unprompted, after long intervals of up to sixteen hours, Panzee let her keepers know where the goodies were. She recalled the locations of more than 90 per cent of them. She had never before had to obtain food by pointing to places outside her enclosure. She got no unconscious help from her keepers, who received no advance information on the whereabouts of the treats. She showed not just that chimps benefit from an instinct for finding food in the wild, but also that they—or at least she—can remember unique events and plan the application of her knowledge.[10] Menzel says 'animal memory systems have always been underestimated—the upper limits are not really known'.[11]

Our memories are bad by comparison with those of other species, at least in some ways. Everyone can summon anecdotal evidence of this fact. My dog is infinitely better than I at remembering how people look (or, I suppose, smell). After seeing Beau, my dachshund, at work, I can believe the Homeric tale of how Odysseus returned home after a twenty years' absence, unrecognized by everyone except his dog.[12] On one occasion, Beau showed he recognized a visitor he had not seen for six years by bringing her a toy he had received from her on her previous visit—having gone to rummage for it in some hidden locality, as he never, to my knowledge, played with it himself. He is also prodigious in remembering routes—a skill I cannot emulate. One need only set out for some destination: even if it is only Beau's second journey along the route concerned, after a long interval since the first, he will bound ahead in utter confidence. We do not have to rely on anecdote. Controlled studies support our conviction that in some respects our memories are feeble by other animals' standards.

Ayuma, a quick-witted chimpanzee in a research unit in Kyoto, became famous in 2008 when she starred in a TV show, beating human competitors in a computerized memory game. The contestants had to recall images of numerals flashed on a screen for 210 milliseconds. Ayuma recalled 80 per cent accurately. Her nine human rivals all scored zero.[13] Some humans have cried 'unfair!' because, with practice, they can ape Ayuma.[14]

'Ape Memory' has become a popular video-game worldwide, as members of our species try to get up to chimpanzee levels of excellence. 'Gorilla Memory' is a comparable game, inspired by King, a gorilla resident of Monkey Jungle, Miami, Florida, who is good at counting. King waves and points to icons printed on cards to communicate with humans. At thirty years of age, he was well stricken with maturity when primatologists picked on him for memory tests, and was well attuned to human peculiarities. He showed that he could master past events in time and array them in order by remembering, with a level of performance significantly well above chance, each of three foods, reversing, when asked to do so, the order in which he ate them.[15] In his memory, he can connect particular individuals with foods they gave him, even when his keepers have forgotten. He would make a far better witness than most humans at a criminal identity parade. Primatologist Bennett Schwartz has led a team performing acts King had never previously seen. They would do physical jerks, or pretend to steal a 'phone, or play a guitar. When they asked King who had done which performance, he got the answer right 60 per cent of the time: the score may seem unimpressive, but few humans could attain it.[16]

It is not necessary for my case to demonstrate the superiority of non-human memories over human ones. I make the comparisons simply to draw attention to human memory's poverty, unreliability, deficiency, and distortions. It is always hard to forfeit self-regard. We prize our memories and take pride in them because they seem so precious for our sense of self—something we are only just beginning to concede to other animals. Memory is one of the mental faculties we deploy in devising and preserving so much human culture—our histories, our myths—and which we call on for our inventiveness, starting, whenever we think or make something new, with what we remember of whatever we thought or made before. Most people recoil when you tell them that human memories are not the best on our planet, but the evidence is suggestive and subversive. It is worth pausing to think about this counter-intuitive notion. Humans have almost always assumed that any faculty that might justify us in classifying ourselves apart from other beasts must be a superior faculty. But maybe we should have been looking at something inferior—at least, inferior in some respects—in us.

How can this forfeiture of human superiority have happened?

Daniel Schacter's explanation is convincing: evolution has given us bad memories, because good ones would make life intolerable.

We have to shift clutter out of the lumber room. We have to be able to discard relatively unimportant data to focus on what we really need.

This fact allies memory closely with imagination. Memory is a faculty of seeing something that is not present to our senses—a description that matches imagination with equally perfect accuracy. To put it succinctly, both faculties make us see what is not there. The fact that our memories distort recollections of events that once really happened shows that memory has creative power: it can recast reality as fantasy, experience as speculation. Work on how the brain works confirms the contiguity of memory and imagination, which, as far as we can tell, 'happen' in overlapping areas. The electrical and chemical activity that goes on in the brain when imagination is at work is almost identical with that which accompanies the registration and retrieval of memory. This should not surprise us: memory works by forming representations of facts and events—which is also what imagination does. Mnemotechnics, the ancient 'art of memory' that Cicero used to deliver speeches in the Roman courts and senate, assigns a vivid image—which may not be a naturally suggestive symbol—to each point the speaker wants to make. A bloody hand might stand for a humdrum point of procedure, a lovely rose or a luscious fruit for the deplorable vices of the speaker's opponent.[17]

Resistance to the fact that memory and imagination overlap has come from two academic communities: philosophers and jurisprudents.[18] Aristotle prejudiced philosophers by insisting, with his usual common sense, that memories must refer to the past—and the past really happened. But life sometimes traduces common sense. In practice memories fuse with imaginings. Instead of recalling that uncorrupted past we mingle it with features it never had. Women who remember faithfully the real pain of childbirth would not be as anxious to repeat it as they commonly are; nor would soldiers return to the trenches, unless they suppressed or romanticized the horrors of war. Old men remember their feats—good authority tells us—with advantages. As well as self-interested modifications, we make outright errors, mistaking imaginatively transformed memories for literal copies of the events we recall. Memories 'recovered' in hypnosis or psychotherapy or psycho-analysis have life-changing power, but sometimes they are really inventions or transformations. The vices that raddle individual memory—the self-interest, the rose-colouring, the sins of transmission, have their part in shaping social memory, too. Propaganda engraves falsehood in monuments, writes it into textbooks, plasters it onto billboards, insinuates it into ritual. It helps make social memory intractable, unresponsive to facts or historical revision. False memory syndrome, which psychology detects in individuals, is detected by history in whole societies. When individual memories are shared and recorded in enduring forms, the outcome is social memory: a received version of the past, which can reach back to times no individual can claim to remember. We can live with the mercurial nature of our individual memories. But they get turned into social memory by dialogue, context, the input and feedback of those around us.

Some people who work in jurisprudence are reluctant to acknowledge that memory and imagination are similar. For the work of law courts, it would be convenient to separate fanciful repicturings of events in question from real accounts of what happened. We know, however, that any two such accounts rarely tally in practice. The text everyone cites whenever the subject crops up is decisive: 'In a Grove', the short story of 1922 by Royonosuke Akutagawa, inspired one of the great works of cinema, Kurosawa's *Rashomon*, which forms part of every bourgeois education in movies. Each witness to a murder gives contradictory evidence from his or her own observations. A shaman releases the testimony of the victim's ghost. But the reader—or the audience of the movie version—remains unconvinced. Every trial, every comparison of testimony, confirms the unreliability of memory. 'You were all in gold,' sings a character in the stage-musical version of *Gigi*. When the lady corrects him ('I was dressed in blue'), 'oh yes,' he says, 'I remember it well'. We all remember equally badly.

Poorly functioning memory is a vital part of what makes humans imaginative creatures. Every false memory is a glimpse of a possible new future—a reconfigured world that we can aim for if we like.

* * *

The distortions of memory help us by enlarging imagination. Memory is not, however, the whole of imagination. Interesting work by a biomedical researcher, Robert Arp, posits what he calls 'scenario visualization', which is really just a fancy name for practical imagination. He links it with a hypothetical psychological adaptation that arose in our hominid history in response to the demands of tool making, such as constructing spear-throwing devices for hunting. He thinks this is a faculty unique to humans—the power of the mind's eye to transform a stick into a javelin, and then, by a further imaginative leap, to add a throwing spear. No other animal, as far as we know, re-envisions a stick quite so radically, but many find practical uses for sticks in solving other problems—building a nest, fishing for termites, enhancing an aggressive charge in a bid for alpha status, smiting nuts. All problem solving surely involves some 'scenario visualization' or capacity for imaginatively foreseeing a solution. When a rat finds its way through a maze, I take it the creature knows where he or she is going. My dog devised an excellent (though ultimately unavailing) strategy for catching squirrels: he took to positioning himself at a point perpendicular to the line between trees, at the mid-point, to maximize his chances of a kill. I am sure he did not do so instinctively, as I watched him learn by trial and error over a period of weeks. I do not class his behaviour as cultural, because he did not acquire it from another dog nor teach it to any of his kind; but I do think he displayed, in small degree, the same kind of foresight that we exhibit in imagination.

He also dreams: the evidence that dogs and cats dream is incontrovertible; they twitch and scrabble with their paws when asleep and make noises consistent with wakeful moods of thrill or agitation. They may be rehearsing or relishing games they have played or look forward to playing, or perhaps they are reliving adventures they have had or hope to have with prey or other food. In any case they are engaged in visions of the unreal. This does not mean they are imaginative in the same sense as humans: sleep is a special, untypical form of consciousness. But it does show some overlap with a visionary property of human minds.[19]

Like Arp's tool makers, my dog hunts. I do not advocate a return to the concept of 'Man the Hunter' as a source of insights in evolutionary psychology, because feminist critics have made the term seem charged with gender (though, to me, 'man' is a term of common gender, with which I am happy). The Human Forager is a better term anyway because hunting is a specialized and extremely demanding form of foraging, and even if hunting has a long history as a preserve mainly of men, we need to examine the behaviour of both sexes. Still, Arp surely did well to look to hunting as an activity that peculiarly stimulates and intensively deploys imaginative powers. It does so, I suggest, because all foraging creatures need to evolve a faculty I call anticipation.

Anticipation, like memory, is the power of seeing what is not there—at least not yet: seeing what danger or opportunity might lurk behind the next clump or tree or hummock, envisaging (if not recalling) where food will be found. I take it to be an evolved faculty. Culture might be able to enhance it, but not to create it. Predators and prey both need it: each needs to anticipate the movements of the other. Some need it more than others. Humans, I suggest, need it most, for two reasons.

First, we are deficient in other evolved faculties that might have made our ancestors competitive as scavengers, gatherers, and hunters. We are relatively slow when it comes to eluding our predators or outstripping the competition in a race to a food source. We are poor climbers, unendowed with tails—which condemns us to a limited range of accessible foodstuffs and denies us a timely refuge from the chase. Our senses of smell and sight are poor compared with those of most of our competitor species. Our fangs and claws are small and weak. To compensate for these deficiencies, I can think of no other physical equipment evolution has given us, except for bipedalism, which frees our hands and hoists our standing bodies to a modest but useful degree of elevation, and a good throwing arm, which gives us the means to kill prey we cannot catch and deter predators who can catch us. But the missile faculty only works in combination with keenly developed anticipation, since the thrower has to be able to track the moving target in advance. Anticipation, therefore, is the key skill that made our foraging ancestors fit to survive.

Second, although all primates seem well endowed with anticipation, we are probably the only surviving primate species with a long history of hunting behind us. Chimpanzees also hunt. But no one observed them doing so until about half a century ago. So maybe it is a relatively new activity for them, induced by the environmental stresses human encroachments inflicted on them. In any case, chimpanzee hunting plays a tiny part in chimpanzees' lives, compared with the role it has had in most human societies for most of the past of our species. Typically, hunting chimps get up to 3 per cent of the calorific content of their diet from the hunt, whereas a study of ten typical hunting peoples in tropical environments similar to those that chimps favour yielded an average figure of nearly 60 per cent.[20] Overwhelmingly, chimpanzee hunters focus on one species, the colobus monkey, whereas every human community has a rich range of prey. It takes up to twenty years for a chimpanzee to learn hunting—chiefly, perhaps, because it is still a relatively infrequent practice and the young have only occasional opportunities to learn—while human children can become proficient after a few expeditions.[21] If hunting hones anticipation, it is not surprising that *homo sapiens* has a more developed faculty of anticipation than other, comparable creatures—even more than our most closely related surviving species. This insight, if it is correct, helps to explain why non-human apes exhibit so much imagination—why, as we have seen, some of them paint pictures, some coin new words, some invent new technologies, some introduce new cultural practices, some adorn themselves—but never take it anything like as far as humans.

Highly developed powers of anticipation are likely to precede fertile imaginations. When we anticipate, we imagine prey or predator behind the next obstacle. We guess in advance the way a threat or chance will spring. But imagination is more than anticipation. It may be, in part, the consequence of a superabundant faculty of anticipation because, once one can envisage enemies or victims or problems or outcomes ahead of their appearance, one can, presumably, envisage other, ever less probable, objects, ending with what is unexperienced or invisible or metaphysical or impossible—such as a new species, a previously unsampled food, unheard music, fantastic stories, a new colour, or a monster, or a sprite, or eternity, or infinity, or a number greater than infinity, or God. We can even think of nothing—perhaps the most defiant leap any imagination has ever made, since the idea of Nothing is, by definition, unexampled in experience.

Imagination is not a faculty that the theory of evolution can predict because, once it reaches beyond the range accessible to anticipation it exceeds the demands of survival and confers no competitive edge. It is, however, a product of the coincidence of two evolved faculties: our bad memories that distort experience so wildly that they become creative; and our overdeveloped powers of anticipation that crowd our minds with images beyond those we need. Culture stimulates imagination further still, partly by rewarding it and partly by enhancing it with psychotropic behaviour. We praise the bard, pay the piper, fear the shaman, obey the priest, revere the artist. We unlock visions with dance and drums and music and alcohol and excitants and narcotics.

'Don't we have imagination because we have language?' a friend asked, who was kind enough to enquire about this book while I was writing it (cf. above, pp. 122–34). The question needs careful parsing, because some people think or claim to think that it is impossible to conceive of anything unless you have a term for it. Jacob Bronowski, the incomparable polymath who, until his death in 1974, was an eloquent spokesmen for the role of imagination in distinguishing humankind from the rest of creation, put it like this: 'the ability to conceive of things which are not present to the senses is crucial to the development of man. And this ability requires the existence of a symbol somewhere inside the mind for something that is not there.'[22] Some kinds of thinking are clearly language-dependent, and the languages we speak have measurable effects on how we perceive the world[23] (though not as much as scholars used to think),[24] but experiments with human infants show that they make systematic choices before they make symbolic utterances.[25] Without broaching the barrelful of studies of the problem of how thought can happen without language, I hope readers will agree that it is at least possible to conceive of a thing first and invent a term or other symbol for it afterwards. So it makes just as good sense to say that language is the result of imagination as that it is a necessary precondition. Of course, once we have a repertoire of symbols the effect on imagination is freeing and fertilizing; and the more abundant the symbols, the more prolific the results. Language (or any symbolic system) and imagination nourish each other, but they may originate independently.

If they are cause and effect, it is at least as likely that language is an effect of imagination than the other way round. Symbols—and language is a system of symbols, in which utterances or other signs stand for their referents—resemble tools. Both are possible because of the ability of the creatures that devise them to see what is not there: to replace absence, to re-envisage one thing as if it were something else. A stick or stone becomes a proxy for an absent limb, or the absent extension of a limb, or a lens for an eye. A sound stands in the place of an emotion or object. A term evokes the entity it denotes, even if no such entity is there. My home, as I write, is hundreds of miles away; so are my wife and my dog; but I can summon their presence symbolically by mentioning it. I possess no wristwatch, but because I have an image of one in my mind, I can conjure the phantasm of it in speech or in writing.

*　*　*

Imagination is the motor of culture. We look around us. We see our world. In our mind's eye we see it differently—improved or made more conformable to some imagined model or pattern, ideal or order; or, if our taste so inclines us, we envision its destruction or reduction to chaos. Either way, we recraft our world imaginatively. We act to realize the world we have re-imagined. That is how and why cultures change.

The first migrants from the cradle-land of *homo sapiens* were pursuing a vision of a life they had never experienced. The first builders saw in advance how they could transform leaves and bones into shelter. The adapters of utterance for communication imagined others' response. The first cannibals anticipated the effects of appropriating their victims' prowess and virtues. The first artists in ochre could envision their bodies adorned. The first cave-painters saw a world inside the rocks. The first shamans imagined themselves as animals, with animals' power over prey. The first magicians imagined themselves manipulating nature. The first mathematicians looked at a plural world and inferred the possibility that numbers might exist independently of their instantiations. The first framers of fields and cities imagined a re-ordered environment, laid out according to an aesthetic that arose in their minds.

I cannot prove any of these speculative reconstructions of the thinking of the long-dead, but I find them convincing—more convincing than locating all these innovations along a putative path signposted by scientific laws. In the formulation of the ingenious French cognitive scientist Dan Sperber, the peculiarities of human culture are the product of humans' 'outstanding meta-representational abilities'[26]—in other words, of imaginations capable of making one thing stand for another.

Another way of putting much the same point is to say that ideas drive cultural change. By ideas I mean thoughts that do not merely represent, or map, or record, or reproduce experience, but exceed it or distort it. Ideas are products of imaginative efforts, because you cannot have them simply by describing the existing world. Ideas have a peculiar property: they 'breed'.[27] Or, to be more exact, they stimulate each other and become more prolific when they interact. Sometimes they reproduce like amoebas, generating their own progeny. More commonly, they issue from the interactions of minds. An interlocutor's distinctive take on a subject inspires a new response. A book or broadcast or image or object ignites a new train of thought. A model from an alien culture alerts recipients to new possibilities for changing direction. Misunderstanding intervenes creatively. We misunderstand someone else's idea: the result is a new idea of our own. Many new ideas are just old ideas misunderstood. The kinds of change thinking ignites—technical innovations, new ways of organizing life—can create conditions propitious for the further multiplication of ideas: this is not to say that technology and social or cultural change cause ideas, but that they help make new ideas possible by facilitating communication or stimulating imaginations.

In consequence, the most culturally productive societies—the most intensely creative, the most innovative, the most dynamic, and the most mutable—tend to be in touch with each other and to experience change most when their contacts are closest. In the early twentieth century anthropologists, mainly working with Franz Boas or in other schools dedicated to fieldwork, accumulated evidence of how cultures develop through borrowing from each other.[28] The proposition is easy to test historically by looking at the circumstances of some of the most spectacular and intensive episodes in the history of ideas in the West: the 'age of sages' of the first millennium BCE in the eastern Mediterranean; the 'renaissance' and intellectual revolution of the high middle ages; and the periods of 'scientific revolution' and European 'Enlightenment' in the seventeenth and eighteenth centuries.

* * *

In about 33 BCE a penniless poet received a gift from the chief minister of the Roman empire: a small farm on the River Tiber, in appreciation of the brilliantly understated verse-satires he had written for Roman salons. It was just what Horace wanted. For the rest of his days he devoted much of his best poetry—some of the cleverest, loveliest work any wordsmith has ever forged—to extolling the simple life of the farm, and praising his patrons. In one poem, he imagined Maecenas, the minister, worrying over what the Chinese might be plotting.

In others, Horace pictured Augustus, the ruler, intimidating them with his power, or engendering a future conqueror of China. This was outrageous flattery: there was no likelihood of the Roman and Chinese empires engaging in conflict, or even having much contact of any kind. In 79 CE, China did send an envoy to Rome, but Kan Ying turned back at the Black Sea, deterred by warnings from local enemies of Rome, who did not want the mission to succeed: 'if the ambassador is willing to forget his family and home, he can embark'. He sent home a favourable report on the Romans: 'the people have an air comparable to those of China.... They trade with India and Persia by sea.'[29] That was probably as close as the Roman and Chinese empires ever got to direct mutual dealings. But the fact that Horace was aware of China, and realized that events at the far end of Eurasia could affect Roman interests, shows how communications had transformed the world of the first millennium BCE, making it 'smaller', as we say now.

Indian world-maps of the period look like the product of stay-at-home minds. Four—then, from the second century BCE onwards—seven continents radiated from a mountainous core. Around concentric rings of rock flowed seven seas, respectively of salt, sugar-cane juice, wine, ghee, curds, milk, and water. One should not suppose, on the basis of this formal, sacred cosmography, that Indians of the time were ignorant of the world: that would be like inferring from the subway map that New Yorkers could not build railways. Real observations are detectable under the metaphors of the maps: a world grouped around the great Himalaya; the triangular, petal-like form of India, with Sri Lanka falling from it like a dewdrop; an ocean divisible into discrete seas, some of which may have been fantastic, imaginary, or little-known, but others of which represented routes to frequented destinations and commercial opportunities: the Sea of Milk, for instance, corresponded roughly to what we now call the Arabian Sea, and led to Arabia and Persia. The Sea of Butter led to Ethiopia. Stories of Indian seafaring from late in the first millennium BCE, or soon after, appear among *Jatakas* or tales of Buddhahood, where pilotage 'by knowledge of the stars' is a godlike gift. The Buddha saves sailors from cannibalistic goblin-seductresses in Sri Lanka. He extemporizes an unsinkable vessel for a pious explorer. A merchant from Benares, following the advice of an enlightened sage, buys a ship on credit and sells the cargo at a profit of 200,000 gold pieces. Manimekhala, a guardian deity, saves shipwreck victims who have combined commerce with pilgrimage 'or are endowed with virtue or worship their parents'.[30]

These are legends (though they only make sense against a background of real navigation). In Persian sources, similar legends are backed by accounts of real voyages. Towards the end of the sixth century BCE, Darius I—an emperor enthusiastic for exploration—ruled Persia. He ordered a reconnaissance of the ocean between Suez and the Indus: this probably extended the range of navigation in the region, since the Red Sea, with its concealed rocks and variable currents, was notoriously hard to navigate. Among the consequences were penal settlements on islands of the Persian Gulf, and a canal from Suez to the Nile: there must have been existing traffic for it to serve, and the result was to increase this further.

To Greek traders, the Seas of Milk and Butter were 'the Erythraean Sea'—source of aromatics and resins, especially frankincense, myrrh, and an Arabian cinnamon-substitute called cassia. Many important ports for long-range trade lined Arabia's shores. At Gerrha, for instance, probably near modern Al Jubayl, merchants unloaded Indian manufactures. Nearby, Thaj also served as a good place to warehouse imports, with its walls of dressed stone, more than a mile and a half in circumference and fifteen feet thick. From Ma'in—one of the south Arabian states conquered by Saba—a merchant supplied Egyptian temples with incense in the third century BCE: we know this because he died in Egypt and his sarcophagus is engraved with the outline of his life. This background explains the death-bed wish of Alexander the Great, the would-be world-conqueror who died in 323 BCE, to launch a conquest of Arabia. Before he died, he sent naval expeditions to explore the Red Sea route to the Indian Ocean, and reconnoitre the way to the Persian Gulf from the mouth of the Indus. Thereafter,

Greek writers began to compile sailing directions, and geographical and ethnographical data for the shores of the Erythraean Sea.

Arabia, in effect, was a fulcrum of long-range commerce, linking the maritime worlds of the Mediterranean Sea and the Indian Ocean. Omani emporia had a glowing reputation among Roman and Greek writers in the two centuries around the birth of Christ. Yemen was a land so rich in spices that men were said to 'burn cassia and cinnamon for their everyday needs'. The author of the a text of the second century CE, the *Periplus of the Eythraean Sea*, believed that 'no nation seems to be wealthier than the Sabaeans and Gerrhaeans, who are the agents for everything that falls under the name of transport from Asia and Europe. It is they who have made Syria rich in gold and have provided profitable trade and thousands of other things to the enterprise of people in the Mediterranean Levant.'[31]

The reason for the long seafaring, sea-daring tradition of the Indian Ocean lies in the regularity of the wind system. Above the equator, north-easterlies prevail in winter. But when winter ends the direction of the winds is reversed. For most of the rest of the year, the winds blow steadily from the south and west, sucked towards the Asian landmass as air warms and rises over the continent. By timing voyages to take advantage of the predictable changes in the direction of the wind, navigators could set sail, confident of a fair wind out and a fair wind home. It is a fact not often appreciated that, overwhelmingly, the history of maritime exploration has been made into the wind: presumably because it was at least as important to get home as to get to anywhere new. This was how the Phoenicians and Greeks opened the Mediterranean to long-range commerce and colonization. The same strategy enabled South-sea Island navigators of this period to begin the long project of exploring and colonizing most of the islands of the Pacific.

Conditions in the Indian Ocean liberated navigators from such constraints. One must try to imagine what it would be like, feeling the wind, year after year, alternately in one's face and at one's back. Gradually, would-be seafarers realized how the changes of wind made outward ventures viable: they knew the wind would change. So they could risk an outward voyage without fearing that they might be cut off from the chance of returning home.

The Indian Ocean has many hazards: it is Sinbad's sea, the setting of countless tales of the mutability of fortune; it is wracked by storms, especially in the Arabian Sea, the Bay of Bengal, and the deadly belt of habitually bad weather that stretches across the Ocean below about 10° south of the equator. But the predictability of a homeward wind made this the world's most benign environment for long-range voyaging. Fixed-wind systems as vast as those of the Atlantic and Pacific were almost uncrossable with ancient technology: we know of no round trips across them. Even compared with other navigable seas, the reliability of monsoon conferred insuperable advantages. No reliable sources record the length of voyages during this period, but, to judge from later statistics, a trans-Mediterranean journey from east to west, against the wind, would take fifty to seventy days: with the monsoon, you could cross the entire Erythraean Sea, between India and a port on the Persian Gulf or near the Red Sea, in three or four weeks in either direction.

In the long run, sea routes were more important for global history than land routes: they carried more goods, faster, more economically, in greater quantities. Nevertheless, in the early stages of the development of trans-Eurasian communications, most long-range trade was small-scale, in goods of high value and limited bulk. It relied on 'emporium-trading'—onward transmission through a series of markets and middlemen—rather than expeditions across entire oceans and continents. In the first millennium BCE, the routes that linked Eurasia by land were at least as important, in the history of cultural contacts, as those by sea.

From around the middle of the period, scattered examples of Chinese silks appeared across Europe, in Athens, in Budapest, and in a series of south German and Rhineland burials. By the end of the millennium, a route for diffusion of Chinese manufactures became traceable, from the southern Caspian to the northern Black Sea, and into what were then gold-rich kingdoms in the south-west stretches of the Eurasian steppe. Meanwhile, starting from Greece, Alexander's armies had used the Persian royal roads to cross what are now Turkey and Persia, conquer Egypt and Mesopotamia, reach the Persian Gulf, and, at the extremities of their eastward march, touch the Pamir mountains and cross the Indus. Merchants could also have used these routes.

The first written evidence of this presumed commerce occurs in the report of Chang Ch'ien, a Chinese ambassador who set out for Bactria—one of the Greek-ruled kingdoms established in central Asia in Alexander's wake—in 139 BCE. His main missions were, first, to recruit allies against the aggression of steppeland imperialists who raided China's northern borders and, second, to obtain horses for the Chinese army from the best breeders, deep in central Asia. His mission was one of the great adventures of history. Captured en route, he remained a hostage with the steppelanders for ten years, before escaping to continue his task, crossing the Pamir mountains and the River Oxus, and returning, without encountering any potential allies, via Tibet. He was captured again, escaped again, and got home, with a steppeland wife in tow, after an absence of twelve years. From a commercial point of view, his reports were highly favourable. The kingdoms beyond the Pamir had 'cities, houses and mansions as in China'. In Ferghana, the horses 'sweat blood and come from the stock of the heavenly horses'. He saw Chinese cloth in Bactria. 'When he asked how they obtained these things, the people told him their merchants bought them in India, which is a country several hundred *li* south-east.' From the time of his mission, 'specimens of strange things began to arrive' in China 'from every direction'.[32]

In 111 BCE a Chinese garrison founded the outpost of Tun-huang—the name means 'blazing beacon'—beyond the western limits of the empire, on the edge of a region of desert and mountains. Here, according to a poem inscribed in one of the caves where travellers sheltered, was 'the throat of Asia', where 'the roads to the western ocean' converged like veins in the neck. We now call them Silk Roads. They skirted the Taklamakan Desert, under the mountains that line it to north and south. It was a terrible journey, haunted, in Chinese accounts, by screaming demon-drummers—personifications of ferocious winds. But the desert was so demanding that it deterred even bandits, and the mountains offered some protection from the predatory nomads who lived beyond them. The Taklamakan took thirty days to cross—clinging to the edges, where water drains from the surrounding mountains. Further west, to get to the markets of central Asia, or to reach India, some of the world's most formidable mountains had to be crossed.

A few years after the founding of Tun-huang, a Chinese army, reputedly of 60,000 men, travelled this road to secure the mountain passes at the western end and to force the horse-breeders of Ferghana to trade. A painted cave shows the general, Wu-ti, kneeling before the 'golden men' that Chinese forces seized. (The painter made them Buddhas, perhaps fancifully.) In 102 BCE, the Chinese invaded Ferghana, diverted a river and obtained 30,000 horses in tribute. Meanwhile, caravans from China reached Persia and Chinese trade goods became common in the Mediterranean Levant.[33]

The routes that bound Eurasia carried vectors of culture back and forth. We only know about a few individual cases. Alexander's armies left colonists strewn across Asia in centres where hybrid art took shape, blending Indian and Greek aesthetics and producing, for instance, a surviving relief of the Trojan horse from Gandhara, with Cassandra flinging out her arms in despair in an image that owes more to the sinuous gestures of Indian *houris* or temple prostitutes than to the ecstasies of a Sybil. Pyrrho went to India with Alexander and conversed with Brahmins. There is no record of direct contacts of this kind in the first half of the millennium, but across Eurasia, from China and India to southwest Asia and Greece, from the fifth century BCE onwards the sages' subjects of debate and their techniques of rational and empirical enquiry had so much in common that it is inconceivable that unaided accident produced the coincidences.[34] Scholarship on the origins of classical Athenian thought has captured the light that the 'east face of Helicon' cast on Greece;[35] the worlds of the Levant and what are now Turkey and Persia, with which Greeks were in constant touch, could mediate thinking and transmit objects from central Asia, India, and China. So could the commerce of the Erythraean Sea.

Partly as a result of the contacts that linked the ends of Eurasia, and put schools and sages in touch with each other, new initiatives in thinking in the first millennium BCE were remarkably similar in Greece, southwest Asia, India, and China. New religions—Zoroastrianism, Buddhism, Taoism, monotheistic Judaism, Christianity, and the beginnings of what became Hinduism—owed something, perhaps, to traditional magic, but they were genuinely new. They upheld the effectiveness of moral practice, alongside formal rituals, as ways to adjust humans' relationship with nature or with whatever was divine: not just sacrificing prescribed offerings fittingly to God or gods, but modifying the way people behaved towards each other. They attracted followers with programmes of individual moral progress, rather than with rites to appease nature. They were religions of salvation, not just of survival. They promised the perfection of human goodness, or 'deliverance from evil'—attainable in this world or, if not, by transfer to another world after death, or by a total transformation of this world at the end of time. The religious teachings of the sages were highlights in a world teeming with other new religions, most of which have not survived. In a period when no one recognized a hard-and-fast distinction between religion and secular life, spiritual ferment stimulated all kinds of intellectual innovation. It is still hard to say, for instance, whether Confucius founded a religion. After all, he ordered rites of veneration of gods and ancestors, but disclaimed interest in worlds other than our own. The other schools of the age in China—so numerous that they were called the Hundred Schools—shared similar priorities, but mixed what we would now think of as secular and religious thinking. Confucius's opponent, Mo-tsu, is a case in point. He called for universal love, on secular grounds, 400 years before Jesus's religious version.

Other innovators of the age formulated techniques that we still use for telling good from evil and truth from falsehood. Similar conflicts ensued over the nature of the state between moral optimists, who wanted to liberate human goodness, and pessimists, who felt the need for the state's restraining force. Thinkers, observers, and experimenters who belonged to the Hundred Schools in China paralleled the achievements of Plato and Aristotle. In India, logicians known as the Nyaya school shared confidence in reason and the urge to analyse it, resolving arguments step by step. Similarities in thinking across Eurasia in the second half of the first millennium BCE suggest that long-range cultural exchanges must have been going on. This was perhaps the critical difference that made Eurasian societies relatively prolific in a period when we know of no comparable achievements in intellectual life anywhere else in the world.[36]

*　*　*

After a long period of disruption in late antiquity and the early middle ages, the routes of communication that linked Eurasia became active again in the twelfth century, when the Song reached westwards from China and crusaders colonized parts of the Levant, and with much greater intensity in the thirteenth and early fourteenth centuries, when the 'Mongol Peace' encouraged trans-Eurasian trade and opened new steppeland routes to long-range travellers. As a result a series of Chinese techniques and ideas reached and reinvigorated Christendom, planting most of the technologies that, in later periods, Westerners misidentified as world-changing inventions of their own. Paper money (the basis of Western capitalism), the blast furnace (the precondition for Western industrialization), the rudder and separable bulkhead (the technologies that made possible the world-ranging shipping of the modern West), and gunpowder (the starting-point for Western supremacy in firepower) were among the arrivals from China during the period. I suspect that the revival of empiricism—the fact-finding technique on which Western scientists congratulate themselves—was also the result of transmission from China, where it had never faded from sages' minds. We know a lot about the individuals who travelled back and forth, carrying ideas and artefacts West from China, and about the travails they underwent: the Polo family, for instance, who crossed Asia in three years' hard pounding, contending with the demons of the Taklamakan; John of Monte Corvino who declared proudly how he faced the daunting mountains of central Asia—'but', he said, 'the Mongols crossed them, and so, with God's help, did I'; or the merchants who travelled with the help of Francesco Balducci Pegolotti's early fourteenth-century guidebook, which told them where along the road to change money, hire transport, get a shave, or employ a prostitute.[37]

The period of interchange between West and East did not last. In 1368, the Ming overthrew the Mongols and China reverted to autarchy. Merchants and monarchs on the Atlantic fringe of western Christendom dreamed of opening a sea route to the East, but the obstacles were formidable and ignorance led Columbus, among others, in the wrong direction. But the first Portuguese mission reached China via the Indian Ocean in 1512 and, little by little, European shippers got a foothold in the lucrative business of supplying the world's richest economy with luxuries from India, south-east Asia, Japan, and the Americas. The great mediators of ideas, the Jesuit missionaries, did not succeed in establishing themselves as part of the acceptance world of the court in China until 1610—and their ascent was laborious, since the Chinese dismissed them at first as barbarians who had nothing to offer 'except a picture of a woman and baby' and dubious, purported relics of 'the Immortals'.[38] They inaugurated, however, a new era of exchange among the great civilizations of Eurasia by interesting the imperial court in their skills, first as cartographers, then as astronomers and experts in arts and engineering. At the same time, artefacts, ideas, and natural and human specimens from other parts of the world reached Europe as a result of the outreach of explorers, *conquistadores*, colonists, and long-range trade, accumulating in the West the raw materials of the world-ranging awareness of opportunities and vision of knowledge that we call the scientific revolution, and incubating—thanks in part to the reports of Jesuits and other European savants in

China, India, and Japan—the new, radical, political and philosophical thinking of the Enlightenment. Some of the most spectacular intensifications of cultural change in the history of the world illustrate the productivity of the avenues of intellectual exchange that bind Eurasia.[39]

*   *   *

This helps explain the effects of a phenomenon Jared Diamond has made familiar: the fact that Eurasia has been an arena of faster change than other parts of the world because its geography favours exchanges of culture between its indigenous civilizations.[40]

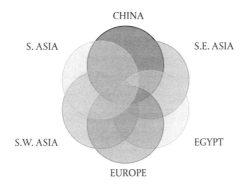

Fig. 6.1 Eurasia

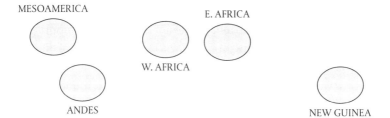

Fig. 6.2 Other civilizations

Geography, like genes, does not determine what we do, but it creates some opportunities and limits or impedes others. Isolation retards change, exchange stimulates it. As Diamond pointed out, New Guinea has a history of farming and sedentary life at least as long-standing as those of most other Asian civilizations, and probably longer than those of Africa, Europe, and the Americas, but isolation slowed or checked subsequent development. We can represent the world-wide difference in the mutual accessibility of civilizations diagrammatically. Civilizations privileged by mutual contacts generate more change than those that isolation obliges to devise their own new ideas. Often, and for protracted periods, Eurasian civilizations have been in close touch with one another, while those of the Americas and sub-Saharan Africa have been sundered by untraversible climatic zones or physical obstacles.

It is legitimate to show Eurasian civilizations as overlapping because mutual accessibility has encouraged cultural exchange between them. Communications shrank the landmass to traversable proportions in the first millennium BCE.

The reach and limits of cultural exchange affect non-human cultures too. On either side of the N'Zo-Sassandra River in Côte d'Ivoire, chimpanzees feed differently. On the west bank they crack open palm-nut kernels with stones to extract the oil. Their east-bank brethren leave the nuts unexploited. There is no environmental difference to explain the cultural divergence. The habitats are, for all practical purposes, identical. One group has discovered the relevant properties of stones and nuts and has enshrined the knowledge in culture. The other has not.[41] The process of passing on the data stopped at the river, just as for millennia the Atlantic prevented European ideas from reaching the Americas, and the geography of Eurasia helped interrupt the sporadic but powerful flow of culture between China and the West.

However that may be, the link between ideas and cultural change is unproblematic. We observe our world. We imagine it differently. We work to realize our imagined world. The best attested reason for the multiplication of ideas is the fertilizing effect of exchange. Ideas multiply as the result of dialogue. That is why we talk to one another. Cultures change, in part, at least, because unfamiliar ideas about how to do things impinge from outside. Cultures change most when they are in touch with other cultures.

Here, I want to suggest, we may have the key to the problem of why cultural change seems to accelerate—or to have accelerated for much of the past and to be accelerating at an unprecedented rate today. No scientific law mandates this. But we observe its pace all the time. Our next task is to try to see why.

7

FACING ACCELERATION

Why cultural change speeds up

I used to think I knew the English. I grew up among them. My father, who spent the Second World War as a foreign correspondent in London, wrote a book about them in an effort to understand them. He depicted them, as all observers did in the 1940s and 1950s, as typically introspective, reserved, untalkative, undemonstrative people, with minds as tightly rolled as their umbrellas. For most of my life I saw no reason to question this received stereotype.

Then, at the end of August 1997, I went to the United States as a Visiting Professor. When I arrived in Providence, Rhode Island, my landlady, mistaking me for an Englishman because she knew I worked in England and she heard me speak the Queen's English, surprised me by commiserating with me on what she called 'the terrible news'. She responded to my bafflement by telling me that Diana, former Princess of Wales, had died in a car accident while I was in the air. I should, I suppose, have had pious thoughts on behalf of the dead woman and the sons she left; but my dislike of Diana choked my sympathy. She was, I thought and think still, a morally abominable person, shallow, meretricious, promiscuous, selfish, exhibitionistic, and talentless.

My first thought was 'how convenient for the Royal Family!', on whom she had heaped obloquy, embarrassment, and misery. My second thought was 'what a career move!' Her death would perpetuate her falsely contrived reputation as 'the people's princess', whereas, had she lived, the truth would have found her out. Rather like the widowed Jacqueline Kennedy, she was already on her way out of Camelot towards a second marriage that the public would have deplored as unworthy of their image of her; her intended, who died with her, was the playboy son of an Egyptian retailer who had 'risen without trace' to enjoy the wealth of a millionaire and a reputation for costly kitsch. Her death forestalled a prospectively unhappy life—unhappy for her, unhappy for her millions of admirers, intolerable to the family she had ditched, and disastrous for England.

I expected her English devotees to remain suckered, but assumed they would respond with characteristically English restraint. How wrong I was! When I 'phoned London daily over the next few days to speak to my wife, I heard of scenes of what sounded like collective insanity: thousands of people gathered outside Kensington Palace, Diana's home, moving on in droves to Buckingham Palace, the Queen's official residence, swelling in numbers to hundreds of thousands, clogging the environs with floral tributes, weeping, wailing, uttering immoderately mawkish expressions of loss, clamouring for the Royal Family to perform public penance, and calling for the death to be marked by a state funeral, with all the panoply of official mourning. The excesses of lamentation, the egregious displays of grief, the madcap encomia, grew in intensity every day for weeks and months. Whenever my wife spoke to me on the 'phone, 'You won't believe what's happening here,' she would say. I barely could. The English had changed, without my even noticing. The reserved generations and traditions that my father described had vanished. The English had become as sentimental and ostentatious as everyone else. The stiff upper lip had gone wobbly. Di's millions of mourners wallowed in what the teachers of my childhood years would have condemned as exhibitionism and emotional slacking.

This was, perhaps, an extreme case of a culture unrecognizably self-transformed but there are many others. The episode was part of a much wider phenomenon of recent history. Cultures experience ever more sudden, extensive, and transmutative fluctuations and lurches. I had already witnessed something similar in the other country I know well, Spain, where, in my boyhood, traditional virtues of austerity, sobriety, dignity, formal courtesy, and a rather dogmatic kind of Catholic piety had commanded the apex of the value system. In 1975 the welcome death of the vicious old cynic, Francisco Franco, who had repressed emotions as determinedly as he repressed opposition during his long dictatorship, seemed to release a lot of pent-up consumerism, self-indulgence, casual manners, and libertinage. Here, of course, the political context changed, but changes in other forms of culture were much more thorough than and in some ways independent of those of politics. Spaniards abandoned a vocation to be 'different' and self-consciously remodelled cultural practices to conform to western European models. The old tourist-board slogan, 'España es diferente', lost its edge as the culture became more and more like those of neighbouring countries. In 1978 pornography appeared suddenly and openly, to the surprise of foreigners, in the kiosks that lined the Rambla of Barcelona. The changes gathered pace as the bridle slackened. Spaniards now tolerate sexual permissiveness and divorce. They drink fastidiously and smoke sparingly in the land of Carmen and Lila Pastia. They talk their regional languages unselfconsciously. They cross the street when they like. Their manners are relaxed. In some parts of the country they have changed the *horarium* of the working day. They dress casually—at least, more casually than before.[1] Two regions have tried to ban bullfighting. Historians have hastened to rewrite Spanish history, excising previously conventional references to exceptionalism in favour of a new characterization of Spain as the outcome of a typical European past.

The self-transformations of Spaniards and English people in the late twentieth century are conspicuous but by no means atypical examples of the accelerations of cultural change. Even in countries that have become exporters of labour, cultural 'westernization' has had similar effects. Everyone can multiply instances from his or her experience. We used to measure such change in centuries or, for more recent periods, generations. Now we do so in decades, years, seasons, and months. A week is now a long time in culture. The next few pages are concerned with the evidence for the acceleration of change and the reasons why we need to understand it. I concentrate on twentieth-century acceleration, because the evidence is abundant and the disquiet it excited is obvious. For contrast, I shall describe the pace of change in the Ice Age, not because other cultures and other periods have been exempt from spells of slow or sporadic change, but because the contrast between Ice Age and i-age is unmissably glaring.

*   *   *

The accelerations we face today began with a sudden spurt. Towards the end of the nineteenth century every measurable kind of change leapt off the graph paper. Globalization, which was already under way with world-encompassing trade and economic interdependence among widely separated regional specializations, made acceleration a genuinely world-wide phenomenon. Observers at the time were keenly aware of acceleration, and theorists rushed to seek explanations—albeit without success. Franz Boas thought 'the rapidity of change has grown at an ever-increasing rate'. In 1917 his student Robert Lowie postulated a 'threshold' beyond which, after 'exceedingly slow growth', culture 'darts forward, gathering momentum'. Fellow-Boasian Alexander Goldenweiser suggested that cultural change 'comes with a spurt' in surges between inert phases, rather like the way Stephen Jay Gould thought evolution happens, 'punctuating' long periods of equilibrium.[2]

By the late twentieth century it was almost impossible for any community to opt out: even resolutely self-isolated groups in the depths of the Amazon rain forest found it hard to elude contact or withdraw from the influence of the rest of the world once contact had been made. The biggest single indicator of acceleration was global consumption, which increased nearly twentyfold in the course of the twentieth century; because people used far more goods in industrialized, urbanized communities (and especially in the United States) than anywhere else, the spread of industrialization and urbanization guaranteed that consumption would continue to hurtle uncontrollably, perhaps unsustainably upwards. World population—an area of growth that excited Malthusian apprehensions and ignited intrusive pro-grammes of population control—hardly kept pace with consumption; but it quadrupled during the century. Production, inescapably, rose in line with consumption in terms of volume, while the range of products multiplied bewilderingly, especially in pursuit of technological innov-ations, medical services and remedies, and financial and commercial instruments.

The world became rapidly unrecognizable to the ageing, whose lives (in regions suitably equipped with physically unstrenuous means of livelihood and death-defying medical technology) were unprecedentedly prolonged. In my boyhood, one of sci-fi's favourite time-travel themes concerned visitors to the present or future from previous centuries and their struggles to adjust to a transformed world. By the end of the century, the BBC was screening a television series about a contemporary projected back in time to the 1970s, depicted as an almost unmanageably primitive era, in which—*horribile dictu*—there were no home computers, games consoles, or mobile 'phones.

The need to explain the origins of change and its recent and current accelerations is acute precisely because the pace of change is so fast today: so fast that even within living memory the world seems to have transformed over and over again, inducing 'future shock', fear, bewil-derment, and resentment. Meanwhile the increasing urgency of the accelerations of change and the ever more disturbing effects on people's sense of security, well-being, and confidence in the future have glared through the headlines. One of the paradoxes of human values is that most of us combine restlessness for change with a strong conservative preju-dice in favour of the familiar. When people feel the threat of change, they reach for security, like a child clenching its grip on a comforter. When they do not understand what is happening to them, they panic. *Grandes peurs* lash society like a flagellant's scourge. Intellectuals take refuge in 'postmodern' strategies: indifference, anomie, moral relativism and scientific indeterminacy, the embrace of chaos, *je m'enfoutisme*.

Change may be good. It is always dangerous. In reaction against uncertainty, electorates succumb to noisy little men and glib solutions.

Religions transmute into dogmatisms and fundamentalisms. The herd turns on agents of supposed change, especially—typically—on immigrants and on international institutions. Cruel, costly wars start out of fear of depleted resources. These are all extreme, generally violent, always risky forms of change, embraced for conservative reasons, in order to cleave to familiar ways of life. Even the revolutions of recent times are often depressingly nostalgic, seeking a golden and usually mythical age of equality or morality or harmony or peace or greatness or ecological balance. The most effective revolutionaries of the twentieth century called for a return to primitive communism or anarchism, or to the medieval glories of Islam, or to apostolic virtue, or to the apple-cheeked innocence of an era before industrialization. Revolutions can be good (though most historical precedents are not encouraging) and there is a time for conservatism as well as a time for every other purpose under heaven. But fear is not the best frame for the future: if we want to respond to change rationally, we have to conquer our fear of it. That is why we need to try to understand its accelerations: when we know why they happen, we will be able to confront them without undue anxiety. We can best confront or cope with the reactions people evince if we can provide a coherent explanation of the rapidity and reach of change in our world. Anyone who visits the British Library, and approaches from the adjoining railway station, passes an inscription attributed to Marie Curie: 'Nothing in the world is to be feared. It is only to be understood.' She exaggerated. There is plenty to fear. Understanding the truly terrifying increases fear. But at least understanding is the first stride towards an effective response.

We can begin by summoning a series of images, so familiar that they need only be mentioned to be visible to the mind's eye, which capture moments of vividly perceived change, when the world in which people of my generation grew up became fearsome to us. As we look in turn at the current accelerations of environmental, moral, political, economic, and deeply cultural change, we should be able to see that the changes in themselves are less menacing than the ways people represent and perceive them. In almost every case, understanding helps by diminishing the threats from fantastic to realistic proportions.

* * *

Eco-anxiety, first, provides plenty of instantly identifiable examples. Some of the most potent images that form today's common stock of horrors document environmental change. No one attentive to world affairs today can forget images of the Greenland ice melting into the sea, the Amazonian rain forest retreating in flames, new viruses inflicting unpredictable plagues upon the world, desertification stranding rusting hulks in what was once the Aral Sea, and cancer and obesity corroding and warping bodies, inside and out. These are peculiarly alarming images of our time; not so much, I think, because of the menace they illustrate for the future, though they certainly do that, as for the way they make vivid the unprecedented nature of change in the recent past. Hitherto, we always thought of environmental change as typically slow—much slower than cultural change. Now the two realms are so thoroughly interpenetrated that the environment seems as unstable as every other sphere of human impact.

Deforestation, for instance, is only one focus of contemporary fears about the rate at which we are depleting vital resources. On scales recently experienced and currently threatened, deforestation excites apprehensions of an unsustainably changed world, because you can see and feel the difference it makes: redrawn maps, manifestly altered satellite images, stressed environments, depleted species, diminished rain, a drier atmosphere. There is nothing new about this. It has happened naturally for as long as there have been trees. Deforestation by human hands has a long history, too, beginning as soon as forest-dwellers adopted agriculture, wherever the availability of manure from livestock liberated them from dependence on leaf-mould for fertilizer. The first protests that I know of occurred in Chinese poetry of the first millennium BCE and in Plato's laments for the nakedness of the landscapes of his day.[3]

Today deforestation is highly visible: in recent decades we have seen forests shrink in the wake of the depredations of loggers, miners, ranchers, holiday makers, and property developers, while, in particular, vast areas of Amazonia have burned before our eyes. Forest fires are essential means of renewing growth, but now they have become the cause of permanent destruction. Rates have improved from somewhat more than 8 million hectares lost annually worldwide during the 1990s to a little over 5 million a year during the first decade of the twenty-first century. Successes, however, have prompted and justified relaxations of controls. In 2011, Brazil and Vietnam—scenes of some of the most madcap deforestation of recent years—eased their regulations. It may be that we can tolerate increasing levels of forest loss; and to some extent, albeit too feebly to compensate, reforestation is happening, unnoticed, in parts of the world where agriculture and urbanization are in retreat. But even false fears have to be addressed, because they can panic people into conflicts.

Desertification is another, closely allied example. It has happened slowly for thousands of years, as the aquatic fossils in many deserts show. It is hard to resist taking fright when one contemplates the way the Aral Sea—genuinely a sea in my childhood—has become a saline wasteland, dotted with the corroding skeletons of ships that desiccation has literally left high and dry. Again, there is nothing new about the encroachments of desert. The spread of the Sahara has been one of the most continuous, relentless processes observable on our planet since the last Ice Age ended 20,000 years ago. Now, however, the problem of the loss of cultivable land unfolds at a pace everyone can witness. In some places in the twentieth century, as so often before— only now on a bigger scale—overexploitation wastes soils, exhausts irrigation resources, and stirs up dust bowls. Marginal land all over the world has become ever less productive as the result of a vicious circle of cause and effect. Farmers have had to force more food from less land, while the spreading deserts edge into their fields. So soils become exhausted, and food supplies precarious. Much of the world is trapped in this cycle. Food output falls, and hunger—or nowadays, more commonly, dependence on foreign aid—spreads. In 2011, the United Nations classified the loss of 12 billion hectares of farmland as the result of desertification.

There was never much land on Earth to begin with—less than 1 per cent of the biosphere. Water, by contrast, is the most plentiful substance on the planet, covering 75 per cent of the surface and filling more than 90 per cent of the cubic capacity. However, if we believe the predictions of some pundits, the likelihood that scarcity will spark violence may soon be greater for water than those for land and oil combined. Allegedly, the Middle East is already tinder-dry, with Israel indicted for 'stealing Arab water'. Are the pundits right? Like most water-related anxiety, except of course clinical hydrophobia, fear of 'water wars' seems exaggerated. In the Middle East, so far, water has been more a pretext for than a cause of conflict. In historical perspective, water rivalries have generally been resolved peacefully, compared with other kinds of dispute. The world's current problems have more to do with uneven distribution and uneconomic abuse than with dearth. As with energy, sustainability is possible if we switch from historic aquifers ('fossil water' if you like) to renewable sources, developing energy-efficient desalination technology. Promising techniques are available, such as precipitating salt by reverse osmosis. The prospects are good that, within a reasonable period, this or other techniques currently under research will put the oceans at our disposal. As with desertification we should worry less about whether the consequences of change are as bad as people fear, and more about how the pace of change excites unsettling apprehensions. If water wars happen, it will not be because there is not enough water, but because increasing consumption rates have made people afraid.

Controversy over the effects of deglaciation and climate change is best understood in a similar light. We can see the Arctic ice-cap retreat before our eyes. We can look at maps of the world's glaciers and recoil in shock at how fast they shrink. We can check periodically on sea levels and notice them rise. We can torture ourselves with predictions of the consequences: a largely submerged 'water world'; a northern hemisphere frozen 'the day after tomorrow' when ocean currents fail or reverse; a planet frying in the glare of global warming. The planet warms and cools periodically in spite of human agency, and none of the trends we fear is new or unprecedented—but no previous generation ever observed the rate of change apparent to us. The pace precipitates panic. Climatic lurches have occurred at intervals in the past, when the Earth's axis tilted, or the planet slipped a little out of its customary orbit; or when massive volcanic eruptions shrouded the sun in ash-clouds; or when, for unknown reasons, sunspots grew or shrank, or multiplied or faltered. Currents periodically go into reverse, or shift capriciously, condemning the areas they wash to extreme fluctuations of heat and cold, abundance and dearth. The additional impact of human profligacy since industrialization is controllable, if we shift energy production away from fossil fuels. And although climate changes will continue irrespective of what we do there has not been a change that humans have not survived or exploited to advantage since the emergence of our species—and as far as we know the last Ice Age of such magnitude as to condemn us to extinction, had our species existed at the time, happened 300 million years ago.

Species extinction multiplies fear. Today, the world faces the loss of more species than at any time since the end of the last Ice Age. One per cent of recorded species of birds and mammals has disappeared in the most recent 100 years. Because of pesticides, invertebrate species, which are less well documented, are likely to have suffered far more. According to the warnings of one of the most eminent authorities, 20 per cent of all invertebrate species were in imminent danger of extinction as the twentieth century drew to a close. The extinction of a species is not an isolated event. Every species is a part of the ecosystem and a link in the food chain. Every extinction threatens other species. Our commitment to some currently fashionable strategies, especially to genetic modification of food and fuel-source plants, makes it almost certain that we shall cause extinctions to accelerate. But, as a result of these problems, there is more concern among humans than ever to nurture biodiversity, and there are more—and more successful—local initiatives than ever. Although some extinctions will harm us, it is fair to say that most present a moral rather than a practical dilemma, and that, on the basis of all the eco-history we know about, we can expect most systems, when species drop out of them, to modify in order to survive.

Urbanization is a related change in our environment that scares us because it is happening so fast that almost everyone can monitor it and feel its effects. In the twentieth century it got increasingly hard to be a peasant, as agriculture grew more uniform and, under the pressure of economies of scale, became a vast business under huge corporations. A few rich countries, such as Germany and France, subsidized their small farmers. In most of the rest of the world peasants abandoned the land and followed the new roads and railway lines towards cities and a promise of prosperity that often remained unfulfilled. This was one of the most dramatic new departures ever in the way people live. For 10,000 years, most people had lived in agricultural settlements. Now centres of industrial manufacturing and services have taken over. Towns and cities have become the normal environments for people to live in. By the end of the century, half the world lived in settlements with populations of 20,000 or more. Cities grew even in countries in which agriculture remained the economically dominant way of life. In Nigeria, typically for regions struggling to escape from a role as primary producers for other people's industries, a fifth of the population lived in towns in 1963. By 1991, the proportion had shot up to a third and by 2010 to more than two-fifths. Now, since 2008, for the first time ever most people in the world live in cities, and many of them in hellish *megalopoles*. A third of urban dwellings are officially classed as slums: in sub-Saharan Africa the figure is closer to two-thirds. We agonize over the results, because we do not know how to eliminate the problems of housing, health, and food supply that accumulate faster than any agency can cope. But most civic societies find ways to make their cities tolerable, and create amenities that enhance life. The rate of urbanization is showing signs of slowing. Urban crime rates, overall, have fallen over the last couple of generations—which is surely a cause or effect of more livable cities. Post-industrial production methods are making huge concentrations of labour uneconomic. Cities will shrink or, if they grow, be better regulated in future.

Pollution is a closely related problem, on a comparably new and noticeable scale. Nineteenth-century agriculture relied on natural fertilizers, especially bird dung or guano. Chemical fertilizers supplied a relatively small market and seem to have had few or no ecological side-effects. That changed in 1909 when Fritz Haber, a German chemist, discovered how to extract nitrogen from the atmosphere and use it to manufacture commercial fertilizer. It was like plucking food from the air and, at first, an undeniable blessing. No other single invention did more to feed the growing population of the world in the second half of the century. In 1940, the world used some 4 million tons of artificial fertilizer. By 1990, it was using about 150 million tons. Phosphate mining provided another source of fertilizers. Agrochemicals manufacturers found ways to double-dose the soil with chemicals to stimulate crops and kill weeds.

The practice had a startling effect on the ecosystems it touched. Although pollution is not recommendable, it has a redeeming grace: carbon emissions and industrial waste are indexes of boosted production and spreading prosperity; in the form of fertilizers and pesticides, pollution averts starvation and saves lives. Yet the intensification of pollution is more fearsome than the remoter threats of climate change or deforestation or deglaciation or desertification, because the world's decisionmakers—the urban dwellers—do not just see it on their screens: they feel it in their lungs and see it in the pores of their skin.

The disease environment also seems to be changing at an unaccustomed rate—though without, as far as I can see, evoking levels of fear comparable with those caused by pollution or even climate change and resource depletion. Periodically in the past sudden microbial mutations have initiated or ended ages of plague. The next such mutation could be our undoing, for we still do not control—nor even adequately understand—the microbial world in which much disease originates. Medical science has developed a kind of rapid response, producing cures or palliatives for many of the new syndromes and sicknesses the microbial world has thrown at us in recent times—polio, AIDS. But although medicine has eliminated old diseases, new ones—or new forms of old ones—have arisen to torment humanity. Pollution, drug abuse, undiscriminating sex habits, and affluence, which condemn the unwary to overindulgence and inertia, are major killers. Far more lethal, however, is the rapid evolution of viruses. In the late twentieth century, Ebola, Lassa fever, the immune-destroying virus known as HIV, and a series of influenzas formerly confined to livestock or wild animals, leaped from the eco-niches in which they had formerly been contained and began to attack humans. A new strain of tuberculosis, which emerged in the late twentieth century, resists every known drug and kills half the people it infects. Bubonic plague has returned to India. New strains of cholera and malaria have emerged. Malaria cases in India rose a hundredfold to 10 million between 1965 and 1977. In sub-Saharan Africa, malaria kills 1 million children a year. Yellow fever—which had almost been eradicated by the mid-century—killed 200,000 people a year in Africa during the 1990s. Measles, a disease that immunization was expected to eradicate, was still killing 1 million people a year at the end of the century. New viruses can defeat antibiotics and other drugs, which decline in effectiveness as a result of overuse.

Other new diseases arose in man-made eco-niches: Legionnaire's disease, which breeds in the dampness of air-conditioning systems, is the prime example. Intensive farming created breeding conditions for salmonella in chickens and accumulated toxins in the food chain. Human-variant CJD, or 'Mad Cow disease', is a brain-killing disease, apparently caused by intensive cattle-farming methods—recycling dead sheep and cattle as fodder—and was transmitted to at least some of its victims in tainted food. Twentieth-century interventions in the environment opened many new eco-niches for disease: in overfertilized soil, stripped of much insect life; in polluted waterways; and in the disturbed depths of the sea, where bacteria multiply in searing hot vents that humans have only lately begun to penetrate. In an increasingly interconnected world, human carriers took diseases far outside accustomed environments. Toward the end of the century, West Nile virus from Africa turned up in New York City. A variant form of influenza from China caused widespread deaths, especially in Canada. Dengue fever from Asia has become endemic in parts of the Caribbean.

Chronic diseases, meanwhile, arose to replace infections as the major menace. 'Lifestyle diseases' and previously unknown mental illnesses replaced the sicknesses we now know how to cure. Cancer and heart diseases grew spectacularly, especially in rich countries, without anyone knowing why. By the 1980s in the United States, one death in every four was blamed on cancer. In Britain, one death in three was ascribed to heart disease, which caused 10 million deaths a year worldwide by the end of the century. Some forms of cancer were 'lifestyle diseases'. Cervical cancer, for instance, is thought to be connected to sexual promiscuity or adolescent sexual intercourse, while smoking, according to most authorities, causes lung, throat, and mouth cancers and contributes to heart disease and stroke. Obesity and its related disorders owe their prevalence, in part, to bad eating habits. In the second half of the twentieth century, evidence began to accumulate that some medical treatments were actually contributing to the disease environment. Doctors prescribed drugs so widely that people were becoming dependent on them, while many viruses and strains of bacteria were developing immunity to them. Even where physical health improved, mental health seemed to get worse. The highly competitive capitalist societies of the developed West became prey to various neurotic disorders collectively known as stress. Worriers 'medicalized' their anxieties and feelings of malaise, classifying them in their own minds as medical problems and taking them to the doctor. Medical services, already hard-pressed, became overburdened.

We find environmental change unsettling, perhaps, because traditionally nature seemed relatively stable, compared with the restless gyrations of culture. On the whole, for most of the past, environmental changes have happened gradually. The rate at which they roll over us nowadays is new—or at least, we experience them with unprecedented terror. We are aware that the environment interlaces and interpenetrates culture: it changes us; but we also change it. However, we may have overestimated our power over it. Nature, according to one of George W. Bush's rare wise utterances, is still the world's greatest superpower; but anthropogenically induced change makes some trends worse, and tinkers with the effects of others. Carbon emissions in the atmosphere, for instance, intensify solar radiation. Hydroelectric projects expose water to evaporation and leech nutrients from soils. Marginal agriculture exhausts land and drains water resources. All kinds of human activity, from innocent travel to reckless sex and unrestrained eating, inflict 'lifestyle diseases' and change the global ecology of disease. Remorseless cultural change exacerbated the problems: increasingly during the twentieth century, most people, in most of the world, overvalued health and crippled their economies in an effort to pay for it.

*   *   *

We expect morals, like the physical environment, to be relatively stable. What makes morals moral is the fact that they are timeless and universal—but much of what we have traditionally supposed to be so turns out to change with the regularity of fashion. In my lifetime sexual morals have succumbed to permissiveness. Instead of a solemn and personal commitment of one man and one woman, marriage has become a temporary fiscal arrangement with the state. In my boyhood, the Queen of the United Kingdom would not receive divorcees, and when her sister fell in love with one her life became a misery. Divorce is now the norm in the British Royal Family. Sexual relationships of every kind enjoy general approval in most of Europe and much of the United States, except—perhaps inconsistently—pædophilia and, in lingering instances, incest and bestiality. Fidelity seems tolerated as an odd aberration when abandoned mistresses evoke at least as much sympathy as abandoned wives. No one up-to-date with the zeitgeist regards homosexuality as morally distinct from any other kind of sexually charged sentiment. As I write, France has recently elected a president who serially abandons women. In the days of monarchy, French heads of state had *maîtresses-en-titre*; so perhaps François Hollande is only reverting to an antiquated custom, but his conduct defies 'republican morality'. Sadism is cool; pinching a choir-boy's bottom is sexual abuse. Public values rate hypocrisy as worse than sexual excess; yet Bill Clinton could graduate to the role of a revered elder statesman after cavorting with an intern and lying about it—abusing power as well as a person. I do not list these changes to complain of them, only to demonstrate the speed of the cultural mutations they represent. Changes in sexual mores are particularly unsettling because they coincide with generation gaps, challenge family solidarity, and have something of the force of violated taboos. In parts of the West, the rapidity with which homosexual alliances have achieved equality or near-equality of esteem with traditional marriage amounts, in effect, to a new morality.

Sex is not the only activity that makes morality mutable. Clinton's successor as US President seems to have been innocent of sexual transgressions in office—he certainly lacked the necessary energy—but got away, so far, with what to me seems the worst imaginable offence against morality: launching a war, inflicting death and misery on a scale inaccessible to most ordinary criminals, on the basis of falsehoods. People nowadays in much of the world have a 'right' to any lifestyle, but abortion victims have no right to life. Suicide and euthanasia—classed as extreme forms of immorality when I was young, because they extinguish a person's prospects of further goodness—are now regarded as moral acts in effect as well as intention. Capitalists in the last generation convinced each other that greed is good. So vice can be classified as a public benefit at one moment and then revert to obloquy when the economic circumstances change. Smoking and recreational drugging have swapped places in the scales of morality. Giving offence—which I grew up to think of as a salutary way of shaking people out of complacency—has become a sin and in some places a crime. It is easy to see why all these moral shifts are unsettling to people who stand on moral ground; but they are not all bad. They have made people, for instance, more compassionate towards women who have abortions not because they are wicked but because they are poor or suffering or ignorant; moral changes have made punishments more lenient for lawbreakers, and have relieved homosexuals from persecution and divorcees from stigma. I think these are benign effects; but the pace with which they have unrolled has contributed to the mass bewilderment and unease of our times.

*   *   *

Other areas of life match or exceed environmental and moral change for pace and perplexity, though we are perhaps more inclined to accept them as part of the normal run of events. Political revolutions—violent and peaceful—are commonplace. In politics, images of the fall of the Berlin Wall recall the surprise of most of those of us who saw it happen. Although some historians and political scientists anticipated the Soviet system's collapse,[4] most people over-estimated its durability. Almost everyone who witnessed the events of 1989–92 in central and eastern Europe was astounded at the scale and suddenness of the end of the Cold War, and the dismantling of a structure that—for all its menace—conveyed the comfort of familiar-ity and, according to the consensus of the experts, preserved the peace of the world. Most people, I suspect, would select the 9/11 destruction of the World Trade Center in New York as another such moment, which reconfigured world politics along with the skyline of the city. The effects of the event have certainly been far-reaching. It contributed to the onset of a new, aggressive era in US foreign policy and to the forfeiture or long postponement of the world's opportunity to create a new order, based on international cooperation and global govern-ance, after the end of the Cold War. But for me the images of destruction and corruption generated by the Iraq War are far more disturbing because they disclose a world I—with all my scepticism and world-weariness—had never previously detected or foreseen. I had naively believed that one of the great merits of democracies is that it is hard to coax them into war, and that they therefore tended to make the world a better and safer place. The Iraq imbroglio has shown us how easy it is for irresponsible governments to start wars even in democracies. The experience has been unsettling for everyone who has thought about it because the world seems an even more dangerous place than formerly: indeed, any comfort we got from the end of the Cold War and the apparent global convergence of political and economic values vanished like a mirage in the shimmer of the desert air. Equally perplexing to everyone raised in the 'American century' are projections of what the world is going to be like as US supremacy wanes. The world order of the last 150 years—such as it is—has been based on Western hegemony. With relative suddenness, a plural, 'multi-civilizational' world has displaced it. China, in most people's image of the future, is on the way to taking over from the USA as the unique global superpower.

Instances like these from the political arena are matched by others from the world of economics: images of panic in the *bourses* and people on the streets, whenever the frightening lurches typical of modern economies topple currencies, break banks, bust businesses, and slash stocks. Economics lurch alarmingly between ill-managed crises. On the whole, however, although these pressures generate far-reaching psychological strains and contribute to the neuroses and psychoses of modern life, I think it is fair to say that economies are surprisingly resilient. When the towers of New York's World Trade Center fell in 2001, even the firms whose headquarters were on the top floors, which bore the brunt of the attack and where all the employees died, were doing business again within a couple of days. The financial 'meltdown' of 2008 caused protracted recession in the USA and Europe, but none of the direst predicted consequences, such as a run on the banks or federal bankruptcy, has yet come to pass, as I write in 2012. The crisis of state debt management in the Eurozone—the group of seventeen member states of the European Union that share a common currency—has conjured scary spectres: governments defaulting, major banks collapsing, the Eurozone breaking up. But a series of short-term expedients has kept all these threats at bay.

The crises have brought to light stunning examples of flagrant dishonesty in banking and investment management at levels of billions of dollars, as well as serious deficiencies in the most basic disciplines of capitalism: executives who pay themselves for failure, whose emoluments are uncontrollable by their shareholders, customers, or governments, and who run businesses in their personal short-term interests. The potential for disaster first became apparent the morning after an earthquake struck Japan on 17 January 1995. The tremor only lasted twenty seconds. But the effect was massive. It killed over 6,000 people in and around the Japanese city of Kobe. It caused 100 billion dollars' worth of damage. By panicking stock markets already concerned about the sustainability of Japanese economic growth, it caused a global financial crisis. For Nick Leeson, a young futures trader in Singapore, it spelled personal disaster.

Nick had always been a big talker, with flashy habits, and a tendency to exaggerate his own merits. Despite a suspiciously misleading job application he had talked himself into a lucrative post with Barings Bank. He had made hundreds of thousands of pounds in legitimate commissions. But for three years he had been making unauthorized speculations, and fraudulently concealing his losses, which by the night of the earthquake amounted to over £200 million. At that point, Leeson was betting on the stability of Japanese stocks. He woke on the fatal morning to news of the tremor. For a few weeks, in increasing desperation, he tried to salvage his position by ever more reckless investments. By late February, his losses had accumulated to a staggering, unconcealable £827 million—double the bank's total capital. 'I'm sorry', he scrawled on the note he left on his desk when he fled. Leeson became infamous as the epitype of the 'Rogue Trader'— the title of the first volume of the bumptious autobiography he wrote in prison. But in some ways he was more a representative than a rogue of late twentieth-century capitalism. His story revealed a lot of what was wrong with the system. In the era of *laissez faire* inaugurated, as we saw in the last chapter, by the policy turns of the late 1970s and early 1980s, huge short-term profits encouraged a get-rich-quick mentality. The ethos 'greed is good', proclaimed by Gordon Gecko, a character in the 1987 movie *Wall Street*, crowded out decency and honesty. Leeson's experience showed how bankers could not be trusted to regulate their own activities, how deregulation eased slackness, how moral constraints had lost effectiveness, and how business growth had come to rely on irrational risk: speculation, overvaluation, and inflated expectations. Leeson's adventures in futures were based on the belief that things would always get better. But, as advertisements for financial products began to warn, 'investments can go down as well as up'.

Deregulation opened socially dangerous wealth gaps, as capitalist 'fat cats' paid themselves unjustifiable salaries and bonuses, while milking their shareholders, dodging their taxes, and restraining their workers' compensation. In 1989 Leona Helmsley, the hotel-millionairess known as the 'Queen of Mean' for her nasty treatment of employees, went to jail for tax evasion in New York, after saying 'only the little people pay taxes'. Fraud, however, was an unnecessary luxury in the era of deregulation, as tax loopholes gave the rich plenty of opportunities for lawful avoidance. Warren Buffett, reputedly the richest man in the world, admitted in 2006 that '400 of us pay a lower part of our income in taxes than our receptionists do, or our cleaning ladies', and that 'there's class warfare, all right, but my class is winning'.

Yet the world failed to heed the accumulated warnings. In some ways, financial shenanigans distracted attention from the fact that the most overvalued market in the world was in real estate—the biggest investment most people at ordinary income levels make. In the three decades that followed the turn to classical economics, the world reaped enormous benefits in enhanced prosperity, productivity, and political freedoms, which spread along with the newly fashionable economics. Eventually, however, it became apparent that the lurch from over-regulated to under-regulated economies had been at best ill-managed and at worst ill-founded. A series of colossal failures among credit institutions in Europe and the USA in 2008–9 showed the results. The collapse of the value of key securities in the USA provoked an uncontainable global credit crisis. International collaboration mitigated the effects. But the failure of the system was so acute that electorates worldwide lost confidence in *laissez faire* and clamoured for a return to regulation. But capitalism had stampeded for a generation over a relatively under-regulated world. Without bit or bridle, it would be hard to rein the broncos in.

The sudden switch from easily available credit to tight conditions triggered recession and mass unemployment—reaching nearly 10 per cent in the USA and 20 per cent in parts of Europe—and threatened the world with economic stagnation. The downward revaluation of real estate and the repossession of mortgaged houses left hundreds of thousands of people homeless. At first, popular indignation blamed greed, which is a universal vice. Gradually, it became apparent that crime, rather than sin, was at the heart of the crisis. When executives milk their shareholders, mislead their clients, abuse the trust placed in them, evade their taxes, and loot their businesses it is more appropriate to call it theft than greed. Most of the fat cats' excesses were beyond prosecution, for reasons of prudence or because of corruption or technicalities. Fred Goodwin, for instance, who ran the Royal Bank of Scotland into a world-record-breaking corporate loss while awarding himself a £16 million pension fund, incurred much abuse but no charges. In most countries that rely on financial services, the law has found no way to stop executives paying themselves excessively— making, as J.K. Galbraith said of executive pay awards, 'a warm personal gesture from the individual to himself'.

In the wake of the 2008 meltdown, however, a few spectacular cases of arraignable misdeeds suggested how far the global financial system had become a criminal playground. In 2009, for instance, Bernie Madoff, whose wealth management business had attracted some of the richest and most respectable clients in America, was imprisoned for 150 years for defrauding them of $65 billion over many years. In 2012 the resignation of Barclays Bank boss Bob

Diamond triggered an international criminal investigation into a widespread conspiracy among major banks to misrepresent how much they paid each other in interest on loans. Despite these trauma-tizing, confidence-shattering facts, the global economy has staggered on, essentially unmodified, partly perhaps because the system is so complex that the failure of any part of it leaves other connexions intact or able to function. 'Emerging markets' have continued to register enough growth to preserve capitalism's credibility. So even the terrible convulsions of economics, which have ruined millions of lives, con-form to the usual pattern of rapid cultural change: the psychological effects are more significant than the material ones.

* * *

Politics and economics are the foam and flecks on the surface of culture. Deep cultural changes, on the other hand, are much harder for society to cope with because when they are rapid and extensive they subvert people's identities and challenge their sense of their place in the world. The current scale of global migration, and its effects on countries with a net intake of migrants, is a prime example. I welcome its enriching effects, but can understand why many people find it disturbing to see their neighbourhoods or even their hometowns changed—the look of buildings and gardens transformed, the shops restocked, the sound of the streets retuned, the places of worship rededicated, the aroma of the food revised. More surprising and more shocking is the fact that cultures can effect self-transmutations as thorough and disturbing, without any outside aid, as the changes migrants make. As the effusions that followed Diana Spencer's death showed, the English abandoned reserve of their own volition, not because foreigners had corroded the culture, but because the English themselves jettisoned it.[5] Spaniards escaped traditional constraints on behaviour eagerly, with no outside prompting, when they threw off Francoism.

Under the surface of political and economic change lurks fear of instability in the most precious sources of identity; what one might call the bedrock of traditions familiarity with which gives their inheritors a sense of their place in the world. I cannot recall a time in which I did not understand the jokes my teachers cracked or the allusions they made to art and literature, because I grew up with the same stock of culture as they did. We all knew the same films, music, comedy sketches, and TV shows, as well as sharing the same schooling in the same canon of high art. Now I have to forgo classroom humour or laboriously explain some of the jokes—which is a sure way of filleting out the fun. Editors bombard me with queries because they—much less the inerudite readers they hope or fear for—do not recognize my references to even the most basic shared texts and icons of Western civilization: not even the Bible or the Greek and Latin classics. There is a temptation to don old fogeys' mourning and blame philistinism or bad schooling. But the real reason for the generational culture gap is surely the pace of change, which now replaces the inherited stock of widely recognizable allusions within a single generation and dilutes or disperses common culture almost as soon as it forms.

One of the most virulent forms of fear of rapid cultural erosion excites movements to retrieve or retain religious, national, or ethnic purity. In the United States, the prospects of adding a second national language to the community's powers of expression and communication seems to me entirely positive; but Spanish is now a real object of fear among monoglots who identify Anglophone speech with their precious national culture. Globalization and mass migrations have spread similar anxieties around the world. The French fear for the attenuation of their cuisine, Muslims and Christians for the integrity of their respective religions, Italians for the inviolability of their language. Britain and the Netherlands are countries with a long tradition of hospitality to refugees and tenacity in the pursuit of cultural pluralism. Now both have extemporized tests of how assimilable to supposed national culture immigrants are. I suspect the tests are silly and that the fears that underlie them are false. In the British case the whole notion is ridiculous since there is no British culture, though there are English, Scots, and Welsh cultures. The only people in the United

Kingdom with a traditionally strong sense of being British are Protestant Unionists in Northern Ireland, and even they have abandoned the notion in recent years, redefining themselves as 'Ulster Scots'.

In general, the effects of pluralism, which are inestimably beneficial, are also unsettling. I think of the widely reproduced photographs of the Pope at prayer in the Agia Sofia Mosque. Catholics of my generation could hardly behold such images without thinking that the world they now inhabit is very different from the one in which they were catechized. Even a young Rip van Winkle would awake today, after a short nap, to a surprising world and a dislocating experience. *Plus ça change* no longer applies: if I can be excused a necessarily paradoxical way of putting it, things can change so much that they are no longer their former selves.

We lurch from one failed solution to its equal, opposite reaction: from overplanning to madcap deregulation and back; between despotism and democracy; between totalitarianism and anarchy; authoritarianism and libertinism; pluralism and ethnocentrism; ideological secularism and irrational religion. Deceptively simple and wickedly 'final' solutions attract electorates convulsed by fear of change. People's willingness to switch between the rival programmes of exploitative demagogues is, I suspect, a measure of their bafflement in the face of apparently uncontrollable change. How much faster can the barrel-organ be wound? How much more frenziedly can grinders' monkeys dance to the manic rhythms?

It was not always thus. So far, as we have seen, non-human cultures have been sluggish. Some human communities have set themselves to resist change and have done a good job, by their own lights, by cherishing their own isolation. For long periods of the past, all human cultures were more or less stagnant. It is worth pausing over that fact: we cannot expect to see accelerating change and the reasons for it clearly except against the background of normal, long-term stasis.

* * *

In 1994, three amateur cave explorers spent their Christmas holiday in the gorges of the Ardèche region in southeastern France. Speleologists had already discovered numerous painted caves in the area, where Ice Age people had decorated deeply concealed rock faces between about 14,000 and 21,000 years ago. But nothing already known about the region prepared the team for the breathtaking find that awaited.

Sensing a draught from behind a rock-fall, they rummaged at earth and stones to create a gap wide enough for the thinnest of them to crawl through. When she realized there was a corridor ahead, she called the others. They shouted into the darkness to get an echo, which would give them a sense of the cave's dimensions. The noise seemed lost in vast emptiness. When they returned with full equipment, they found that the corridor led to the biggest cavern ever discovered in this part of France. Yet more astounding was their discovery in an adjoining chamber: a portrait in red ochre of a bear, rearing over a metre high—preserved for who knew how many thousands of years? It soon became apparent that the Chauvet cave—as the explorers named it, after their team leader—was one of the most extensive collections of Ice Age art in the world.

Furthermore, carbon-dating from many of the images led to an inescapable conclusion. These were the world's oldest-known paintings, yielding three dates of over 30,000 years, and none less than 23,000.

Sculpture of comparable antiquity had been discovered, but paintings that yielded such early dates by carbon-dating had been too few and far between to provide consistent, convincing evidence of their age. Moreover, such paintings had been too fragmentary to disclose anything about the minds that made them. Suddenly a huge gallery of data had been added to the sources.

As if the age and extent of the discovery were not astonishing enough, Chauvet held one more surprise: the paintings subverted everything people formerly thought about Ice Age art. Previous scholarship had assumed that 'primitive' sketches by the earliest artists gradually yielded to the sublime images painted towards the end of the Ice Age in the caves of Altamira in Spain and Lascaux in France—two sites that, though created thousands of years ago, had long commanded special respect from modern artists.

The Chauvet paintings exhibit distinctive styles that can be linked to particular painters but, in technique and skill, the work is equal to paintings done in similar environments 10- or 15,000 years later. If Lascaux painters had seen them, they might have been as astonished as we are by the similarity to their own style: broadly the same images, made with the same technology.

In one respect, the images in the Chauvet caves seem somewhat less mature than their successors in southwest France and northeast Spain. There are numerous 'signs' in the form of lines, dots, and stylized sexual organs. The conventional symbols of the late Ice Age—squares, rectangles, and triangles—are not present.[6] But the Chauvet finds fit with a number of other recent discoveries that, taken together, reveal a remarkably continuous level of skill from the earliest discoveries to the latest. Even more surprising than the continuities of technique are those of subject matter. Some of the scenes could be transferred to late-Ice Age settings without appearing out of place. There are storming bison and aurochs, stampeding horses, grazing or gazing reindeer, running ibex, creatures fleeing the hunt or falling victim to it. The Chauvet painters' favourite subjects, however, were rhinoceroses, which hardly figure in the later period (there is only one in Lascaux). They are followed by lions—often shown stalking, like fellow-hunters—and mammoths, both of which are relatively rare subjects in the later period. On the other hand, human figures are as rare as at other sites. Not until the ice began receding did human figures multiply considerably. The only exceptions are disembodied sexual organs and a shaman-like figure, half human, half bison. As at later sites, the organs seem to be used to give certain scenes a gendered or at least a sexual significance. A carving similar to the shaman-form and of the same age has also recently come to light. Does this suggest that shamanistic religion was already part of the world of Ice Age people 30,000 years ago, and has endured, in effect, ever since?

The evidence we have, such as it is, suggests that the Chauvet caves served the same function as the late examples. There is no sign of habitation. These caves were reserved for special activities, not for providing housing or places where the people of the time ate their meals or buried their dead. The only surviving footprints are—again as at later sites—of bare feet and, in disproportionate numbers, childishly small.

It seems therefore that if we look to a sufficiently remote past—say, to the Ice Age—we find that cultures changed with almost imperceptible slowness. To paleoanthropologists, the changes that we can measure in cave art of the paleolithic era were revolutionary—evidence of supposedly enhanced cognition, new technologies, accumulating prosperity, and emerging social complexity—that distinguish *homo sapiens* from preceding and contemporary hominid species. But the evidence, such as it is, of the emergence of these innovations covers a period of scores of thousands of years, succeeded by a further period of relative stagnation that lasted for at least ten millennia more.

Art is the mirror of society. It discloses for us the way our predecessors saw their world. Anyone who wants to understand the past should look at its art, which is where our predecessors recorded their perceptions, visions, and relationships to each other and to the world around them. When other cultural changes happen, art reflects them. New political culture changes the way artists depict power. New religions modify the structures of patronage and the representation of transcendence. New economic practices force their way into artists' views of the landscape and of the species they exploit. The continuities that link the art of Chauvet and Lascaux are proof that society changed little over the period encompassed by the paintings in these two caves. Nowadays, when we experience a convulsive new 'ism' in artistic fashion almost every week or month, and artists thrive rather by reacting against each other than by imitating their forebears, it is improbable that today's art will anticipate tomorrow's, and unthinkable that art should be recognizably the same in subject matter, technique, or concept, as paleolithic painters' was, after a lapse of ten years—let alone ten thousand.

This is not to say that Ice Age societies were stagnant. On the contrary, in many ways they were highly dynamic—nomadic or transhumant, restless, conflictive. Overall, however, they changed much less than later ones. In some respects the slow or sporadic pace resembled the way chimpanzee cultures can be observed in change today. Conspicuous areas of stability for paleolithic people included food and basic technologies for obtaining it.

Religion, too, was relatively stable. As far as we know, there were only two kinds of religion in the Ice Age: shamanism, detectable in images of dancing figures, clad in animal disguises as if captured in a moment of magical self-transformation, and the veneration or idealization of steatopygous figures—'Earth Mothers', as some commentators speculatively call them—found carved in reliefs or statuettes. As far as the evidence illuminates the politics of the era, it looks as if the only ways of organizing political life were under chiefs, along lines of kinship or totemic fraternity. Everyone's economics were alike: based on foraging, with a limited range of technologies. If globalization, in the strong sense of the word, means having a single, world-wide way of life, the most globalized era in history was the paleolithic.

First, these processes of cultural volatility and mutual cultural differentiation have occupied a relatively brief period of the human past: they really got going only during the latter part of the last great Ice Age. Until then, most human communities had much the same way of life, the same technologies and, as far as we know, other common features of culture, such as the same or similar religions and aesthetics. We simply do not know why the normal continuities of human life were interrupted in favour of the rapid, revolutionary changes that have gathered pace ever since: in part, presumably, climatic instability and environmental diversity helped to set change in motion;[7] and change, like appetite, *vient en mangeant*, as changes provoke other changes. It should be remembered, however, that rapid change—viewed in the context of the entire human past—is still an exceptional circumstance. The period of our cultural differentiation (though not of the mutability of our culture) now seems to be over, as globalization imposes, world-wide, a convergent model of how to live.

Second, even during the period in question, some human societies have remained largely exempt from change: some forest and desert peoples have attained the stunning achievement of resisting change and conserving tradition with amazing tenacity. If we ask 'which have been the world's most successful societies?' we tend to leap to the glib, self-flattering assumption that change is the brand of success; societies that have achieved spectacular progress, expansion, and environmental transformation are hailed as 'great civilizations' and models to copy, even if they have run out of stream or crumbled to ruins. But if survival is the goal, the most successful societies are really those that have changed least—that have preserved their traditions and identities intact, or that have perpetuated their existence by rationally limiting the exploitation of their environments. The longest-enduring societies—those that have successfully resisted the risks of change—are those that still lead the forager's way of life: the San or Bushmen of South Africa, Australian aboriginals, some rarely encountered forest peoples. This social longevity—as we might call it—aligns them with most non-human social animals.

In the ten millennia or so after the ice began to recede big changes—unprecedented divergences of culture from place to place—are discernible in the archaeological record. Previously, humans had led lives of a similar kind, wherever they lived—fed by the same methods of scavenging, foraging, and hunting; awed by the same kinds of gods and spirits; guided spiritually by shamans who experienced similar ecstasies; organized along similar lines into societies constructed of clans and totemic fraternities. Amid tremendous convulsions of climate, however, arose opportunities or exigencies to imagine and implement different ways of life.

Human cultural change speeded up at an unprecedented rate. The inescapable inference is that social and cultural change is an historical subject, susceptible of historical explanation. The peculiar mutability of human society has its origins not in 'human nature'—whatever that is—but in the circumstances of the relatively recent past. The increasing pace of change, moreover, is not an inherent property of change, but an historical phenomenon. It has occurred—for the most part—within a relatively well-known and relatively well-documented period, which can be said to have coincided roughly with the Holocene, and to have quickened spectacularly in the last few centuries.

* * *

As far as I know, no explanation for the increasing pace of change is available, other than the assumption that change is cumulative—which is no explanation, but merely an alternative way of describing the phenomenon we have to explain. Expectations of cumulative change—or gathering 'reiteration', or a 'ratchet effect' as some people like to call it, appropriating a term anthropologist Michael Tomasello coined to denote incremental improvements in the innovations that drive cultural change[8]—may be delusive. The model in biological evolution is of 'arms races' between contending species, or a 'Red Queen' process, named after the dictum of Lewis Carroll's character, in whose country 'it takes all the running you can do to stay in one place'.[9] Each species has to evolve ever more rapidly to break even. But Carl Bergstrom and Michael Lachmann have pointed out that antagonistic relationships are not necessarily typical and that collaborative evolution favours slow rates of change. Acceleration can be fatal. 'Fast evolution does not allow a species to outrun a partner,' they argue. 'It simply causes this species to yield to whatever threats are made.'[10] Their model fits culture remarkably well: cultures thrive on collaboration. They collapse when they 'ratchet up' changes.

At this point, some reader may call to mind the work of a great genius of the late twentieth century, the French polymath, René Girard, whose writings I always recommend to students, although I see his books as belonging in the category of 'great but wrong'. He did not set out to explain the accelerations of culture, but rather its origins. His theory no longer commands much assent as an account of how culture came about, but it does include a way of understanding how and why changes accumulate. Girard formulated it before learn-ing the lessons of primatology,[11] but in a series of interviews, first published in 2007, with João-Cezar de Castro Rocha and Pierpaolo Antonello he did a good job of aligning his views with the latest data and responding to his critics. He accepted a characterization of his views as Darwinian, on the grounds that he proposed a universal dynamic that drives culture, just as Darwin proposed general laws of organic change.[12] But he was not really a Darwinian: on the contrary, he aimed to free the study of culture from determinism of every kind. He did, however, detect an evolved faculty, supposedly unique to humans, underpinning culture: what he called 'mimetic desire'—definable in brief, though Girard would probably not endorse a brief summation, as the urge to appropriate observed virtues and advan-tages by imitation.

Syntactically, at least, the structure of Girard's theory resembles my insistence on evolved faculties of anticipation and memory impelling cultural change. In substance, however, Girard dispenses with the need for a creative act to precipitate culture: imitation is by definition not creative. But mimesis must have something to imitate. And imagin-ation must be prior to mimetic desire, because all imitation involves an imaginative act: that of seeing oneself as resembling or supplanting the creature one seeks to imitate. Without imagination, Girard's pro-posal would not work; with it, 'mimetic desire' seems superfluous. Still, even if 'mimetic desire' seems unsatisfactory as a prerequisite of culture, it is surely true that covetousness is a deeply ingrained source of human behaviour, and it is worth accompanying Girard further along his way in order to appreciate his possible contribution to the understanding of cultural acceleration.

The way he saw it, imitation tends to trigger conflict. One of its most common manifestations is the imitation of aggressive behaviour. Violence breeds mimetic violence. At some point in the exchange of violence a pair or group of an ancestor-species of ours initiated culture as a means of escape from the cycle of violence. This part of Girard's argument was evidently itself mimetic and unoriginal—cribbed from social contract theory, reminiscent, in particular, of Hobbes's view of society as a device to resolve 'the war of every man against every man' that scarred the state of nature. He added, however, an entirely new and utterly brilliant insight: that mutual aggressors deflect their violence against a common scapegoat in what he called 'the convergence of anger and rage towards a random victim'.[13]

Sacrifice was therefore, for Girard, the founding act of culture, in two senses. First, a scapegoat is a symbol, and symbolism, in Girard's opinion, is the ingredient of human thinking that distinguishes it from that of other animals; but, as we have seen, there is plenty of evidence that non-human creatures can grasp the nature of symbols; and in any case, Girard came to realize, on the basis mainly of primatological evidence, that culture is not exclusively human. Even if it were, there is no evidence to support the assertion that sacrifice preceded other forms of symbolism, including language, which Girard saw as a consequence of collaborative violence. Still, Girard's second reason for identifying sacrifice as the beginning of culture was that it is a ritual, and culture is definable in terms of ritual, which encodes learning. Again, however, to claim that sacrifice was the first ritual is to invite only very tentative and conditional assent, at best, even though Girard defined sacrifice worryingly widely—including every collaborative slaughter, such as conspiratorial murder for gain; infanticide in circumstances of extreme stress; and hunting, which, Girard insisted, must have originated for more than simply gathering food.

Girard always realized that the origins of culture must be sought in a dimly remote era—perhaps before the emergence of *homo sapiens*, among ancestral hominids. He came to appreciate that chimpanzees practise collective violence very similar to those previously thought peculiarly human, but he clung to the belief that chimpanzee culture is fundamentally different from ours on the grounds that 'their brains aren't developed enough' for symbolism.[14] That assumption was simply wrong. Girard betrayed his underlying unease when he recalled a passage about Konrad Lorenz's beloved geese (above, p. 81), which evaded combat when approaching one another in mutually imitated hostility by redirecting their violence against a third party.[15] No one has ever supposed that geese are cultural.

Still, mimesis is cumulative—it 'spirals', as Girard said. He used the concept brilliantly to explain the twentieth-century explosion of consumerism. Every time a new consumer acquires a commodity or indulgence as a consequence of envy of someone else, the example becomes accessible to more potential consumers. Every time a consumer sees a rival imitate him successfully he has to consume more to maintain his advantage. The convolutions of mimetic desire can explain some accelerations at some times, but if they alone were responsible for all cultural change, the pace of acceleration would be uniform and universal.

Mimesis can only help us if we also invoke a further context. Of course, there is a ratchet effect in culture. We see it at work whenever, for example, a new solution to an old problem has unforeseen consequences that demand further new solutions in their turn, or when a single idea breeds like an amoeba, releasing or inspiring further innovation. But the ratchet effect is an image more descriptive than explanatory. We can accept that culture accumulates. A complete explanation of the peculiarities of cultural change demands more: it has to account for why accumulation happens at different rates in different times and places; and why, in some cultures, changes accelerate more than others. The historical evidence—which is as near to empirical data as we can get for the study of culture—shows a correlation between change and exchange. The examples in Chapter 6 located experiences of acceleration in cultures exposed to reciprocal contacts, and in periods when mutual access eased. The madcap, worldwide changes of the twentieth century coincided with what we call globalization, in the most active period of intercultural traffic ever.

8

TOWARDS THE PLANET
OF THE APES

How change itself might change

The pace of contemporary change has changed historians. Historical writing narrates the past but reflects the present. In my time in the profession, the most conspicuous change—to me, at least, though fellow historians have left it unremarked and perhaps thought it unworthy of notice—has been what I call the collapse of the *longue durée*. When I was a student, gradualism was the vogue. My contemporaries and I were taught to see the origins of changes in the grinding structures of competing kinds of determinism. Now it is accepted that great events can arise from small causes that vary randomly;[1] everything can be understood or is even best understood in its immediate context. Contingencies and chaos make the difference between what happened and what might equally well have turned out otherwise. In Pascal's famous image 'had Cleopatra's nose been shorter, the whole face of the world would have been different'.[2]

When we seek to explain the decline and fall of the Roman Empire, for instance, we do not return, like Gibbon, to the Antonine age, when the Empire was doing rather well, but confine ourselves to the circumstances of the barbarian invasions of the late fourth and fifth centuries CE. When we want to understand the English Civil War, we no longer appeal, as Macaulay did, to 'the Whig interpretation' or to supposed long continuities of England's traditions of freedom, stretching back to the Germanic woods; much less to the long, supposedly inexorable rise of the bourgeoisie. We concentrate instead on the few years preceding the outbreak of hostilities, and in particular on the disruptive effects of the Scottish war of 1638. When we explore the causes of the French Revolution, we no longer reach back, as Tocqueville did, to the era of Louis XIV, when France was remarkably successful and in no apparent need of revolution, but explore a relatively brief crisis that began with the depletion of French resources in the American Revolutionary War. When we discuss the origins of the First World War, we no longer do as Albertini did, and cite the defects of the nineteenth-century diplomatic system, which actually kept the peace, but look at the breakdown of that system in the years just before the war, or even, in an extreme case, at the impetus of the railway timetables of August 1914. And so on. The examples are innumerable. In other words, as the pace of change in our own times has increased, the willingness of historians to believe in long continuities in the past has declined.

It is not surprising that academics should be sensitive to the rhythms of the world they study, even to the point of readjusting accordingly. Historians, perhaps because they try to avert their gaze from the distorting allure of hindsight, have been rather slow to adapt to changed circumstances, compared with other practitioners, and have followed the examples of colleagues in other departments. The irresistible trend of most new departures in science, philosophy, anthropology, mathematics, and linguistics throughout the twentieth century was towards a random, unpredictable model of how change happens. The jolt administered by Poincaré, Saussure, and the other *méchants* discussed in Chapter 3 above became a series of shudders, toppling traditional certainties with volcanic force. In what seemed increasingly to be a chaotic cosmos—indescribable with exactitude, unconformable to laws—academics in all disciplines lost confidence in their own ability to explain or even, in some respects, to describe what happened around them satisfactorily.

Between 1911 and 1913, for example, work on atomic structures revealed that electrons appear to slide erratically between orbits around a nucleus. Findings that followed from the attempt to track the elusive particles of sub-atomic matter informed the new discourse of 'quantum mechanics'. Its forms were paradoxical, like those employed by the Danish Nobel Prize-winner Niels Bohr, who described light as both waves and particles simultaneously. By the middle of the third decade of the twentieth century, more contradictions piled up. When the motion of sub-atomic particles was plotted, their positions seemed irreconcilable with their momentum. They seemed to move at rates different from their measurable speed and to end up where it was impossible for them to be. Working in collaborative tension, Bohr and his German colleague Werner Heisenberg enshrined these incompatible values in a principle they called 'Uncertainty' or 'Indeterminacy'. Their debate provoked a revolution in thought. Hugo von Hoffmannsthal, the fashionable and often prophetic Austrian poet who despaired of the power of language to express anything coherently, had already noticed that 'the nature of our epoch is multiplicity and indeterminacy...Foundations that other generations believed to be firm are really only sliding.' Scientists who thought about it realized that the world of big objects is continuous with the sub-atomic world: experiments in both spheres are vitiated by the same limitation. The observer is part of every experiment and there is no level of observation at which his or her findings are objective. The Uncertainty Principle threatened to put scientists back on par with their predecessors, the alchemists, who, because they worked with impractically complex distillations under the mercurial influence of the stars, could never repeat the conditions of an experiment and, therefore, never predict its results.

This was of enormous importance because practitioners of other disciplines tended to treat science as a benchmark of objectivity. Historians, anthropologists, sociologists, linguists, and even some students of literature called themselves scientists in proclamation of their intention to escape their status as subjects. It turned out that what they had in common with scientists, strictly so-called, was the opposite of what they had hoped: they were all implicated in their own findings.

Even after the formulation of the Uncertainty Principle, it was still possible to pick a way among the pits dug in the graveyard of certainty. Mathematics and logic, at least, seemed uncorrupted by the sub-lunar, sub-atomic world of quantum contradictions. Kurt Gödel believed in mathematics, but the effect of work he published in 1931 was to undermine the faith of others. He accepted Kant's view that numbers are known by apprehension, but he helped inspire others to doubt it. He felt certain—as certain as Plato or Pythagoras—that numbers really exist as objective entities, independent of thought, but he gave succour to those who dismissed them as merely conventional. He excited doubts as to whether they are known at all, rather than just assumed. He undermined a traditional way of understanding arithmetic as a formal system of reasoning similar to or identical with logic, and he inspired an unintended effect, encouraging philosophers of mathematics to devise new arithmetics in defiance of logic—rather as non-Euclidean geometries had been devised in defiance of traditional physics. He thought the truths of mathematics are non-negotiable, but by severing them from logic he encouraged a trend towards 'intuitionist' mathematics, which he abhorred. Intuitionist mathematics comes close, at the extremes, to saying that every man has his own mathematics and that a theorem proved is proved to the satisfaction of the prover. Potentially, it undermines the traditional view, as Plato expressed it: 'that which puts its trust in measurement and reckoning must be the best part of the soul', and the study of numbers 'obviously compels the mind to use pure thought in order to get at the truth'.[3]

To lose that trust and forgo that compulsion was a terrible forfeiture. The effect of Gödel's demonstrations on the way the world thinks was comparable to that of termites on a vessel formerly regarded as watertight by those aboard it: the shock of the obvious. If maths and logic were leaky, the world was a ship of fools.[4]

Contributions later in the century only seemed to put more space between subject and object. After the Second World War, the most significant boost to the tradition came with the publication of

Wittgenstein's *Philosophical Investigations* in 1953. The printed pages still have the flavour of lecture notes, full of unresolved prompts and queries, and anticipated questions or dialogue from the audience. In them roams a potentially annihilating virus. For those of us who want to tell the truth, language is an attempt to refer to things. After reading Wittgenstein's last work, one finds it hard to go on believing that this is possible. His argument that we understand language not because it corresponds to reality but because it obeys rules of usage seems unanswerable. Therefore, when we understand language, we do not necessarily know what it refers to, except on its own terms. Wittgenstein imagined a student asking 'so you are saying that human agreement decides what is true and what is false?' and again, 'aren't you at bottom really saying that everything except human behaviour is a fiction?' These were forms of scepticism anticipated by pragmatists and existentialists respectively. Wittgenstein tried to distance himself from them: 'if I do speak of a fiction, it is of a grammatical fiction'. The impact of a writer's work, however, often exceeds his intention. When he drove a wedge into what he called 'the model of object and name', Wittgenstein parted language from meaning. He even anticipated the absurdity in which postmodern pedagogy revels: 'my aim', he told his students, 'is to teach you to pass from a piece of disguised nonsense to something that is patent nonsense'.[5]

* * *

Scientific certainty was among the casualties of this era of subverted confidence. In 1960, in one of the most influential works ever written by a philosopher about science, Thomas Kuhn argued that scientific revolutions are identifiable with what he called 'paradigm shifts': changing ways of looking at the world and new imagery or language in which to describe it. Kuhn always repudiated the inference that most people drew: that the findings of science depend not on the objective facts but on the perspective of the enquirer. Yet increasingly in the twentieth century ordinary people and non-scientific intellectuals lost confidence in science. Faith that it could solve the world's problems and decode the secrets of the cosmos evaporated. In part, this was the result of science's practical failures: every technological advance activated its own problems and unleashed side-effects. Science seemed best at devising horrors and engines of destruction. In part, however, the process was one of intellectual disintegration as uncertainty corroded the 'hard facts' with which science had formerly been associated. To some extent, if one leaves health and defence spending out of the account, the trend in the public funding of science in the late twentieth century reflected public disenchantment. Even in the United States, where science commanded huge prestige and where the culture generally favoured investment in research and development, and especially in 'basic research'—untargeted on practical ends—total spending never reached 3 per cent of GDP. It concentrated increasingly on funding the practical demands of defence, industry, and health; total public expenditure on science peaked in the 1960s, when a 'space race' to beat the Soviet Union to the moon was under way.[6] Overall, with some fluctuations, it has declined, relatively speaking, ever since.

Over the three or four decades following the peak, postmodernism modified intellectual practices. A postmodern sensibility responds to the elusive, the uncertain, the absent, the undefined, the fugitive, the silent, the inexpressible, the meaningless, the unclassifiable, the unquantifiable, the intuitive, the ironic, the inexplicit, the random, the transmutative or transgressive, the incoherent, the ambiguous, the chaotic, the plural, the prismatic: whatever hard-edged modern sensibilities cannot enclose. Postmodernists typically abjured such hallowed values as creativity, originality, uniqueness, meaning, and form. In ethics postmodernism came to mean, or at least to include, advocacy of moral relativism; in epistemology, it suggested favouring scepticism about the validity of the concepts of reality and truth. In the humanities generally it referred to the adoption of methodologies affected by the 'linguistic turn'. And what was said to be postmodern science was 're-enchanted', or 'organicist', or deflected by the 'oriental turn' into an attempt to incorporate the insights—holistic and mystical—of supposedly eastern wisdom into Western thought.[7] All disciplines registered the effects; not least, the practice of history.

Postmodernism mounted an epistemological challenge that once seemed to threaten to subvert historians' dearest traditional quests: for truth and for the language in which to express it. For an extended moment, which lasted for most of the last quarter of the twentieth century, historians feared that librarians of the future would consign history to the same shelves as fiction. This would not, in my opinion, have been a bad thing: my books would have joined the company of good literature. Postmodernism, however, proved to be a paper tiger of fearful asymmetry. University history departments now have token postmodernists, as once they had token women and token blacks. But even as the tide receded, postmodernism left a rich residue on the shore, encouraging historical beachcombing. 'Virtual' histories, histories of the counterfactual, the ambiguous, the implicit, the liminal, the transgressive, the self-reflexive, the semiotic, the representational, the unconscious, and the dreamed have become fascinating and irresistible or, at least, interesting and acceptable to almost everybody.

Meanwhile, increasingly in the 1960s and 1970s, the growing power of computers revealed new dimensions of disorder in the world. In 1972 the meteorologist Edward Lorenz gave a paper to the American Association for the Advancement of Science on 'Predictability: does the flap of a butterfly's wings in Brazil set off a tornado in Texas?' The 'butterfly effect' became the universally adopted name for a chaotic system, in which causes are untrackable and effects unpredictable. The more specialists searched other areas of life for chaos, the more they found. In 1974, the Polish-born French mathematician Benoit Mandelbrot who, in under-appreciated work, had already demonstrated that financial and commodity markets are chaotic, published *Les Objets fractals*, showing to most readers' satisfaction that the particles of which the universe is composed, and the patterns they seem to exhibit, are irregular and do not correspond to the easily described shapes of traditional geometry. Deregulated economies mirror the unregulated universe. When I was schoolboy, and even, to some extent, when I read history at university in the late 1960s and early 1970s, everyone who taught me saw the world as a tissue of cause and effect, and causation as the order of the cosmos and the motor of change. Now that I am an ageing professor, I find that most of my colleagues are no longer sure. The world is now describable, according to one's taste, as delightfully surprising or dangerously volatile. Predictions have yielded to prophecies—accurate only if inspired. The search for the underlying or overarching order of the cosmos seems only to lead to chaos, which has replaced causation as the cement of the universe. History as a system, if you like, resembles the weather, in which the flap of a butterfly's wings can raise a storm. The flapping also fans Cleopatra's nose.

At least two positive effects have ensued. First, it no longer seems realistic to demand a predictable cosmos, ruled by definitive, unbending laws and bound by links of cause and effect. The causes may still be there, but are often untraceable. The effects may still be there but are often untrackable. Second, science has come to seem more approachable and more intelligible from the perspectives of other disciplines: less hard-edged, more yielding; less cocksure, more flexible; less definitive, more open-ended; less confident of solutions, more entranced by problems. After a long period in which humanities and social studies have tried to be more scientific, science has begun to look more like art. Science has let its hair down and become more arty. But, until now, circumstances have still kept the disciplines apart.

*   *   *

Toward the end of the century, divisions—sometimes called culture wars—opened between apologists of science and advocates of alternatives. 'Life is scientific,' says Piggy, the doomed hero of William Golding's novel of 1959, *Lord of the Flies*. The rest of the characters prove him wrong by killing him and reverting to instinct and savagery. Golding died in 1993, hailed as one of the great storytellers of the century, largely because of the impact of this one novel, which seemed to be an allegory of its times. Science—in most people's judgement—soared and failed. It sought to penetrate the heavens and ended by contaminating the Earth. Among its most influential inventions were bombs and pollutants. Instead of a universal benefit to humanity, science was a symptom or cause of disproportionate Western power. The expansion of knowledge added nothing to wisdom. Science did not make people better. Rather, it increased their ability to behave worse than ever before.

Under the influence of these feelings, and in response to the undermining of science by scepticism, an antiscientific reaction set in in the late twentieth century. It generated conflict between those who stuck to Piggy's opinion and the vast global majority who turned back to religion or even magic to help them cope with the bewildering world of rapid change and elusive understanding. Modern Japan is a land of high-tech Shinto, where spirits infest computers and where an office tower of steel and plate glass can be topped off with a shrine to Inari, the fox-god. Quantum science encouraged a revival of mysticism—a 're-enchantment' of science, according to a phrase the British theologian David Griffin coined.[8] Even religious fundamentalism—one of the most powerful movements in the late twentieth-century world— owed something to science (above, pp. 65–6).

The last wave of revulsion from science—or, at least, from scientism—in the twentieth century was a form of humanism: a reaction in favour of humane values. Science seemed to replace genies with genes, as it blurred the boundaries between humans and other animals, or even between humans and machines. It seemed to make freedom impossible and reduce moral choices to evolutionary accidents or genetically determined options. It turned human beings into subjects of experimentation. Ruthless regimes abused biology to justify racism and psychiatry to imprison dissidents. Scientism denied all non-scientific values and became, in its own way, as dogmatic as any religion. Humanists who responded to it in the era that followed the Second World War saw humans whole: as combinations of hard matter and chemical processes that science could illumine, with elusive feelings and dreams and intuitions and sympathies and hatreds and irrational temptations that remain dark even under the most brilliant flares of the Enlightenment. The movement was much more, however, than an antiscientistic reaction. Most of its leading figures, such as Bertrand Russell, or Isaiah Berlin, or Jean-Paul Sartre, in their several ways, tended to blame religion—or, at least, religious conflicts—as much as science for the failures of history, and humanistic thinkers and practitioners of the era commonly sought a morality based on universal or potentially universal values without reference to God. More than either science or religion, the barbarities of the political history of the twentieth century stimulated the resurgent humanists. Sartre summed it up: he had abandoned belief in God, but amid the horrors of the Second World War he had learned to believe in men.[9]

*   *   *

The culture wars divided students of culture into antagonistic camps, whose visions of their subject resembled respectively abstract and pointillist canvases: in one were those determined to make cultures conform to universal models, abstracted from the evidence, and in the other those unwilling to hide real diversity, beguiling complexity, and the unpredictability of events behind monolithic theories. In a long and bitter controversy in the late 1960s with Marvin Harris (his materialist colleague or rival in anthropology), Elman Service denounced the search for a 'prime mover' behind cultural change. Contingency—the play of circumstance, making every change explicable in its own terms—became beloved of historians who appreciate the vividness of conjuring the uniqueness of the events they narrate.[10] Historians reconstructed 'lost moments', re-imagining pasts that never happened but might have ensued from slightly reconfigured chance.[11] Cultural anthropologists formally dissociated themselves from their former colleagues who continued to work on physical anthropology—even to the point of splitting many university departments. Leading figures in late twentieth-century anthropology, archaeology, and sociology repudiated the very word 'evolution', including Edmund Leach, Adam Kuper, Anthony Giddens, Ernest Gellner, and Colin Renfrew.

Some of the older generation grew restive in the face of what Lewis Binford, one of the discoverers of 'Stone Age affluence' called 'weird humanism—"we're just appreciating the glories of mankind in its variability"—and nobody's trying to explain anything'.[12] Biology was the most widely backed prime mover going. A countermovement in the study of culture by seekers after predictability and submission to scientific laws started, more or less, with a famous and brilliant paper by William Hamilton in 1964, providing for altruism the Darwinian explanation that had eluded Darwin: altruism is explicable as a genetically evolved trait.[13] The uncompromisingly scientistic accounts of culture by Edward Wilson and Richard Dawkins (above, pp. 88–93) followed. Those who thought biology explains culture and those who did not disengaged—hardly talking to each other, hardly understanding each other when they did communicate.

No one who loves learning or values the lessons of unfamiliar disciplines could be satisfied with the gap between the 'two cultures' or the mutual silence of science and arts. Late twentieth-century hostility between scientistic and religious dogmas has been especially frustrating to rationally religious people, who want religion to be informed by science and consistent with reason (like Pope Benedict XVI, who tried to induce the Pontifical Academy to face scientific challenges to faith, as we shall see [below, pp. 258–9]). The problems of effecting reconciliation, however, have been daunting. Academic specialization is a terrible device that divides us among ghettoes of the like-minded. Ever-multiplying journals and web-rooms cram ever smaller sodalities into ever-tighter niches. It is literally impossible to talk regularly to all one's own colleagues in the big departments most of us inhabit in modern universities. There is too much work in any one discipline for an individual to keep up with all of it, even before he or she thinks about reading the latest findings in other fields. Everyone in academia prates about interdisciplinarity: practising it is harder.

Most late twentieth-century efforts to reconcile science and non-science were infelicitous. Edward Wilson advocated what he called consilience—which sounded well but amounted to a *putsch*, in which science would take over everything else. In my youth, the clamour among historians who envied science was for 'cliometrics'—an attempt to make the past calculable. Graduate students of my vintage had to fill our dissertations with tables and graphs, most of which turned out to be decorative or deceitful, because human vagaries are beyond quantification. Econometrics, meanwhile, drove many economists into rebellious refusal to accept that everything in the discipline is reducible to mathematical formulae. Even literature succumbed to the computer for a while, as students became fascinated with counting images—following the lead of Caroline Spurgeon, who before the Second World War had reckoned up the incidence of words and terms in the works of Shakespeare with an adding machine. Scientific imperialism underpinned most of the efforts, narrated in Chapter 5 above, to crush culture into explicability, or coax it into predictability, by means of biological laws or calculations of energy consumption.

Now, however, as science gets fuzzy at the edges, embraces absurdity, acknowledges the role of the random, and despairs of hard-and-fast answers, circumstances are more propitious in some ways for the humanities to absorb the sciences, rather than the other way round. Meanwhile, though some scientific triumphalists have not given up the attempt to conquer the arts with the armoury of science, scientists dedicated to the advocacy of evolutionary explanations of culture have retreated into a bunker, exchanging recriminations and accusations of heresy—which is usually a sign of defeat—as advocates of group selection and selfish genes sound off against each other. Richard Dawkins has decided that E.O. Wilson is 'erroneous' and 'perverse'. P.Z. Myers, who edits a popular evolutionist blog, thinks David Sloan Wilson 'needs a good punch in the balls'.[14] This is almost as nasty as any *odium theologicum* rival religious dogmatists have ever exchanged.

* * *

Meanwhile, scientists committed to talking about culture in evolutionary language are struggling to escape from their own quarrels and conciliate advocates of the autonomy of culture—another sign, I think, that scientistic imperialists have lost their battle to engorge the study of society and replace history with biology. Two excellent recent textbooks have tried to pilot students between the Sirens, but both start from aboard the evolutionists' bark and barely get beyond the shore. The anthropologist, Agustín Fuentes, my admired colleague at Notre Dame, warns that 'extra-somatic' behaviour limits the scope of biological explanations of culture;[15] but he exercises his skills as an academic broker almost entirely between rival forms of evolutionism and advocates 'true Darwinian anthropology...as culturally sensitive as any other kind of anthropology'.[16] His fellow textbook-writers, Kevin Laland and Gillian Brown (above, p. 92), are even more austere in ignoring work from anthropologists, philosophers, and historians, and excluding that by Fuentes himself. They concede that there is more to culture than biology, and that evolutionary explanations might not encompass everything in culture; but they arbitrate only among quarrelsome fellow-evolutionists. In scholars sceptical of some evolutionist excesses they diagnose 'post-modernist malaise' and 'a fashionably anti-science negativism'.

One of the heroes of the effort to re-align science and social study is the deservedly influential British sociologist, Walter Runciman (above, pp. 92–3, 119). He used his position as President of the British Academy to put his fellow members in ever-closer touch with their scientific counterparts in the Royal Society, a few doors down the street in Carlton House Terrace.[17] He thought the application of Darwinian models of change in the humanities would help forge a new synthesis, or at least a workable interdisciplinary programme, but he never elevated Darwinism to the ranks of a dogma. He acknowledged the difference between biological inheritance and cultural transmission. The latter, he wrote, is 'different from the transmission of information passively copied in the receiving organism with only the possibility of occasional and limited mutation'.[18] He appreciated that 'natural science cannot by itself account for the diversity of collective human behaviour-patterns'.[19] Selectionist narratives, he was happy to allow, 'leave room for many others'.[20]

He pointed out some valuable truths about the usefulness of evolutionary facts for the understanding of culture: for instance, 'that there are some innate, species-wide dispositions, capacities and susceptibilities', of which he cited love and anger as incontestable cases, 'which impose some inescapable limits on the possible extent of variation between one culture or society and another'. That is a valid warning to any student of culture who thinks our evolved faculties are irrelevant to his or her work. He was right to say that 'our biological inheritance includes...the innate capacities which enable us to display a far greater variety of behaviour than any other species'. I think what I have said about memory and imagination helps us identify those capacities. He identified 'an innate predisposition to conformity' in humans, and while I should prefer to see that claim reformulated, it is true that culture is inherently stable—the long periods of relative stagnation in the history of most cultures, human and non-human, pretty well proves that; hence the need to explain the accelerations of change that were the subject of the previous chapter.[21] He was right to say that some of what people do together is a direct, 'evoked' response to the environment.[22]

Runciman overestimated, however, the power of evolution to explain what he called 'acquired behaviour'—culture in the sense adopted in the present book—and behaviour 'imposed' by 'institutional inducements or sanctions'. He distinguished 'imposed behaviour' as social rather than cultural, but I think imposition is best understood as one means of acquisition—by stick and carrot, rather than Socratic winkling or learning in freedom. Runciman became zealously prescriptive, insisting that 'sociologists have...to identify and trace the heritably variable and competitively selected information without which... cultures...would not have evolved into what they are', and that sociologists 'can answer the questions which concern them by directly applying the models which have served the theory of natural selection so well to the very different, although in some ways analogous, mechanisms by which cultural and social evolution are driven'.[23] The pre-emptive language disclosed Runciman's assumptions: that culture is or closely resembles a system of descent with modification (above, p. 148), that it therefore evolves, and that heritability and selection between them account for the range of variation. Runciman was right to urge fellow students of culture to take evolution into account, wrong to assert that Darwinian models could answer 'the questions that concern them'. As we have seen, cultures often adopt competitively ill-adapted practices. The analogies between cultural and biological change are weak and often misleading; evolution is an infelicitous designation for cultural change; and such change has no 'mechanisms' and is not always well described as 'driven'.

*   *   *

There is now a chance to break the barriers between science and the rest on the basis of equality. The two cultures are reconverging as indeterminacy and re-enchantment dapple science and as interdisciplinarity and curricular reform entice academics across demarcation lines. The opportunity for rapprochement is worth exploring: real consilience, which acknowledges that nothing explains everything, and that the potentialities of culture are as unconstrained as the imaginations that drive change.

I have been in two places where science and humane letters, and what one might call evolutionism and culturalism, have coexisted amicably and contentedly, exchanging honour and learning with each other, in constructive repose: once in an academic team, and once in a garden. The academic experience was in a collaborative project housed at the Radcliffe Institute at Harvard, and organized by the Harvard historian Daniel Smail and the Michigan sociologist Andrew Shryock. The aim of the project was to get representatives of every relevant discipline, including history, anthropology, linguistics, genetics, primatology, sociology, and biology, to join in convincing historians generally to extend the range of their work back into the 'deep past' before the beginning of history, as conventionally and traditionally conceived, into what has hitherto been excluded as 'prehistory' or 'natural history'— including the hominid background from which *homo sapiens* emerged.[24]

The garden was, perhaps, a more likely place for peace, in the tranquil, damp, gently undulating Scottish lowlands, where Charles Jencks, the architect and philosopher, created what is surely the biggest and most ambitious work of art of the twentieth century world: the Garden of Cosmic Speculation. Jencks began his garden in 1989 and gradually recrafted thirty acres with the snaking, spiralling shapes of soliton waves, helical twists, and fractal wonderlands, lapping and linking landforms and sculptures and water-courses that represent, simultaneously or contiguously, the history of the Earth and the history of how people have thought about it. In an abrupt fault in the ground, Jencks built a cascade, which the visitor can mount by steps that represent the æons of the Earth, each embedded with geological specimens that correspond to each age, and all of different breadths and height in proportion to the length of time each period lasted. From the summit, you see a garden of the history of science, with sculptures that recall great insights from antiquity through the renaissance and the Enlightenment and onwards. Particular gardens portray and tease each of our senses, and mimic ingeniously the way sub-atomic particles seem to move. Another captures the dislocation one might feel when witnessing the implosion of a black hole. The programme is impartial and realistic. The destructive tendencies of both science and religion are obvious in a sculpture that combines an image of Shiva with a mushroom cloud. A nonsense garden nestles amid the clear-headed representations of scientific fact and celebrations of reason. Passion beyond science flows under the whole composition like lava, sometimes bubbling up to disturb scientific self-assurance, sometimes provoking a sense of seismic quakes, dizzying and jolting the beholder. The paths through the garden seem to straddle science and meta-science.

*　*　*

One leaves the Garden of Cosmic Speculation with faith that science can be humane and a resolve to overleap academic narrows. Basic to entente between biology and history is the acknowledgement of three facts: that culture is not uniquely human; that the existence of culture depends on evolution in the sense that we can only do anything with the physical and cerebral equipment evolution has given us; but that culture also changes independently of evolution, which should not be expected to have infinitely elastic powers of explanation.

We need to espouse pluralism among contending disciplines, just as much as among mutually jostling cultures and civilizations: dialogue in place of strife, respect before rejection, reciprocal learning instead of reciprocal hectoring. Pluralism became the late twentieth century's best means of keeping the peace of the world—or at least some peace in some of it—as the inescapable consequence of global change. Most of history had favoured unitary states, with one religion, ethnicity, and identity. Large empires had always been multicultural, but they usually had a dominant culture, alongside which others were, at best, tolerated. In the twentieth century, this would no longer do. The aftermath of the era of global empires, the range and intensity of migrations, the progress of ideas of racial equality, the multiplication of religions, and the large-scale redrawing of state boundaries made the toleration of diversity essential to the peace of most states. Those states that rejected toleration in the late twentieth century faced traumatic periods of 'ethnic cleansing'. Meanwhile, democracies could only contain the intense competition of rival ideologies by embracing political pluralism—that is, the admission to the lawful political arena, on equal terms, of parties representing potentially irreconcilable views.

What was true of individual states was true of the entire world. 'Shrinkage' brought peoples and cultures into unprecedented proximity. The peace and future prosperity of the world at the end of the century demanded a new global consensus in favour of pluralism, and an effort to accommodate plurality of cultures— religions, languages, ethnicities, communal identities, versions of history, value systems—on terms of equality in a single global community.

Isaiah Berlin explained how such a consensus and such an effort are possible:

> There is a plurality of values which men can and do seek…And the difference it makes is that if a man pursues one of these values, I, who do not, am able to understand why he pursues it or what it would be like, in his circumstances, for me to be induced to pursue it. Hence the possibility of human understanding.

This position differs from cultural relativism. It does not say, for instance, that all cultures can be accommodated. One might exclude Nazism, say, or cannibalism. It leaves open the possibility of peaceful argument about which culture, if any, is best. It claims, in Berlin's words, 'that the multiple values are objective, part of the essence of humanity rather than arbitrary creations of men's subjective fancies'.[25]

In a world where globalization made most historic communities defensive about their own cultures, it has been difficult to persuade them to coexist peacefully with the contrasting cultures of their neighbours. Still, pluralism is obviously the only practical future for a diverse world. Paradoxically, perhaps, it is the only truly uniform interest that all the world's peoples have in common.

Pluralism, however, is not perfect freedom. Pluralism entails proscriptions, or at least self-denying ordinances. It is not possible, for instance, to be a pluralist Nazi. Similarly, in a world of academic coexistence, it is not possible to be pluralist and to demand submission to a single dogma, or crush disparate phenomena into one uncomfortably inelastic explanatory matrix. I should not want to proscribe talk of cultural evolution—but I do want to forgo it. The term does not describe accurately the way culture changes, any more than any of the other mythic and archaic models of cultural change people formerly espoused, such as that it is cyclical, or static, or in a permanent state of decline. It is fair to say that increasing elaboration or increasing complexity dominate the history of many cultures, just as they dominate the natural history of many organisms; but the interesting exceptions subvert any temptation to turn generalization into grand theory. The mutations that make for a multiplicity of culture are different from those that kick off organic changes: they are capricious, but not random; they are devised by minds, not spontaneous; typically, they do not replicate according to the incidence of any advantage, nor does their success or failure respond necessarily to environmental constraints or opportunities. The study of how our lives change has to involve a dialogue between history and biology, because humans behave with the limbs and brains and bones and organs that evolution has given us. But culture crafts itself, and once it transcends bodily constraints, anything can happen.

*   *   *

So what might happen next? It may be helpful now to have a look back at the main lines of the argument so far, before I offer some speculations about possible futures.

Human cultures are conspicuously mutable. In trying to understand why, it is tempting to look to the two influences that have proved most reliable in explaining change in non-human species (including most behavioural change and at least some change properly classified as cultural): evolution and environment. But neither of these is satisfactory in accounting for the frequency and volatility of cultural change in humans. The critical gap between human and non-human cultural species demands a further, peculiarly human explanation. The environment, in any case, is relatively inert compared with human culture, and although there are occasional cases, such as large-scale volcanic eruptions or the sudden evolution of a new and powerful micro-organism, when the rhythms of environmental and cultural change coincide, these are too infrequent to account for all the lurches of culture.

Evolution, too, though it can and does unfold with amazing rapidity at intervals, seems generally too slow-working a mechanism to meet the case. Even the syncopations of 'punctuated equilibrium' are too slow and too rare. We can measure the pace of human evolutionary divergence in our DNA: the results do not stand comparison with the cultural divergence historians record. Although our species encompasses a wide range of DNA, the variation is infinitesimal, compared with the enormous diversity of our cultures.

Those are not decisive considerations in themselves; but such evidence as we have supports a conclusion incompatible with the normal operations of evolution, as organic change discloses them: the most adaptive cultures are not those best fitted for survival, but the most prone to catastrophe. Successful survival cannot therefore account for the replication of traits of culture, in the way that it explains physiological traits. A system that, independently of human choice, imposed cultures equipped to survive would select for foraging, for instance. Cultures that have stuck to that strategy have survived for scores of millennia, while those that have substituted sedentarism, urbanization, agriculture, and all the other adaptations we associate with 'civilization' are one with Nineveh and Tyre. Our adaptations bear the fingerprints of free will precisely because, so far, just about all of them have been unsuccessful. Their increasing pace looks like a measure of increasing desperation.

We can at least be confident in asserting that, although evolution and the environment create the framework of contingencies within which everything in history happens, and some features of cultures may be explicable in evolutionary and environmental terms, specific cultural changes do happen independently of evolution and environment. For culture is a projection of the human mind, and cultural changes originate in the realm of ideas. The theory of memes is valueless for all the reasons we have noted (above, pp. 90–3)—and not just because there is no evidence for the existence of memes, in the sense of evolved 'units' of culture, or of any mechanism by which evolution could select them for transmission to other cultures, but also because empirical evidence suggests that culture spreads by means of imaginative creation and conscious adoption among individuals. I do not mean to assert that the mind—or, to focus on exactly what I mean by 'mind' in the present context, the capacity for generating ideas—is unaffected by evolution. If it is true, as we suppose on the basis of our present knowledge, that humans have an exceptional capacity for generating ideas, evolution should have played some part in endowing us with it. But while the faculty of thinking up ideas is a product of evolution, the ideas that ensue flow and shift with a dynamic of their own, unpredictable, unquantifiable, ungoverned by laws, and with no necessary advantage to man or 'meme'.

Put it like this: once we have identified the evolved faculties that make culture possible and mutable, there is no need, no reason, to seek further evolutionary preconditions for particular features of culture. Once we know how evolution has equipped cultural animals to teach and learn, there is no need, no reason to seek a gene, say, or group advantage for washing sweet potatoes, or religion, or agriculture, or space travel, or any of the other things those animals teach and learn from each other. Much less is there any call to concoct evolutionary explanations for the divergences of culture—for the multiplication, say, of food-gathering strategies, or the varieties of language, or the diversity of religions, or the multiplicity of political and social systems, or the vagaries of taste.

We do not know for certain what in evolution made culture possible. It may be a gene or combination of genes, or a group advantage, or a spandrel, or even a trait inherent in 'the lowest forms of bacteria'. As we are still only beginning to identify cultural animals and sort them out from the rest, it is premature to expect clear results from the search for the biology that underpins culture in general. It is worth trying, however, to identify the evolutionary prerequisites that make some cultural animals more innovative than others, because we know which animals they are: cetaceans, maybe; primates, certainly; and, above all, by a long way, humans.

As a working hypothesis, I have suggested that the ideas that make human cultures exceptionally malleable and strikingly divergent by comparison with other cultural species are a by-product of prodigious imagination—which in turn is the issue of well-developed powers of anticipation, such as humans possess to an exceptional degree, combined with the relatively unreliable memories with which evolution has equipped humans (above, pp. 167–78). Evolution selects for anticipation especially in the case of hunting animals, which need to be able to anticipate the behaviour both of prey and of rival predators, often in environments that occlude the senses. *Homo sapiens* needs a relatively rich range of anticipation to make up for the feebleness of body, slowness of gait, and weakness of sight and smell that disadvantage us as hunters. Exceptionally productive imaginations are probably a side-effect, an evolutionarily useless outcome of superabundant anticipation. Although many people nowadays—especially feminists in recoil from the concept of 'Man, the hunter', or readers in rebellion from the oversimplifications of evolutionary psychology, or advocates of the unquestionable parity of other food-garnering strategies, such as scavenging or gathering, in the deep past of our hominid ancestors—deprecate the influence on us of a hunting past, we cannot overlook its importance. It explains, I suspect, why humans have so many more ideas than other primates. Non-human apes resemble us closely in so many other respects; but rarely, in the chimpanzee and bonobo cases, or never, among other great apes, do they eat meat, and typically they do not go hunting, or have only a short and limited experience as predators, compared with humans and human ancestor-species of the last couple of million years or so. Of course, there are plenty of hunters outside the primate family—but we have to leave them out of the comparison until we know whether they have culture and until we have more data on their faculties of anticipation and memory.

*   *   *

Suppose my argument is right so far. Suppose change issues from imaginations. Suppose human imaginations are in part a side-effect of the long evolution of anticipation as a faculty predators need. Suppose the cultures of non-human apes change slowly because of relatively deficient imaginations. It follows that once other apes embark on hunting as a food-garnering strategy they might evolve the same faculty of anticipation as humans have, and acquire increasingly flexible imaginations as a consequence.

As we now know, chimpanzees do hunt. We do not know for how long they have done so, but the earliest observations date from the 1960s. So it is possible, at least, and likely, I think, that hunting is a recent innovation in chimpanzee culture, induced by the stresses human competition has caused, and the shrinkage of traditional foraging grounds. In any case, as we have seen hunting so far forms a minuscule part of the economy of chimpanzee societies: it could grow. Predictably, it will grow as human pressure on chimpanzees' environments increases. Now that chimpanzee communities have embraced the ecology of hunters, I do not think it is fanciful to speculate that their trajectory of change could eventually draw closer to ours, as hunting becomes more important in their economies, evolution responds accordingly, and chimps get ever more imaginative. The long-term outcome—or, maybe, *reductio ad absurdum*—animates one of the most successful movie franchises of the late twentieth century: *Planet of the Apes*.

The story seems almost indescribably nonsensical. In the book on which the movie-makers based their concept, honeymooners stumble on a screed and extract it from the bottle in which it was sealed. They read of how, after an æons-long journey of exploration in search of a distant galaxy, astronauts emerged from a spacecraft onto a planet where chimpanzees, gorillas, and orang-utans collaborated in the creation of a technically well-equipped civilization. The human population, confined to harsh, marginal environments, seemed under-evolved by comparison with the non-human apes, and intellectually deficient—fit only to be caged in gorilla-run zoos, or killed for fun, or appropriated as victims of enslavement or vivisection. Chimp scientists treated the newly arrived specimens of *homo sapiens* as curiosities, testing their intelligence, teasing them as Pavlov teased his dogs, and—in a satirical echo of Noam Chomsky's debates with primatologists—arguing over whether the humans' ability to talk was mere mimicry or evidence of a genuine language faculty. At the end of the movie version, which captivated cinema audiences in 1968, the planet in question is revealed to be Earth in the distant future. The original novel, *Le Planète des singes* by Pierre Boulle, has a further twist. The honeymooners who discover the tale turn out to be chimpanzees.

We shall not end up, like Boulle's time-travellers, in the Planet of the Apes, because more than hunting is involved in the evolution of human imaginations. Non-human apes would have to follow the human historical trajectory in other respects to join us in facing the perils and pleasures of our tantalizingly, terrifyingly unstable cultures. They would have to live in ever-larger societies to develop human-style memories, equipped with blessed defects that filter out an unbearable burden of data. That is not impossible, though there is no sign of it in primatologists' observations so far. But chimpanzees would not have to evolve in the biological sense—they would not need different genes or brains or bodies—for their culture to experience transmutative changes. Walter Runciman once imagined a primatologist returning from a visit to a group of chimpanzees who told ancestral myths, ran their affairs through a council of elders, and built monumental architecture. He immediately banished the thought: such creatures, he supposed, could not be chimpanzees but 'other primates with a critical difference ... in their genetic inheritance and the design of their brains'.[26] Runciman's reasoning was obviously fallacious. Suppose we replace his primatologist with an extra-terrestrial anthropologist, and substitute the early humans of Herto for his chimpanzees. Would the visitor be right to suppose that the objects of its fieldwork must belong to different species from the denizens of the University of Cambridge, or even the caves of Altamira?

The development of hunters' imaginations, without new biological mutations, is a consequence rationally predictable among chimpanzees on the basis of current evidence. If it were to occur, how long would it take to have an effect on the rate of change in chimpanzee culture? In the human case, the hunting imagination seems to have taken a long time to emerge and get to work. Our hominid ancestors took up the practice perhaps as much as between 2 and 2.5 million years ago. The rate of change in the cultures of hunting hominids only began to exceed that measurable among chimpanzees about 800,000 years ago, when *homo erectus* began to penetrate unfamiliar environments and engage in wide-ranging migrations. The same kind of change began for *homo sapiens* only about 100,000 years ago. Even in the time of the cave-painters of the paleolithic, as we have seen, as recently as 20–30,000 years ago, cultural continuity was amazingly consistent, and change staggeringly slow, by comparison with the accelerations of the last 10- or 15,000 years. It is one of the privileges of a predictor to locate his prophecies in a future so remote as to make them unfalsifiable until he is long dead. So I daresay, on the basis of comparison with the human past, that after at least 100,000 years of hunting, or perhaps as many as 1 million, chimpanzees' imaginations, which are already precocious and productive in impressive ways, may rival ours—though if I am right about the role of memory in imagination chimpanzees might be too good at remembering accurately to have quite the same imaginations as we do. We shall not be in the Planet of the Apes, but our descendants, if there are any, may share their world with comparably volatile cultural species.

* * *

Whatever the chances of such a future, comparison of human with non-human cultures helps us to understand the past: why, for so much of it, cultural change was so slow—among humans, as we have seen, barely exceeding the rate of change in other cultural species; why it has accelerated recently out of all comparison with other creatures.

I have insisted on repudiating any notion that history can be encompassed in a single, simple story: that it is 'about' cultural evolution, or increasing complexity or elaboration, or progress, or providence, or cycles or stages. But there is one overall characterization of the past of cultural species that holds good for humans in particular. The story has been, for most of the time, one of divergence, as human communities migrated across the globe and in many cases lost touch with one another. In such cultural changes as occurred during the period of divergence, adaptations to the different environments human migrants encountered played their part. Subsequently, at first very gradually or fitfully, as sundered communities re-established contact, ideas oscillated with increasing frequency across newly established frontiers, generating or contributing to the generation of accelerating change. Among the changes were projects for extending the reach of exploration and exchange, and technologies to effect them: striking examples of re-imaginings of the world, realized in practice.

Convergence and divergence are always going on together, tugging at each other, and overlapping. But in the last half-millennium or so, convergence has replaced divergence as the dominant trend in global history. Enhanced powers of travel and communication, the reach of trade and migration, the creation of vast imperial arenas for the exchange of culture and biota, and the gradual adscription even of the shyest and remotest peoples to the global community have all combined to make cultures in every part of the world resemble all the others in ways unprecedented since paleolithic times. The beginning of a new and so far relatively short period of convergence therefore coincided with a quickening of change of all kinds. The most marked feature of the very recent past—which we call globalization—is, from one point of view, intensified exchange. To put it crudely: change grows out of exchange; the more exchange, the more change. Inter-cultural contacts do not just reshake the kaleidoscope of the world; they also multiply the crystals that it contains.

Is the quickening of the pace of change limitless? We could muddle along, at least for a while. We have done so during more than a century of unprecedented acceleration. Changes in the way people behave outwardly have kept pace with the shift and drift of ideas. As we have seen, for instance, for people who experienced the unprece-dented rate of progress in the early twentieth century, utopia seemed attainable. A world improved or perfected seemed within reach. Ambitions inherited from the past seemed briefly realizable, before disillusionment or realism set in. Massacre was just one way to get there: re-creating a world without enemies. The new power of technology at the disposal of governments constituted an opportunity to reforge society for the better. The social history of the century was largely a story of projects that failed, as chaos undid plans and overpowered progress. Wartime solidarity was an emergency response for most of the societies that experienced the Second World War. It was bound to disappear into the generation gap that opened up in the 1950s and 1960s. As young people grew up without shared memories of wartime, they turned to libertarianism, existentialism, or mere self-indulgence.

The twentieth-century trajectory, in short, was of well-meaning utopias that became living hells, and of social and economic planning, espoused in enthusiasm and abandoned in disgust. The global economic crisis of the 1970s was a turning-point: state control proved incapable of supplying shortages, arresting inflation, or meeting social costs. Some of the most over-planned societies of the era that followed the Second World War—in the Soviet Union and Soviet-dominated eastern Europe—became effectively uninhabitable and succumbed to liberalizing revolutions. In most of the rest of the world, public preferences shifted from admiration of highly regulated life, Scandinavian-style, to the US model of unrepentant *laissez faire*. Chicago economics displaced Keynesianism. In the tawdry utopias that modern architecture created, citizens recoiled from the dreariness of over-planned societies. Much, perhaps most, rationalist housing of the 1960s, erected wherever governments or municipalities or philanthropic foundations could afford it, has now fallen to the wrecking ball. Within a generation or so of their construction, the projects became the targets of campaigns for demolition. Utopia, it seems, has been demolished—or at least, as the hugely popular English lawyer John Mortimer put it in a novel of 1986, paradise was postponed. People felt let down by progress and deceived by their leaders. By the 1980s, they began to lose faith in the viability of economic public sectors. As we have seen, economies lurched from over-regulation to under-regulation, with even more disastrous consequences, as the old Adam reappeared in the guise of Gordon Gecko. How could societies prevent the alienation and sufferings of the victims of failed utopianism?

Traditions had to struggle to survive the quickening pace of change, which made social and political relationships unrecognizable to successive generations and bewildering to those whose lives spanned the transformations. Science drove change, inspiring new technology, reforging the way people saw the world. The relentless growth of global population, which wars did not interrupt, increased the pressure on the world's resources. But, even more than population growth, spiralling desire—consumerism, lust for abundance, impatience to enjoy the rewards of economic growth—made people exploit the planet with increasing ruthlessness.

Broadly speaking, towards the end of the twentieth century a frail consensus in favour of pluralism emerged as the only workable strategy for a globalizing world, with intermingled cultures. Economic consensus, too, seemed easy to establish after the failures of over-planned, rigidly regulated, or state-run economies, as the world turned back to the prescriptions of classical economics. Political convergence towards democracy seemed bound to accompany widening economic freedoms. The new consensus has lasted into the twenty-first century. It might equip us to cope with even faster, more variegated change, because pluralism makes a virtue of diversity. But the consensus now seems to be breaking down under the strain of competition for diminished resources and the resentments, frustrations, and hatreds that issue, as we have seen, from a world of uncontrollable change.

If we do not muddle through, we could hurtle towards entropy, like a crazily accelerating machine that explodes with the force of its own output of energy, or ice that melts as it warms, or a star that collapses on itself. Implicit in 'Big History' (above, pp. 160–1) is the prospect that civilization will run out of energy. Or we could collapse, engorged by our unrestrained consumption or spiralling desire, or exhaust vital resources by ecological mismanagement. Or we might immolate ourselves in nuclear violence. Or environmental changes beyond our control might fry us in a warmed world or freeze us in a new

Ice Age or drown us in a 'waterworld' or exterminate us in a new age of plague.

Historians properly base their predictions of the future on the experience of the past and tend to be surprised when the normalcy of the world fails to restore itself. If my train of thought is valid so far, we should expect change to slow and even cease; it will slow. It will not cease: people like it too much; those hyper-active imaginations and warped memories, which are part of human nature (above, pp. 167–81) will go on inducing visions of possible futures and provoking efforts to realize them. But if we ever achieve a truly globalized world, in which we share a common, globalized culture, we shall have reverted to a form of isolation more extreme than any our ancestors experienced. We shall be alone in the universe, having no other cultures—except those of putative beings in other galaxies—with which to communicate. There will be no intercultural exchange to spawn rapid innovation. In the meantime, however, we shall continue to live in 'interesting times' and suffer the corresponding curse.

So, in the meantime, until immolation sets in, or entropy exhausts us, or we perish in any of the other terminal disasters that threaten, if indeed they ever come to pass, we have to find ways of living at ease in a disturbingly alchemical world of rapid, total transmutations of culture. In particular, we have to be on our guard against the forms of political and religious extremism that thrive in revolutionary circumstances.

One strategy is to emphasize that there are still continuities to cling to, and that some features of tradition can endure even hectic change. Change is now so pervasive that we should be more surprised that any continuities survive, than that the transformations we observe are so sweeping. In part, I suspect, those continuities remain possible as a paradoxical effect of change. For change usually tends to increase complexity because it is inseparable from and multiplies the connective elements in the system: the world of today is connected by innumerable links between its dazzlingly varied elements. In some instances, complex systems are highly fragile because their parts are interdependent, and failure in one area can cause total arrest; but in general they tend to be surprisingly robust, especially if they are undesigned, with far more links than are strictly necessary, because some links can perish without jeopardizing the continuity of functions. That is probably the kind of system we live in now. Its lurches are disturbing, but it also conveys a kind of comfort. For its very momentum, its very mutability, are becoming its increasingly familiar features. If they were to cease, that change—the last change—would be the most unsettling of all.

IN THE VATICAN GARDEN: AFTERWORD AND ACKNOWLEDGEMENTS

There are nymphs in the Vatican Garden. You will find them painted on the walls of the delightful little renaissance pavilion that houses the Pontifical Academy of Sciences. The night before my lecture to that august body, I slept in the Domus Sanctae Marthae, where cardinals are housed when they gather in conclave to elect a pope. Dark greenery waved at me in the wind through the high window, as I lay between sheets rigid with starch, on a bracingly hard bed. The walls were undecorated except for a crucifix nailed high above my head. The room had gravity: heavy furnishings of chestnut and solid fittings of glowing brass. It proclaimed grandeur with austerity, cost without comfort.

It gleamed with purity. I have never been in such a spotless environment, and the only hint of how it got to be so clean was the occasional wisp of the hem of a nun's habit, disappearing around a corner of the corridor. In the public spaces of the Domus, the same aesthetic prevailed: vast, marbled, spotless, joyless. The austerity extended to the food.

To get to the Academy from the Domus, one winds one's way along paths that curl through the gardens and create a sense of spaciousness inside the Vatican's cramped walls. Abruptly, the track turns to reveal the elegant Casina Pio IV, the Academy's home. Sudden new sensations almost make one swoon at the promise of luxury. Pius IV had the pavilion stuccoed, carved, and painted in the mid-sixteenth century, at a time when popes could enjoy themselves unashamedly. Secular, pagan themes jostle narratives of the powers of the papacy and the justice of the Church. Everything is designed for delicacy and ease, in contrast to the monumentality and chastity of the Domus. In the elliptical *cortile*, when visitors are received, the table groans with every kind of food and drink—the expert confections (on the days I visited) of Tuscan caterers. While the clergy endure the austerity of the Domus, the Academicians, most of whom are laymen, seem to do themselves rather well.

I was shown into an angular little meeting-chamber with ranks of reverberant microphones and a hostile, echoing acoustic, to give a talk that became one of the starting-points of this book. Pope Benedict XVI, who is an inexhaustibly curious intellectual, wanted the Church to be informed about every discovery of science and scholarship that might have implications for doctrine. Accordingly, with the support of the John Templeton Foundation the Academy assembled a conference of researchers who could perhaps throw light on one of the key sources of problems: changes in our understanding of the difference between humans and other creatures. Christianity has always posited a special relationship between God and humankind, involving lordship or at least stewardship of creation, but almost every newly disclosed fact about the continuum that links humans with other creatures challenges traditional thinking about the distinction. As I work for a university that seeks 'to do the Church's thinking', the project was intensely interesting and important to me.

I took the opportunity to broach what I thought was an exciting prospect: how the study of non-human cultures—of which, I pointed out, there are many, with more being discovered all the time—can help us understand humankind. It was obvious that the Academicians present generally found the subject disturbing. Questions from the audience included 'what does Aristotle say about this?' and 'what does Aquinas say about this?' But unless we revise our notion of ourselves and locate humans where we belong, among other cultural animals, we shall have no hope of understanding our lives, how they change, how we change them, and how much the changes are the outcomes of processes beyond our control.

The proceedings of the get-together in Rome led to a collection of studies, edited by Malcolm Jeeves, on *Rethinking Human Nature*, published by Eerdmans in 2010. The John Templeton Foundation also sponsored another conference out of which this book grew: a gathering in London in 2007, which yielded a volume edited by Donald Yerxa, on *British Abolitionism and the Question of Moral Progress in History*, published by the University of South Carolina Press in 2011. Underlying my contributions to both undertakings was my long-standing and perhaps rather idiosyncratic interest in the history of the limits of the human moral community—the subject of an earlier essay of mine, *So You Think You're Human* (published in the United States as *A Brief History of Humankind*), which appeared with Oxford University Press in 2007. Between them, these three projects turned my thoughts to the problems that animate the present book.

I am grateful to the John Templeton Foundation, to colleagues who took part in the discussions in Rome and London, and especially to Malcolm Jeeves and Donald Yerxa for guiding the results as masterful editors, and to readers of *So You Think You're Human* who helped by sending useful comments. I benefited immeasurably from being part of a collaborative project at the Radcliffe Institute, Harvard University, organized by Daniel Smail of Harvard and Andrew Shryock of the University of Michigan, on locating history in the deep past of humankind, and to the colleagues who collaborated in producing the book that emerged from our efforts, *Deep History*, published by the University of California Press in 2011. Sarah Radcliffe of Cambridge University magnified my chances of thinking about the problem of the limits of evolution by organizing a collaborative panel on determinism for the periodical *Human Geography* in 2009. My colleague Julia Thomas was kind enough to talk to me ahead of publication about a proposed forum on history and biology in the *American Historical Review*. I was also lucky to have opportunities to air some other work towards the present book in forums where I benefited from invaluable criticism and comment, including, roughly in alphabetical order, the Universidad de los Andes (Bogotá), the University of Arkansas (Fayetteville), Arkansas Tech University, the University of Bristol Interdisciplinary Seminar, the Universidad Complutense de Madrid, the University of Notre Dame Institute of Advanced Study, Oxford University's Stubbs Society, the University of Vermont, and Western Michigan University; I am especially grateful to the Institute of Archaeology, University College, London, where the Director, Steven Shennan, and many staff are strongly committed to the search for ways to apply evolutionary language and lessons to cultural change, without compromise of kindness and forbearance in entertaining a heterodox guest lecturer. The readers of Oxford University Press provided much helpful advice, as did the Press's excellent editorial team, especially Luciana O'Flaherty. The support of colleagues, students, and selfless staff at the University of Notre Dame is an invaluable treasure.

Notre Dame, Indiana,
June 2015

NOTES

Introduction

1. P. Coates, *Nature: Changing Attitudes since Ancient Times* (Cambridge, Polity Press, 1998); J.-M. Drouin, *Réinventer la nature: l'écologie et son histoire* (Paris, Desclée de Brouwer, 1991), especially 171–93; P. Descola and G. Pàlsson, eds, *Nature and Society: Anthropology in Perspective* (London and New York, Routledge, 2003).

2. K. Laland and G. Brown, *Sense and Nonsense: Evolutionary Perspectives on Human Behaviour* (Oxford, Oxford University Press, 2011); A. Whiten *et al.*, *Culture Evolves* (Oxford, Oxford University Press, 2012). Below, I cite material in this collection from the previous version, which appeared in *Philosophical Transactions of the Royal Society* in 2011.

3. A. Mesoudi, *Cultural Evolution: How Darwinian Evolutionary Theory Can Explain Human Culture and Synthesize the Social Sciences* (Chicago, University of Chicago Press, 2011), 2.

Chapter 1

1. J.D. Lewis-Williams, 'Harnessing the brain: vision and shamanism in upper palaeolithic Western Europe', in M.W. Conkey *et al.*, eds, *Beyond Art: Pleistocene Image and Symbol* (Berkeley, CA, University of California Press, 1996), 321–42; J. D. Lewis-Williams and J. Clottes, *The Shamans of Prehistory: Trance Magic and the Painted Caves* (New York, Abrams, 1998).

2. J. Needham, *Science and Civilisation in China*, ii (Cambridge, Cambridge University Press, 1956), 36–41.

3. H. Diels and W. Kranz, eds, *Die Fragmente der Vorsokratiker*, 3 vols (Berlin, Weidmann, 1952), i, 101.

4. W.K.C. Guthrie, *History of Greek Philosophy*, i (Cambridge, Cambridge University Press, 1979) 403n.

5. *Fragments*, ed. P.E. Wheelwright, *The Presocratics* (New York, Macmillan, 1966), fr. 50.

6. Ibid., fr. 89; G. Vlastos in *American Journal of Philology*, 1955, 344–7.

7. Ibid., frr 51, 67, 84a.

8. Plato, *Parmenides*, 127 a–c.

9. *Fragments*, ed. A.H. Coxon, *The Fragments of Parmenides* (Assen, Van Gorcum, 1986), fr. 8; *Parmenides*, ed. L. Tarán (Princeton, Princeton University Press, 1965); A.P.D. Mourelator, *The Route of Parmenides* (New Haven, CT, Yale University Press, 1970), 74–135.

10. Plato, *Phaedrus*, 261d; W.C. Salmon, *Zeno's Paradoxes* (Indianapolis, IN, Hackett, 1970).

11. *De Rerum Natura*, V, 5.

12. M. Myerowitz Levine, 'Ovid's evolution' in R. Gibson *et al.*, eds, *The Art of Love: Bimillenial Essays on Ovid's Ars Amatoria and Remedia Amoris* (Oxford: Oxford University Press, 2007), 252–78.

13. A.J. Toynbee, *A Study of History*, ii (Oxford, Oxford University Press, 1957), 213; J. Masefield, *ODTAA* (New York: Macmillan, 1926).

14. H. Chadwick, *Augustine of Hippo* (Oxford, Oxford University Press, 2009), 9.

15. *Confessions*, XI, 8.

16. Ibid., XI, 14.

17. Ibid., 16.

18. J.L. Borges, *The Aleph* (1945), tr. N.T. Giovanni, available at <http://www.phinnweb.org/links/literature/borges/aleph.html>.

19. *Confessions*, XI, 23.

20. D. Johnson, *Nuer Prophets* (Oxford, Oxford University Press, 1997).

21. J. Chevalier, *Henri Bergson* (Paris, Plon, 1926), 40.

22. Ibid., 62.

23. H. Bergson, *La Perception du changement* (Oxford, Oxford University Press, 1911), 12.

24. Chevalier, *Bergson*, 53.

25. *Données immédiates de la conscience* [1889] in *Œuvres* (Paris, Presses Universitaires de France, 1970), 67.

26. *Perception du changement*, 18–37.

27. T. Love Peacock, *Headlong Hall* (1816), ch. 1.

28. *Essais de Théodicée* (Amsterdam, Chagniol, 1739).

29. M.J.A. de Condorcet, *Sketch for a Historical Picture of the Progress of the Human Mind*, tr. J. Barraclough (London, Weidenfeld, 1955), 201.

30. G.K. Chesterton, *The Annotated Innocence of Father Brown*, ed. M. Gardner (Mineola, NY, Dover Press, 1988), 148.

31. *The Two Cultures* (Cambridge, Cambridge University Press, 1965), 14–15.

Chapter 2

1. A. Roger Ekrich, *At Day's Close: a History of Nighttime* (London, Weidenfeld, 2005).

2. D. Everett, *Don't Sleep: There are Snakes: Life and Language in the Amazon Jungle* (New York, Pantheon, 2009), p. v.

3. *The Expression of Emotions in Man and Animals*, ed. P. Ekman (Oxford, Oxford University Press, 1998), p. xxviii.

4. M. Mead, *Coming of Age in Samoa* (New York, Morrow, 1928), 10, 88–109, 135–40, 146–57; D. Freeman, *The Fateful Hoaxing of Margaret Mead: an Historical Analysis of her Samoan Research* (Boulder, CO, Westview, 1999); P. Shankman, *The Trashing of Margaret Mead: Anatomy of an Anthropological Controversy* (Madison, University of Wisconsin Press, 2009).

5. Mead, *Coming of Age in Samoa*, 195–248.

6. *Kinesics and Context: Essays on Body Motion Communication* (Philadelphia, University of Pennsylvania Press, 1970), 78.

7. A. Kroeber, *Anthropology: Culture Patterns and Processes* (New York, Harcourt, 1948), 63.

8. A.W. Crosby, *Ecological Imperialism: the Biological Expansion of Europe* (Cambridge, Cambridge University Press, 2004).

9. S.D. Levitt and S.J. Dubner, *Freakonomics: a Rogue Economist Explains the Nature of Everything* (New York, Morrow, 2005), 118.

10. M.F. Ashley-Montagu, *Culture and the Evolution of Man* (Oxford, Oxford University Press, 1962); *Culture and Human Development: Insights into Growing Human* (Upper Saddle River, NJ, Prentice Hall, 1974).

11. R.E. Nisbett and D. Cohen, *Culture of Honor: the Psychology of Violence in the South* (Boulder, CO, Westview, 1996).

12. K.T. Kishida *et al.*, 'Implicit signals in small group settings and their impact on the expression of cognitive capacity and associated brain responses', *Philosophical Transactions of the Royal Society*, ccclxvii (2012), 704–16; E. G. Bruneau, N.Dufour, and R. Saxe, 'Social cognition in members of conflict groups: behavioural and neural responses in Arabs, Israelis and South Americans to each other's misfortune', in ibid., 717–30.

13. E.W. Fish *et al.*, 'Epigenetic programming of stress responses through variations in maternal care', *Annals of the New York Academy of Science*, mxxvi (2004), 167–80; I.C. Weaver *et al.*, 'Epigenetic programming by maternal behavior', *Nature Neuroscience*, viii (2004), 147–54.

14. D. Reich *et al.*, 'Reconstructing Indian population history', *Nature*, cccclxi (2009), 489–94.

15. S. Mead *et al.*, 'A novel protective prion protein variant that colocalizes with kuru exposure', *New England Journal of Medicine*, ccclxi (2009), 2056–65.

16. *Science*, ccciv (2004), 814.

17. S. Chevalier-Skolnikoff, 'Spontaneous tool use in cebus compared with other monkeys and apes', *Behavioural and Brain Sciences*, xii (1989), 561–627.

18. T. Matsuzawa, 'Spontaneous sorting in human and chimpanzee', in S. Taylor Parker and K.R. Gibson, eds, *'Language' and Intelligence in Monkeys and Apes: Comparative and Developmental Perspectives* (Cambridge: Cambridge University Press, 1990), 451–68.

19. M. Morwood and P. van Oosterzee, *A New Human: the Startling Discovery and Strange Story of the 'Hobbits' of Flores, Indonesia* (Washington, DC, Smithsonian Books, 2007).

20. R. Dunbar, 'Neocortex size as a constraint on group size in primates', *Journal of Human Evolution*, xxii (1992), 469–93; *Grooming, Gossip, and the Evolution of Language* (Cambridge, MA, Harvard University Press, 1998); 'The social brain hypothesis', *Evolutionary Anthropology*, vi (1998), 178–90.

21. R.L. Holloway, 'The evolution of the primate brain: some aspects of quantitative relationships', *Brain Research*, vii (1968), 121–72; 'Brain size, allometry and reorganization: a synthesis', in M.E. Hahn, B.C. Dudek, and C. Jensen, eds, *Development and Evolution of Brain Size* (New York: Academic Press, 1979), 59–88.

22. *The Cultural Origins of Human Cognition* (Cambridge, MA, Harvard University Press, 1999).

23. P.J. Richerson and R. Boyd, *Not by Genes Alone: How Culture Transformed Human Evolution* (Chicago, University of Chicago Press, 2005); P.J. Richerson, R. Boyd, and J. Henrich, 'Gene-culture coevolution in the age of genomics', *Proceedings of the National Academy of Sciences*, cvii (2010), 8995–92.

24. A.R. Pagden, *The Fall of Natural Man* (Cambridge, Cambridge University Press, 1982), 38.

25. D.M. Goldenberg, *The Curse of Ham: Race and Slavery in Early Judaism* (Princeton, NJ, Princeton University Press, 2005).

26. C. Lévi-Strauss, *The Elementary Structures of Kinship* (Boston, Beacon, 1971), 46.

27. F. Fernández-Armesto, *So You Think You're Human* (Oxford, Oxford University Press, 2007).

28. St Augustine, *City of God*, ed. R. Dyson (Cambridge, Cambridge University Press, 1998), 710 (Book XVI, ch. 8); A.T. Davidson, 'The horror of monsters', in J. Sheehan and M. Sosan, eds, *The Boundaries of Humanity* (Berkeley, CA, University of California Press, 1991), 36–67.

29. D. Bindman, *Ape to Apollo: Aesthetics and the Idea of Race in the Eighteenth Century* (London, Reaktion, 2002), 201–9.

30. D. Pick, *Faces of Degeneration: a European Disorder* (Cambridge, Cambridge University Press, 1989), 22.

31. N.L. Stepan, *Picturing Tropical Nature* (New York, Reaktion, 2006).

32. A. Gerbi, *The Dispute of the New World* (Pittsburgh, PA, University of Pittsburgh Press, 1973), 31–3.

33. Ibid., 48.

34. J. Cañizares Esguerra, *How to Write the History of the New World* (Stanford, CA, Stanford University Press, 2002); 'New World, new stars: patriotic astrology and the invention of Indian and Creole bodies in colonial Spanish America', *American Historical Review*, civ (1999), 33–68.

35. E.C. Semple, *Influences of Geographic Environment on the Basis of Ratzel's System of Anthropo-geography* (New York, Holt, 1911), 2.

36. Ibid., 25.

37. Ibid., 620.

38. K. Marx and F. Engels, *The German Ideology* (Amherst, NY, Prometheus, 1976), 65.

39. C. Darwin, *Journal of Researches into the Natural History and Geology of the Various Countries Visited During the Voyage Round the World of HMS Beagle* (London, Murray, 1890), 225, 242–3.
40. C. Darwin, *The Descent of Man and Selection in Relation to Sex* (London, Murray, 1871), ii, 388–9.
41. R.C. Bannister, *Social Darwinism: Science and Myth in Anglo-American Social Thought* (Philadelphia, PA, Temple University Press, 1989), 40.
42. *An Autobiography*, 2 vols (London, Murray, 1902), i, 502; ii, 50.
43. M. Hawkins, *Social Darwinism in European and American Thought* (Cambridge, Cambridge University Press, 1997), 81–6.
44. R. Weikart, *Hitler's Ethic: the Nazi Pursuit of Evolutionary Progress* (New York, Palgrave Macmillan, 2009), 50.

Chapter 3

1. *Bertie's Guide to Life and Mothers* (Edinburgh, Polygon, 2013), 164.
2. R. Lowie, *Primitive Society* (New York, Boni, 1920), 441, quoted in R. Darnell, *Along Came Boas: Continuity and Revolution in Americanist Anthropology* (Amsterdam, Benjamins, 1998), 287.
3. K. Armstrong, *The Battle for God* (New York, Knopf, 2000).
4. R. Seidelman, *Disenchanted Realists: Political Science and the American Crisis* (Albany, NY, SUNY Press, 1985), 31; L. Ward, *Glimpses of the Cosmos*, v (New York, Putnam, 1917), 234.
5. *Pure Sociology* (New York, Macmillan, 1903), 17.
6. Ibid., 29.
7. *Outlines of Sociology* (Norwood, MA, Norwood Press, 1898), 91.
8. F. Boas, *The Mind of Primitive Man* (New York, Macmillan, 1913), 113.
9. Ibid., 208–9.
10. R.H. Lowie, 'The determinants of culture', in H. Applebaum, ed., *Perspectives in Cultural Anthropology* (Albany, NY, SUNY Press, 1987), 85–99 at 85.
11. L.L. Bernard, 'Neuro-psychic technique', *Psychology Review*, xxx (1923), 437, quoted in H. Cravens, 'The abandonment of evolutionary social theory in America: the impact of academic professionalization upon American sociological theory', *American Studies*, xii (1971), 5–20, at p. 14.
12. T. Dantzig, *Henri Poincaré, Critic of Crisis* (New York, Scribner, 1954), 11.
13. H. Poincaré, *The Foundations of Science* (Lancaster, PA, Science Press, 1946), 42.
14. Ibid., 208, 321.
15. F. Fernández-Armesto, 'Pillars and Post: the Foundations and Future of Post-Modernism', in C. Jencks, ed., *The Post-Modern Reader* (Chichester, Wiley, 2011), 125–37.
16. G. Holton, *Einstein and the Cultural Roots of Modern Science* (Cambridge, MA, Harvard University Press, 1997), 8.

17. C. Hockett, 'Biophysics, linguistics, and the unity of science', *American Scientist*, xxxvi (1948), 558–72.
18. D. Worster, *Nature's Economy: a History of Ecological Ideas* (Cambridge, Cambridge University Press, 1994); A. Bramwell, *Ecology in the Twentieth Century* (New Haven, CT: Yale University Press, 1989).
19. Darnell, *Along Came Boas*, 261–9.
20. B. Montgomery, *A History of Warfare* (New York, Morrow, 1983), 13; M. Mead, 'War is only an invention, not a biological necessity', in D. Hunt, ed., *The Dolphin Reader* (Boston, MA, Houghton, 1990), 415–21; cf above, 154.
21. *The Territorial Imperative* (New York, Athenæum, 1966), 5.
22. Ibid., 26.
23. R. Wrangham and D. Paterson, *Demonic Males* (Boston, Houghton, 1996), 6.
24. J.C. Mitani *et al.*, 'Lethal intergroup aggression leads to territorial expansion in wild chimpanzees', *Current Biology*, xx (2010), 507–8.
25. C. Boesch and H. Boesch-Ackermann, *The Chimpanzees of the Tai Forest* (Oxford, Oxford University Press, 2000).
26. H. Cravens, *The Triumph of Evolution: American Scientists and the Heredity–Environment Controversy, 1900–41* (Philadelphia, University of Pennsylvania Press, 1978), 251.
27. A. Jensen, 'How much can we boost I.Q. and scholastic achievement?', *Harvard Educational Review*, xxxix (1969), 1–123.
28. *The Bell Curve: Intelligence and Class Structure in American Life* (New York, Free Press, 1996).
29. *The Astonishing Hypothesis: the Scientific Search for the Soul* (New York, Scribner, 1994), 6–7.
30. 'Science and ideology' in *Academic Questions* (1995), 73–81, at 80.
31. *Sociobiology* (Cambridge, MA, Harvard University Press, 1975), 547.
32. Ibid., 548.
33. Ibid., 560.
34. Compare R. Fox and L. Tiger, *The Imperial Animal* (New York, Transaction, 1998).
35. R. Dawkins, *The Selfish Gene* (Oxford, Oxford University Press, 1976), 202–15.
36. 'Human cultural evolution and its relationship to organic insect societies', in H.R. Barringer *et al.*, eds, *Social Changes in Developing Areas: a Reinterpretation of Evolutionary Theory* (Cambridge, MA, Schenkman, 1965), 56.
37. L. Cavalli-Sforza and M.W. Feldman, 'Models for cultural inheritance', *Theoretical Population Biology*, iv (1973), 42–55.
38. C.J. Lumsden and E.O. Wilson, *Genes, Mind and Culture: the Coevolutionary Process* (Cambridge, MA, Harvard University Press, 1981).
39. G. Mitman, *The State of Nature* (Chicago, University of Chicago Press, 1992), 160.
40. J. Tooby and L. Cosmides, 'The psychological foundations of culture', in L. Barkow *et al.*, eds, *The Adapted Mind: Evolutionary Psychology and the Generation of Culture* (New York, Oxford University Press, 1992), 137–59.

41. *The Selfish Gene*, 206, 214.
42. D.L. Smail, *On Deep History and the Brain* (Berkeley, CA, University of California Press, 2008), 96–7.
43. D. Dennett, *Darwin's Dangerous Idea: Evolution and the Meanings of Life* (London, Penguin, 1995); S. Blackmore, *The Meme Machine* (Oxford, Oxford University Press, 1999).
44. *Sense and Nonsense*, p. v, 197.
45. Cambridge, Cambridge University Press, 2009, p. 5.
46. E. Rogers, *Diffusion of Innovations* (New York, Free Press, 1993), 150–1.
47. Ibid., 246–9.
48. Ibid., 341–2.
49. Ibid., 216.
50. Ibid., 1–5.
51. Ibid., 8–10.
52. Ibid., 48–51.
53. Ibid., 256.
54. Ibid., 268.
55. Ibid., 138–9.
56. F. Fernández-Armesto, *Civilizations* (New York, Free Press, 2002).
57. Rogers, *Diffusion of Innovations*, 407.
58. *The Shock of the Old: Technology and Global History since 1900* (Oxford, Oxford University Press, 2009).
59. M. Harris, *Good to Eat: Riddles of Food and Culture* (New York, Simon and Schuster, 1985), 56–66.
60. M. Douglas, *Purity in Danger* (London, Routledge, 1966), 55.
61. K. Kiple and C. Ornelas, *The Cambridge World History of Food*, 2 vols (Cambridge, Cambridge University Press, 2000), ii, 1505–7; F. Fernández-Armesto, *Food: a History* (London, Macmillan, 2001), 37.

Chapter 4

1. F. Fernández-Armesto, 'How to be human: a historical approach', in M. Jeeves, ed., *Rethinking Human Nature: a Multidisciplinary Approach* (Grand Rapids, MC, Eerdmans, 2010), 11–29.
2. F. de Waal, *The Ape and the Sushi Master* (New York, Basic, 2001), 199–202.
3. M.A. Huffmann, 'Stone-play of *macaca fuscata* in Arashiyama B troop: transmission of a non-adaptive behavior', *Journal of Human Evolution*, xiii (1984), 725–35.
4. J. Goodall, 'Cultural elements in a chimpanzee community', in E. Menzel, ed., *Precultural Primate Behavior* (Basel, Karger, 1973), 144–84.
5. D. Quammen, 'Fifty years at Gombe', *National Geographic Magazine*, October 2010, <http://ngm.nationalgeographic.com/2010/10/jane-goodall/quammen-text>.

6. R.W. Wrangham *et al.*, eds, *Chimpanzee Cultures* (Cambridge, MA, Harvard University Press, 1994); A. Whiten and C. Boesch, 'The cultures of chimpanzees', *Scientific American*, cclxxxiv (2001), 60–7; A. Whiten, 'The scope of culture in chimpanzees, humans, and ancestral apes', *Philosophical Transactions of the Royal Society*, ccclxvi (2011), 997–1007.

7. A. Whiten *et al.*, 'Cultures in chimpanzees', *Nature*, cccxcix (1999), 382–5.

8. A.J. Marshall, R.W. Wrangham, and A.C. Arcadi, 'Does learning affect the structure of vocalization in chimpanzees?', *Animal Behavior*, lvii (1999), 825–30; 'Charting cultural behaviour in chimpanzees', *Behavior*, cxxxviii (2001), 1481–516.

9. C.B. Stanford, *Chimpanzee and Red Colobus: the Ecology of Hunter and Prey* (Cambridge, MA, Harvard University Press, 2001).

10. C. Boesch, 'Is culture a golden barrier between human and chimpanzee?', *Evolutionary Anthropolgy*, xii (2003), 82–91.

11. T. Nishida, 'Individuality and flexibility of cultural behaviour patterns', in F. de Waal and P.L. Tyack, eds, *Animal Social Complexity* (Cambridge, MA, Harvard University Press, 2003), 392–413.

12. C.P. van Schaik *et al.*, 'Orangutan cultures and the evolution of material culture', *Science*, ccxcix (2003), 102–5.

13. C.P. van Schaik, 'Local traditions in orang utans and chimpanzees: social learning and social tolerance', in D.M. Fragaszy and S. Perry, eds, *The Biology of Traditions: Models and Evidence* (Cambridge, Cambridge University Press, 2003), 288–328; A.E. Russon, 'Developmental perspectives on great ape traditions', in ibid., 329–64.

14. J.J. Rousseau, *Discours sur l'origine de l'inégalité*, ed. J.M. Tremblay (Paris, Bordas, 1985), 27–30, 73–8.

15. *Science News*, 3 April, 2004. In northeast Brazil they teach each other to bang stones together as a signal. Antonio Moura and S. Perry, 'Social traditions and social learning in capuchin monkeys', *Philosophical Transactions of the Royal Society*, ccclxvi (2011), 988–96.

16. A. Paulkner *et al.*, 'Capuchin monkeys display affiliation towards humans who imitate them', *Science*, cccxxv (2009), 880–3.

17. M. Dindo, A. Whiten, and F. de Waal, 'In-group conformity sustains different foraging traditions in capuchin monkeys (*Cebus apella*)', available at <http://journals.plos.org/plosone/article?id=10.1371/journal.pone.0007858>.

18. S. Perry and J.H. Manson, 'Traditions in monkeys', *Evolutionary Anthropology*, xii (2003), 71–81.

19. A. Fuentes, 'Being human and doing primatology: national, socioeconomic, and ethnic influences on primatological practice', *American Journal of Primatology*, lxxiii (2011), 233–7.

20. H.O. Box and K.R. Gibson, eds, *Mammalian Social Learning: Comparative and Ecological Perspectives* (Cambridge, Cambridge University Press, 1999).

21. K.N. Laland *et al.*, 'From fish to fashion: experimental and theoretical insights in the evolution of culture', *Philosophical Transactions of the Royal Society*, ccclxvi (2011), 958–68.

22. A. Thornton and T. Clutton-Brock, 'Social learning and the development of individual and group behaviour in mammal societies', in ibid., 978–87.

23. K.W. Pryor, 'A dolphin–human fishing cooperative in Brazil', *Marine Mammal Science*, vi (1990), 77–82; L. Rendell and H. Whitehead *et al.*, 'Culture in whales and dolphins', *Behavioural and Brain Sciences*, xxiv (2001) and accompanying debate, 309–82; R. Smolker *et al.*, 'Sponge carrying by dolphins (*Delphinidae, Tursiops* sp.): a foraging specialization involving tool use?' *Ethology*, ciii (1997), 454–65; R.S. Wells, 'Dolphin social complexity: lessons from long-term study', in de Waal and Tyack, *Animal Social Complexity*, 32–56; J. Owen, 'Dolphin moms teach daughters to use tools', *National Geographic News*, 7 June 2005.

24. P. Lee, 'Early social development among African elephant calves', *National Geographic Research Journal*, ii (1986); C. Moss, H. Croze, and P.C. Lee, *The Ambroseli Elephants: a Long-term Perspective on a Long-lived Mammal* (Chicago, University of Chicago Press, 2011); K. Payne, 'Sources of social complexity in three elephant groups', in de Waal and Tyack, *Animal Social Complexity*, 57–85.

25. K. Laland and W. Hoppitt, 'Do animals have culture?' *Evolutionary Anthropology*, xii (2003), 150–9.

26. Laland and Brown, *Sense and Nonsense*, 150–1.

27. F. de Waal, *Good Natured* (Cambridge, MA, Harvard University Press, 1997), 6–7.

28. R.A. Gargett, 'Grave shortcomings: the evidence for Neanderthal burial', *Current Anthropology*, xxx (1989), 157–90.

29. J.D. Sommer, 'The Shanidar IV "Flower Burial": a re-evaluation of Neanderthal burial ritual', *Cambridge Archaeological Journal*, ix (1999), 127–9.

30. D. Falk, 'Comparative anatomy of the larynx in man and the chimpanzee: implications for language in Neanderthal', *American Journal of Physical Anthropology*, xliii (1975), 123–32; E. Callawy, 'Neanderthals speak out after 30,000 years', *New Scientist*.com, 15 April 2008.

31. E. Trinkhaus, 'Bodies, brawn, brains and noses: human ancestors and human predation', in M.H. Nitecki and D.V. Nitecki, eds, *The Evolution of Human Hunting* (New York, Plenum, 1987), 107–45; rebuttal in C.B. Stanford, *The Hunting Apes: Meat-eating and the Origins of Human Behavior* (Princeton, Princeton University Press, 1999), 133.

32. J.J. Hublin *et al.*, 'A late Neanderthal associated with Upper Paleolithic artefacts', *Nature*, ccclxxxii (1996), 224–6.

33. M. Hamai, 'New records of within-group infanticide and cannibalism in wild chimpanzees', *Primates*, xxxiii (1992), 151–62.

34. J.Goodall, 'Infant killing and cannibalism in free-living chimpanzees', *Folia Primatologica*, cclxxxiv (1977), 259–89.

35. W.G. Runciman, *The Theory of Cultural and Social Selection* (Cambridge: Cambridge University Press, 2009), 89.
36. Stanford, *The Hunting Apes.*
37. T. Nishida, *Chimpanzees of the Lakeshore: Apes and Culture at Mahale* (Cambridge, Cambridge University Press, 2011), 275.
38. R.W. Shumacher *et al.*, *Animal Tool Behavior* (Baltimore, MD, Johns Hopkins University Press, 2011), 73–203.
39. W. Grainge White, *The Sea Gypsies of Malaya* (New York, AMS, 1922), 208.
40. D. Morris, *The Biology of Art: a Study of the Picture-making Behaviour of Great Apes and its Relation to Human Art* (London, Taylor and Francis, 1962); T. Lenain, *Monkey Painting* (London, Reaktion, 1997).
41. R. and D. Morris, *Men and Apes* (New York, McGraw-Hill, 1966), 221–4.
42. *Theory of Cultural and Social Selection*, 89.
43. T.A. Seboeck, 'Prefigurements of art', in T. Maran *et al.*, eds, *Readings in Zoosemiotics* (Berlin, DeGruyter, 2011), 195–245, at 207.
44. R.W. Byrne, 'Social and technical forms of primate intelligence', in F.B.M. de Waal, ed., *Tree of Origins* (Cambridge, MA, Harvard University Press, 2002), 145–72, 167.
45. Boesch, 'Is culture a golden barrier?'
46. C.B. Stanford, 'A comparison of social meat-foraging by chimpanzees and human foragers', in C.B. Stanford and H.T. Bunn, eds, *Meat Eating and Human Evolution* (Oxford, Oxford University Press, 2001), 134.
47. Runciman, *Theory of Cultural and Social Selection*, 89.
48. G. Radick, *The Simian Tongue: the Long Debate about Animal Language* (Chicago, University of Chicago Press, 2007), 16.
49. C. Kenneally, *The First Word: the Search for the Origins of Language* (New York, Penguin, 2007), 231; A. Cangelos and D. Parisi, eds, *Simulating the Evolution of Language* (London, Springer, 2002).
50. N. Chomsky, *Knowledge Of Language: Its Nature, Origin, And Use* (Westport, CT, Praeger, 1986), 55.
51. Ibid., 137.
52. N. Chomsky, M. D. Hauser, and W.T. Fitch, 'The faculty of language: what is it, who has it, and how does it evolve?' *Science*, ccxcviii (2002), 1569–79.
53. D.L. Everett, *Language: the Cultural Tool* (New York, Pantheon, 2012), 290–8; Kenneally, *The First Word*, 263.
54. W. McGrew, '*Pan symbolicus*: a cultural anthropologist's viewpoint', in C.S. Henshilwood and F. d'Errico, eds, *Homo Symbolicus* (Amsterdam, Benjamins, 2011), 1–12.
55. Radick, *The Simian Tongue.*
56. J. Vauclair, 'Primate cognition: from representation to language', in Taylor Parker and Gibson, '*Language' and Intelligence*, 312–29.
57. *Essays* (1893), ii, 145.
58. Radick, *The Simian Tongue*, 108.
59. Ibid., 325.

60. A. Desmond, *The Ape's Reflection* (London, Quartet, 1979), 38–57, 101–3.

61. P. Marks Greenfield and E.S. Savage-Rumbaugh, 'Grammatical combination in *pan paniscus*: processes of learning and invention in the evolution and development of language', in Taylor Parker and Gibson, *'Language' and Intelligence*, 540–78.

62. S. T. Boynsen and G.G. Bernton, 'Development of numerical skills in the chimpanzee', in Taylor Parker and Gibson, *'Language' and Intelligence*, 435–50.

63. M.K. Temerlin, *Lucy: Growing Up Human* (Palo Alto, CA, Science and Behavior Books, 1975), 68–9, 113–16.

64. D. Premack, 'Language in chimpanzee?', *Science*, clxxii (1971), 808–22.

65. S. Savage-Rumbaugh and R. Lewin, *Kanzi: the Ape at the Brink of the Human Mind* (Toronto, Wiley, 1994).

66. H.L.W. Miles, 'The cognitive foundations for reference in a signing orangutan', in Taylor Parker and Gibson, *'Language' and Intelligence*, 511–39; 'Language and the intellectual abilities of orangutans', in W.A. Haviland *et al.*, eds, *Cultural Anthropology: the Human Challenge* (Belmont, CA, Wadworth, 2011), 107–8.

67. I. Pepperberg, 'Some cognitive abilities of an African Grey parrot', in P.J. B. Slater *et al.*, eds, *Advances in the Study of Behavior* (New York, Academic Press, 1990), 357–409.

68. C.T. Snowdon, 'From primate communication to human language', in de Waal, *Tree of Origins*, 193–227.

69. *Unravelling the Evolution of Language* (Bradford, Emerald, 2003).

70. D. Northrup, 'Globalization and the Great Convergence: Rethinking World History in the Long Term', *Journal of World History*, xvi (2008), 249–67. F. Fernández-Armesto, *Pathfinders* (Oxford, Oxford University Press, 2007).

71. *Chimpanzee Politics* (Baltimore, MD, Johns Hopkins University Press, 1982), 19.

72. Ibid., 87.

73. *Chimpanzee Politics* (2007), pp. xv–xvi.

74. J. Goodall, *The Chimpanzees of Gombe*, (1986), 424–9; 'Behavior of free-living chimpanzees of the Gombe stream', *Animal Behavior Monographs*, i (1968), 163–319.

75. R.M. Sapolsky and L.J. Share, *A Pacific Culture among Wild Baboons: its Emergence and Transmission*, available at <http://journals.plos.org/plosbiology/article?id=10.1371/journal.pbio.0020106>.

76. J. Mercader *et al.*, '4,300-year-old chimpanzee sites and the origins of percussive stone technology', *Proceedings of the National Academy of Sciences*, cix (2007); M. Haslam *et al.*, 'Primate archaeology', *Nature*, ccccvi (2009), 339–44.

77. Laland and Brown, *Sense and Nonsense*, 99.

78. E.A. Kelley and R.W. Sussman, 'An academic genealogy on the history of American field primatologists', *American Journal of Physics and Anthropolgy*, cxxxii (2007), 406–25.

79. 'Ten dispatches from the chimpanzee culture wars', in de Waal and Tyack, *Animal Social Complexity*, 424.

80. Strassmann et al., 'Altruism and social cheating in the social amoeba', *Nature*, ccccviii (2000), 965–7.

81. J.T. Bonner, *The Evolution of Culture in Animals* (Princeton, NJ, Princeton University Press, 1980), 54, 72–3.

82. C. Darwin, *The Descent of Man and Selection in Relation to Sex* (New York, Hurst, 1874), 88.

Chapter 5

1. J. Dupré, 'Reflections on biology and culture', in Sheehan and Sosan, *The Boundaries of Humanity*, 130.

2. G. Snooks, *The Collapse of Darwinism* (Lanham, MD, Lexington, 2003).

3. 'Billions and billions of demons', *The New York Review of Books*, 9 January 1997.

4. R.C. Lewontin, *Biology as Ideology: the Doctrine of DNA* (New York, Harper-Collins, 1993).

5. J. Fracchia and R.C. Lewontin, 'Does culture evolve?' in D. Pomper and D. G. Shaw, eds, *The Reurn of Science: Evolution, History, and Theory* (Lanham, MD and Oxford, Rowman, 2002), 233–64.

6. 'Science and ideology', *Academic Questions*, viii (1995), 73–81; U. Segerstrale, *Defenders of the Truth: the Battle for Science in the Sociology Debate and Beyond* (Oxford, Oxford University Press, 2000), 35–51, 164–9.

7. M. Tomasello, 'The human adaptation for culture', *Annual Review of Anthropology*, xxviii (1999), 509–29.

8. 'History *versus* science: the evolutionary solution', *Canadian Journal of Sociology*, xxii (1997), 345–64.

9. 'Gene-culture coevolutionary games', *Social Forces*, lxxxv (2006), 151–66.

10. C. Holden and S. Shennan, 'How tree-like is cultural evolution?' in R. Mace *et al.*, eds, *The Evolution of Cultural Diversity: a Phylogenetic Approach* (Walnut Creek, CA, Left Coast Press, 2005), 13–29.

11. P. Gagneux *et al.*, 'Mitochondrial sequences show diverse evolutionary histories of African hominoids', *Proceedings of the National Academy of Science*, xcvi (1999), 5077–82; N.A. Rosenberg *et al.*, 'Genetic structure of human populations', *Science*, ccxcviii (2002), 2381–5.

12. G. Kodama *et al.*, 'Global landscape of recent inferred Darwinian selection for *Homo sapiens*', *Proceedings of the National Academy of Sciences*, ciii (2006) 135–40; G. Coop *et al.*, 'The role of geography in human adaptation', *PLoS Genetics*, 5 June 2009, available at <http://journals.plos.org/plosgenetics/article?id=10.1371/journal.pgen.1000500>; G.R. Brown *et al.*, 'Evolutionary accounts of behavioural diversity', *Philosophical Transactions of the Royal Society*, 2nd series, ccclxvi (2011), 313–24.

13. Brown *et al.*, 'Bateman's principles and human sex roles', *Trends in Ecology and Evolution*, xxiv (2009), 294–304.

14. S. Pääbo, *Neanderthal Man: in Search of Lost Genomes* (New York, Basic, 2014).

15. D. Dediu and D.R. Ladd, 'Linguistic tone is related to the population frequency of the adaptive haplogroups of two brain size genes, ASPM and Microcephalin', *Proceedings of the National Academy of Sciences*, civ (2007), 10944–9.

16. J. Taylor, *Not a Chimp: the Hunt to Find the Genes that Make us Human* (Oxford, Oxford University Press, 2009), 58–67; R.C. Lewontin *et al.*, *Biology under the Influence* (2007).

17. W.D. Hamilton, 'The genetical evolution of social behavior', *Journal of Theoretical Biology*, vii (1964).

18. E. Sober, *Philosophy of Biology* (Boulder, CO, Westview Press, 2000), 85.

19. G.F. Miller, 'Sexual selection for cultural displays', in R. Dunbar *et al.*, eds, *The Evolution of Culture: an Interdisciplinary View* (New Brunswick, NJ, Rutgers University Press, 1999), 71–89.

20. R. Williamson, *The Triumph of Human Empire: Verne, Morris, and Stevenson at the End of the World* (Chicago, University of Chicago Press, 2013), 306–7.

21. Fernández-Armesto, *Food: a History*, 91–7.

22. Gen Yamakoshi and Yukimaru Sugiyama, 'Pestle-pounding behavior of wild chimpanzees at Bossou, Guinea: a newly observed tool-using behavior', *Primates*, xxxvi (1995), 489–500.

23. R. Lewontin, 'Adaptation', *Scientific American*, ccxxxix (1978), 212–28; Guglielmo *et al.*, 'Cultural variation in Africa: role of mechanism of transmission and adaptation', *Proceedings of the National Academy of Sciences*, xcii (1995), 7585–9.

24. Fernández-Armesto, *Civilizations*.

25. J. Goudsblom and B. de Vries, eds, *Mappae Mundi: Humans and their Habitats in Long-term Ecological Perspective* (Amsterdam: Amsterdam University Press, 2002); I.G. Simmons, *Global Environmental History* (Chicago: Chicago University Press, 2008); J.R. Diamond, *Collapse: How Societies Choose to Fail or Succeed* (New York: Viking, 2005).

26. R. Lewontin, 'Is nature probable or capricious?' *Biological Science*, xvi (1966), 25–7; 'Annotation: the analysis of variance and the analysis of causes', *American Journal of Human Genetics*, xxvi (1974), 400–11.

27. D. Campbell, 'Variation and selective retention in socio-cultural evolution', in Barringer, Blanksten, and Mack, *Social Change in Developing Areas*, 19–49.

28. *Progress: Its Law and Cause in Essays Scientific and Speculative* (New York, Appleton, 1915), i, 8–62, 10.

29. E. Chaisson, *Cosmic Evolution: the Rise of Complexity in Nature* (2001); D. Christian, *Maps of Time* (2004); F. Spier, *Big History and the Future of Humanity* (Oxford, Wiley-Blackwell, 2010).

30. L. White, *The Evolution of Culture* (1959).
31. Ibid., 366.
32. R. McElreath and J. Henrich, 'Dual inheritance theory: the evolution of human cultural capacities and cultural evolution', in R. Dunbar and L. Barrett, eds, *Oxford Handbook of Evolutionary Psychology* (Oxford: Oxford University Press, 2007).
33. H.C. Koerper and E.G. Stickel, 'Cultural drift: a primary process of culture change', *Journal of Anthropological Research*, xxxvi (1980), 463–9.
34. R.A. Bentley *et al.*, 'Random drift and culture change', *Proceedings of the Royal Society*, 2nd series, cclxxi (1980), 1443–50.
35. M.W. Feldman and L. Cavalli-Sforza, *Cultural Transmission and Evolution: a Quantitative Approach* (Princeton, Princeton University Press, 1981), p. v.
36. Laland and Brown, *Sense and Nonsense*, 168.
37. R. Boyd and P.J. Richerson, 'Memes: universal acid or better mouse trap?', in R. Aunger, ed., *Darwinizing Culture: The Status of Memetics as a Science* (Oxford: Oxford University Press, 2000), 143–62.
38. 'Culture, adaptation, and innateness', in in P. Carruthers, S. Stich, and S. Laurence, eds, *The Innate Mind: Culture and Cognition* (New York, Oxford University Press, 2006), 23–38.
39. B.G. Miner *et al.*, 'Ecological consequences of phenotypic plasticity', *Trends in Ecology and Evolution*, xx (2005), 685–92.
40. *Philosophie zoologique*, ed. C. Martins, 2 vols (Paris, Savy, 1873), i, 71–96, 220–65.
41. *The Future of Man* (New York, Basic Books, 1960).
42. L. Gabora, 'Five clarifications about cultural evolution', *Journal of Cognition and Culture*, xi (2011), 61–83.
43. Medawar, *The Future of Man*.
44. Fracchia and Lewontin, 'Does culture evolve?', at 258.

Chapter 6

1. M. Halbwachs, 'The social frameworks of memory', *On Collective Memory* (Chicago, 1992), 96–124. See also P. Burke, 'History as social memory', in T. Butler, ed., *Memory: History, Culture and the Mind* (Oxford, Blackwell, 1989), 97–113.
2. A. Baddeley, *The Psychology of Memory* (London, 1992). See also D. Rubin, ed., *Autobiographical Memory* (Cambridge, 1986); J. Prager, *Presenting the Past: Psychoanalysis and the Sociology of Misremembering* (Cambridge, MA, 1998).
3. 'The Consequences of Literacy', *Comparative Studies in Society and History*, v (1963), 304–45.
4. D.L. Schacter, ed., *Memory Distortion: How Minds, Brains and Societies Reconstruct the Past* (Cambridge, MA, 1995), p. x.

5. Prager, *Presenting the Past*, 185; Schacter, *Memory Distortion*, 17–18.

6. E. Tulving, *Elements of Episodic Memory* (Oxford, Oxford University Press, 1985).

7. W.A. Roberts, 'Introduction: cognitive time travel in people and animals', *Learning and Motivation*, xxxvi (2005), 107–9.

8. N. Dickinson and N.S. Clayton, 'Retrospective cognition by food-caching western scrub-jays', in ibid., 159–76; H. Eichenbaum *et al.*, 'Episodic recollection in animals: if it walks like a duck and quacks like a duck . . .', in ibid., 190–207.

9. C.D.L. Wynne, *Do Animals Think?* (Princeton, NJ and Oxford, Princeton University Press, 2004), 230.

10. C.R. Menzel, 'Unprompted recall and reporting of hidden objects by a chimpanzee (*pan troglodytes*) after extended delays', *Journal of Comparative Psychology*, cxiii (1999), 426–34.

11. B.P. Trivedi, 'Scientists rethinking nature of animal memory', *National Geographic Today*, 22 August 2003.

12. Compare I. Adachi, H. Kuwahata, and K. Fujita, 'Dogs recall their owner's face [*sic*] upon hearing the owner's voice', *Animal Cognition*, x (2007), 17–21.

13. Taylor, *Not a Chimp*, 11; *Current Biology*, xvii (2007), 1005.

14. A. Silberberg and D. Kearns, 'Memory for the order of briefly presented numerals in humans as a function of practice', *Animal Cognition*, xii (2009), 405–7.

15. B.L. Schwartz *et al.*, 'Episodic-like memory in a gorilla: a review and new findings', in ibid., 226–44.

16. Trivedi, 'Scientists rethinking nature of animal memory'.

17. F. Yates, *The Art of Memory* (Chicago, University of Chicago Press, 1966).

18. K. Danziger, *Marking the Mind: a History of Memory* (Cambridge, Cambridge University Press, 2008), 188–97.

19. S. Coren, *How Dogs Think* (New York, Free Press, 2005).

20. M. Gurven *et al.*, 'Food transfers among Hiwi foragers of Venezuela: tests of reciprocity', *Human Ecology*, xxviii (2000), 175–218.

21. H. Kaplan *et al.*, 'The evolution of intelligence and the human life history', *Evolutionary Anthropology*, ix (2000), 156–84; R. Walker *et al.*, 'Age dependency and hunting ability among the Ache of eastern Paraguay', *Journal of Human Evolution*, xlii (2002), 639–57, at 653–5.

22. J. Bronowski, *The Visionary Eye* (Cambridge, MA, MIT Press, 1978), 9.

23. G. Deutscher, *Through the Language Glass: Why the World Looks Different in Other Languages* (New York, 2010).

24. S. Pinker, *The Language Instinct* (New York, Morrow, 1994), 57–63.

25. E. Spelke and S. Hespos, 'Conceptual precursors to language', *Nature*, ccccxxx (2004), 453–6.

26. D. Sperber, *Explaining Culture: a Naturalistic Approach* (Oxford, Blackwell, 1996), 149.

27. M. Ridley, *The Rational Optimist: How Prosperity Evolves* (New York, Harper, 2010).

28. R. Lowie, *Primitive Cultures* (New York, Boni, 1920), 440.

29. J. Mirsky, *The Great Chinese Travelers: an Anthology* (Chicago, University of Chicago Press, 1974).

30. Fernández-Armesto, *Civilizations*, 260.

31. L. Casson, ed., *The Periplus Maris Erythraei* (Princeton, NJ, Princeton University Press, 1989).

32. J. Needham, *Science and Civilisation in China*, i (Cambridge, Cambridge University Press, 1956), 173–99.

33. R. Whitfield, ed., *Cave Temples of Mogao: Art and History on the Silk Road* (Malibu, CA, Getty, 2000), 48.

34. G.E.R. Lloyd, *Ancient Worlds, Modern Reflections: Philosophical Perspectives on Greek and Chinese Science and Culture* (Oxford, Oxford University Press, 2004); J. Hobson, *The Eastern Origins of Western Civilisation* (Cambridge, Cambridge University Press, 2004).

35. M.L. West, *The East Face of Helicon: West Asiatic Elements in Greek Poetry and Myth* (Oxford, Oxford University Press, 1999).

36. F. Fernández-Armesto, *The World: A History* (Boston, etc., Prentice Hall, 2011), 130–58.

37. Fernández-Armesto, *Pathfinders*, 74–83.

38. J.D. Spence, *The Memory Palace of Matteo Ricci* (New York, Penguin, 1984).

39. Fernández-Armesto, *The World*, 129, 356–9, 633–43.

40. *Guns, Germs and Steel* (New York, W.W. Norton, 1997), especially 354–75.

41. C. Boesch *et al.*, 'Is nut-cracking in wild chimpanzees a cultural behavior?' *Journal of Human Evolution*, xxvi (1994), 325–38.

Chapter 7

1. J. Hooper, *The New Spaniards* (2003); G. Tremlett, *Ghosts of Spain* (2006).

2. R.L. Carneiro, *Evolutionism in Cultural Anthropology: a Critical History* (Boulder, CO, Westview, 2003), 169–70.

3. Fernández-Armesto, *Civilizations*, 124–7.

4. A. Dallin and G. Lapidus, eds, *The Soviet System from Crisis to Collapse* (1995).

5. F. Fernández-Armesto, ed., *The Folio Society History of England*, xii (London, Folio, 2000), 509–47.

6. J.-M. Chauvet *et al.*, *Chauvet Cave* (1996).

7. R. Potts, 'Sociality and the concept of culture in human origins', in R. W. Sussman and A.R. Chapman, eds, *The Origins and Nature of Sociality* (New York, De Gruyter, 2004), 249–69.

8. Tomasello, 'The human adaptation for culture', 509–29.

9. R. Dawkins and J.R. Krebs, 'Arms races between and within species', *Philosophical Transactions of the Royal Society*, ccv (2005), 489–511.

10. 'The Red King effect: when the slowest runner wins the coevolutionary race', *Proceedings of the National Academy of Sciences*', c (2003), 593–8.

11. R. Girard, *Violence and the Sacred* (Baltimore, Johns Hopkins University Press, 1977).

12. *Evolution and Conversion* (London, Continuum, 2008), 96.

13. Ibid., 64.

14. Ibid., 106.

15. Ibid., 101.

Chapter 8

1. M. Howard, *The Causes of Wars and Other Essays* (1984), 14.

2. D. Boorstin, *Cleopatra's Nose: Essays on the Unexpected* (New York, Vintage, 1995); G. Lively, 'Cleopatra's nose, Naso, and the science of chaos', *Greece and Rome*, xlix (2002), 27–43.

3. *Republic*, ed. D. Lee (Harmondsworth, Penguin, 1974), 333.

4. F. Fernández-Armesto, *Truth: a History* (New York, St Martin's Press, 1997), 188–90.

5. Ibid., 200; L. Wittgenstein, *Philosophical Investigations* (Oxford, Blackwell, 1953), 88, 100, 102–3, 133, 241, 293, 307, 464.

6. J.V. Kennedy, 'The sources and uses of science funding', *The New Atlantis*, 36 (Summer 2012), 3–22.

7. F. Fernández-Armesto, 'Pillars and posts: the foundations and future of post-modernism', in C. Jencks, ed., *The Post-modern Reader* (Chichester, Wiley, 2011), 125–37.

8. D.R. Griffin, *The Reenchantment of Science* (New York, SUNY Press, 1988).

9. *Les Mots* (Paris, Gallimard, 1964), 213.

10. Carneiro, *Evolutionism in Cultural Anthropology*, 185–9.

11. H. Trevor-Roper, 'The lost moments of history', *The New York Review of Books*, 27 October 1988.

12. Carneiro, *Evolutionism in Cultural Anthropology*, 264–76.

13. Hamilton, 'Genetical evolution of social behavior', 1–52.

14. T. Bartlett, 'Dusting off God', *The Chronicle of Higher Education*, 13 August 2012.

15. *Evolution of Human Behavior* (New York, Oxford University Press (2009), 184–6.

16. Ibid., 248.

17. See for instance W. Runciman, J. Maynard Smith, and R.I.M. Dunbar, eds, *Evolution of Social Behaviour Patterns in Primates and Man: a Joint Discussion Meeting of the Royal Society and the British Academy* (Oxford, Oxford University Press, 1996).

18. *Theory of Cultural and Social Selection*, 109.
19. Ibid., 3.
20. Ibid., 192.
21. Ibid., 65–74.
22. Ibid., 8.
23. Ibid., 7–9.
24. D.L. Smail and A. Shryock, eds, *Deep History* (Berkeley, CA, University of California Press, 2011).
25. *The New York Review of Books*, xlv (1998); *The Power of Ideas*, ed. H. Hardy (London, Chatto, 2000), 11–14.
26. *Theory of Social and Cultural Selection*, 88.

INDEX